Where We Came In

Where We Came In

SEVENTY YEARS OF
THE BRITISH FILM INDUSTRY

BY

C. A. OAKLEY

London
GEORGE ALLEN & UNWIN LTD
RUSKIN HOUSE   MUSEUM STREET

PRINTED IN GREAT BRITAIN
in 10 on 11 point Times Roman type
BY SIMSON SHAND LTD
LONDON, HERTFORD AND HARLOW

INTRODUCTION

The Tough 'Un

••

One of the titles considered for this book was *The Tough 'Un*. It was
called after an expositional documentary film made by Mary Field
and Percy Smith, winner of many awards at festivals in the late
1930s. The subject was the dandelion, the thesis indestructibility.

You can trample on the dandelion, kick it around, decapitate it,
haul it out by the roots, torment it in every conceivable way. But
there is no getting rid of it. Or you can subvert it by kindness, by
satiating its appetite for fertilizing delicacies, so that, after prodigious
gorging, it bursts asunder. But up it will come again.

In many respects the British film-making industry takes after that
resurgent plant. It has been virtually written off several times. But
the industry's recuperative powers asserted themselves. Something
stirred, somewhere, somehow, and there it was once more.

To take this analogy further would ill-advisedly invite a retort
that what came up each time was just another dandelion. This would
not be a wholly justified aspersion. Over the years the British cinematic horticulturists have created bigger and certainly more expensive dandelions. A remarkable variety of able and earnest men of
different temperaments and backgrounds have striven, often to their
considerable financial loss, to make British films worthy of a place in
the world's markets. Many fine narrative feature films have been
produced and it would not be difficult to name a score of international importance. We might have made more but for the Hollywood's practice of enticing away our promising directors, actors,
actresses and technicians.

It is in the field where the poaching has been least noticeable, producing documentary films, that our reputation has been consistently
highest. And on the exhibiting side of the industry the British have
been second only to the Americans in their keenness for going to
the pictures. As judged by the capital invested and by the personnel
employed, showing films was really big business during most of the
first sixty years of this century. Mention should perhaps be made
also of the quite outstanding contributions that were made in Great

Britain to the development of television; but that is not a subject for this book.

The history of the British film industry was never written. Many books appeared about the American industry and most libraries have volumes on their shelves about the Danish, French, German, Italian, Japanese, Russian, Swedish, and other industries, all of which have been smaller than ours. This does seem all the more strange because, although the story is not a particularly happy one, it is, as Dilys Powell has remarked, romantic as well as sprawling.

Oliver Bell, when Director of the British Film Institute, was concerned to fill the gap and in 1946 set up a committee under Cecil Hepworth's chairmanship to prepare a history of the British cinema. After three volumes had been published, covering the early days (by Rachel Low and Roger Manvell), 1906-14 and then 1914-18 (both by Rachel Low), the series came to an end, at least temporarily, when Rachel Low went abroad.

With the approach of the Institute's twenty-fifth anniversary, James Quinn, the present Director, revived the project and an arrangement was made for a fourth volume, covering the 1920s, to be taken in hand. Unfortunately this work has not yet made much progress.

It became clear that years would pass before the completion of the series and, during the discussions that followed this disclosure, the suggestion was made that I should write a shorter book covering the whole period of seventy years. As the Institute had no research workers or others to do the 'devilling', a plan was adopted, resembling one which I have twice used for books of a historical character. I was to rely on my memory, refreshed by references to the books in my library; and the Institute's Information Department would endeavour to answer questions I put to them. The draft chapters would then be sent to knowledgeable people inviting correction and amendment, and seeking sources of additional information. After that the revised script would be prepared.

The aspect most discussed when the project was first being considered was the manner in which the various films should be treated. Some thought it best for only a few films, 'typical of their period', to be selected so that could be considered fairly fully. Others shared my view that there is no such thing as a typical fiim of any period and that in a history it is essential to mention the many rather than the few—although the necessity was appreciated for preventing the book from turning into a catalogue, even though it does contain no fewer than 450 titles.

There was a further complication in that my own interests have been in production and in exhibiting. Except for taking part in a few BBC programmes I have never engaged in film criticism and have not the least suggestion of a file available recording my reactions to the innumerable films I have seen over the decades.

So in dealing with all major films I have drawn on views expressed by leading critics. This gives some measure of objectivity to the references, although the point must be conceded that in the choice of the critic I disclose my own attitude. Furthermore, it must be admitted that the critics tend to use their more arresting phrases when running down a film rather then when praising it; and perhaps they caught my eye most often when in this mood. I have striven, however, to prevent the general feeling of this book from being either 'down-beat' or 'jingoish'.

The draft script was read, as was hoped, by several of the leading members of the industry, and by members of the staff of the British Film Institute. To them I express my great indebtedness.

I have consulted innumerable papers and many books in the British Film Institute's Information Department. Having abandoned the prodigious taks of drawing up a full bibliography, I would advise inquirers to seek out these papers and books in that Department.

I have prepared a short bibliography, however, and must make particular reference to:

The History of the British Film (1896-1906). Rachel Low and Roger Manvell. George Allen & Unwin. 1948.

The History of the British Film (1906-1914). Rachel Low. George Allen & Unwin. 1949.

The History of the British Film (1914-1918). Rachel Low. George Allen and Unwin. 1950.

Twenty Years of British Film. The Falcon Press. 1945.

Films Since 1939. Dilys Powell. The British Council. 1947.

Michael Balcon's 25 Years in Films. World Film Publications. 1947.

The Elstree Story. Clerke and Cockeran. 1948.

The Film Till Now. Paul Rotha. Vision. (1949 edition.)

Came the Dawn. Cecil Hepworth. Phoenix. 1951.

Films, 1945-50. Denis Forman. The British Council. 1952.

Mr. Rank. Alan Wood. Hodder & Stoughton. 1952.

The British Film Industry. PEP. 1952.

Sir Alexander Korda. Ian Dalrymple. British Film Academy. 1956.

Flashback. George Pearson. George Allen & Unwin. 1957.

The House that Stoll Built. Felix Barker. Frederick Muller. 1957.

Alexander Korda. Paul Tabori. Oldbourne. 1959.

The Decline of the Cinema. John Spraos. George Allen & Unwin. 1962.

A Guide to British Film Production. British Film Producers' Association. 1963.

The Kinematograph Weekly (and particularly its Diamond Jubilee Number, 1956).

Sight and Sound (and particularly its Festival of Britain Number, 1951, and its Twenty-fifth Anniversary Number, 1958).

The British Film Institute's *Monthly Film Bulletin*.

C. A. OAKLEY

CONTENTS

••

ILLUSTRATIONS

The Sequence of Events

....

1895   Birt Acres photographs several 'topical' items, including the the Oxford and Cambridge boat race.

1896   Films shown commercially for the first time in London (February 25) by Louis Lumière in a Regent Street Polytechnic hall.

R. W. Paul commissioned by the Alhambra music hall to photograph the Derby and to show the film on the night of the race. Other music halls adopt the idea of showing animated pictures as the concluding item of their shows.

1897   Film record of *Queen Victoria's Jubilee Procession* shown throughout country. It introduces the public to the amazing new magic lantern.

1898- Fairground proprietors take over the cinematograph and
1912   many sideshows are replaced by booths exhibiting films.

Films are substituted for individual 'turns' at professional concerts. Enterprising promoters hire public halls on Saturdays for film-concerts. Subsequently many halls are leased for conversion into cinemas, with the pictures steadily taking up more of the time at the expense of the living performers.

1898   Leon Gaumont forms his British company.

Cecil M. Hepworth opens his printing laboratory at Walton-on-Thames.

Charles Urban founds the Warwick Trading Company.

1899   The Brighton School becomes R. W. Paul's principal competitor in supplying films.

1900   Will Barker begins making films at Stamford Hill.

1901   R. W. Paul transfers his studio to Muswell Hill.

Col. A. C. Bromhead opens his studio at Loughborough.

Charles Pathé establishes his British branch in London.

1904   Clarendon Film Company founded with studios at Croydon.

Sir Ambrose Fleming announces the invention of the thermionic valve, and so opens the way for radio, the sound film and television.

1905   Cecil H. Hepworth's *Rescued by Rover*.

B

1906 First shop (in Oxford Street) converted into a cinema (for Hale's Tours). This marks the beginning of the genteel 'Bijou' type of cinema.

A. C. Bromhead organizes the first continuous film shows (in Bishopsgate).

1907 The Kinematograph Film Makers' Association (KMA) constituted.

The Kinematograph Weekly begins in its present form.

Walter Haggar's *The Salmon Poachers.*

A truce is declared in the United States to end disputes over patent rights. American film production shoots ahead.

1909 A flood of American as well as French films overwhelms British cinemas, and the *first cinematograph crisis* develops when film-making in Great Britain collapses.

Dr Ralph T. Jupp founds PCT (Provincial Cinematograph Theatres) to establish a circuit of 'picture palaces' in large towns.

Charles Pathé begins his British edition of Pathe Gazette.

1910 The first Cinematograph Films Act. Welcomed as the 'Showman's Charter', which would make the industry respectable, it is soon viewed with hostility. Local authorities interpret their powers for ensuring public safety as affecting mental as well as physical well-being, and try to censor programmes.

The Incorporated Association of Film Renters (the precursor of the KRS) formed.

Charles Urban contributes materially in restoring the reputation of British films with his factual productions, including the *Delhi Durbar,* made in Kinemacolor.

1911 Will Barker directs a lengthy episodic film, *Sixty Years a Queen,* for special and highly profitable performances throughout the country.

Cecil M. Hepworth's *Rachel's Sin.*

Herbert J. Ponting's film record of the *Scott Antarctic Expedition.*

1912 The film industry, through the KMA and with Government approval, sets up the British Board of Film Censors.

The Cinematograph Exhibitors' Association (CEA) founded with ten members.

1913 Dr Ralph Jupp founds the original London Film Company to make 'feature films' in new studios at Twickenham. He engages American directors, technicians and players. Their first film is *The House of Temperley.*

Florence Turner, one of the leading stars, leaves the United States with her staff to make films in London. Other

American companies survey Great Britain for studio sites.

The Bijou cinemas, with insufficient accommodation to make the showing of 'feature films' economically possible, give way to larger and more luxurious picture houses.

British studios are fully occupied again. Leading players, Pimple, The Tilly Tomboys, Lieutenant Rose and Lieutenant Daring.

1914 Gaumont Studios opened at Shepherd's Bush.

At the outbreak of the war there are thirteen circuits in this country owning ten or more cinemas.

The British industry responds to the Government's injunction, 'Business as Usual', and film-making is stepped up. Americans begin, however, to withdraw to the United States.

1915 Dr Jupp's illness brings about the virtual closing-down of London Films. Their principal director, George Loane Tucker, returns to Hollywood.

Cecil M. Hepworth establishes himself as the leading British film-maker. His principal associates are Henry Edwards and Tom Bentley. Alma Taylor is the most popular British star.

Will Barker produces the spectacular film, *Jane Shore*.

The McKenna Duties imposed on imported film stock.

1916 The Chancellor of the Exchequer introduces the Entertainments Tax.

The first feature-length documentary film of the war, *The Battle of the Somme*, directed by Geoffrey Malins and J. B. McDowell, is widely shown.

1917 Ideal Films produces its series of prestige films, including *Masks and Faces*, directed by Fred Paul.

Welsh-Pearson Company formed.

T. P. O'Connor appointed Film Censor.

The Government's Department of Information forms a Cinematograph Branch under the direction of (Sir) William Jury.

1918 During last stages of the war, studio production in Great Britain virtually ceases, and the industry faces its *second crisis*.

The Kinematograph Renters Society (KRS) established.

Sir Oswald Stoll sets up a film-making company.

1919 British film production is slow to recover and the American predominance on British screens continues.

Cecil M. Hepworth embarks on his ill-fated expansion policy.

H. Bruce Woolfe forms British Instructional Films.

1920 The PCT group extend their circuit to sixty-eight cinemas.

There are 4,000 cinemas in Great Britain and the trade estimates that 2,000 more are needed.

The Stoll Company produce the Guy Newall-Ivy Duke society dramas, including *Duke's Son*.

Wireless broadcasting of entertainment programmes begins.

1921 The 'crisis' meeting held in the Connaught Rooms at which W. Friese-Greene dies.

Concern expressed about people staying at home to listen to the radio.

Hepworth Picture Plays make their most successful film, *Alf's Button*.

Welsh-Pearson produce the first of the *Squibs* comedies and Betty Balfour becomes the most popular British star.

J. Stewart Blackton produces *The Glorious Adventure* in 'natural colour'.

Stoll studios opened at Cricklewood.

1922 New Era Films founded by (Sir) Gordon Craig.

Cinematograph Exhibitors Association's membership 2,000.

Jack Graham Cutts directs *The Wonderful Story* for Herbert Wilcox.

Lilian Hall Davies becomes another leading British star.

1923 The Entertainments Tax Abolition League set up.

Sir Oswald Stoll presents his major film, *The Prodigal Son*, in the Royal Opera House, Covent Garden.

Graham-Wilcox Productions formed.

1924 Reductions made in Entertainments Tax, particularly affecting the cheaper seats.

Hepworth Picture Plays bankrupt.

British Films Week campaign inaugurated by the Prince of Wales. It is a failure. Alarm grows at the British public's preference for American films.

British producers meet their *third crisis* as film-making completely collapses in November.

Michael Balcon, John Freedman and Victor Saville form an independent unit which engages Jack Graham Cutts to direct *Woman to Woman*, one of the most successful British silent films. Alfred Hitchcock and Clive Brook are associated with the production.

The Tivoli in the Strand, the West End's first super cinema, opened.

1925 The Slump continues. The Federation of British Industries urges the Government to adopt a quota system and to form a Government-controlled finance corporation to assist British film production.

Oscar Deutsch becomes financially interested in film exhibition.

The London Film Society holds its first meeting in the New Gallery Cinema.

1926   British films now occupy only 5 per cent of British 'screen time'.

British National Studios built at Elstree.

The KRS organize the transport of films by road during the General Strike. This continues as the established method of distributing films.

1927   The (second) Cinematograph Films Act institutes Renters' and Exhibitors' Quotas, restricts 'block and blind' booking, and appoints the Cinematograph Films Advisory Committee. The consequence is an immediate revival of film-making in Great Britain.

There are now twenty-three circuits in Great Britain owning ten or more cinemas, but their control extends to no more than 12 per cent of all the cinemas in the country. The largest circuits are PCT (eighty-five cinemas) and Gaumont-British (twenty-one cinemas).

John Maxwell acquires the studios at Elstree and forms British International Pictures (BIP).

Dr Lee de Forest makes and shows sound films commercially in London.

J. L. Baird projects a motion picture by television from London to Glasgow.

The Shaftesbury Avenue Pavilion opens to show foreign and other unusual films.

Alfred Hitchcock's *The Lodger.*

1927- Has been described as the 'watershed between mediaeval and
1930   modern cinematography in Great Britain'.

1928   John Maxwell forms the ABC circuit with forty cinemas, and establishes the first major vertical combination (production, distribution and exhibition) in Great Britain.

Gaumont-British acquire the PCT circuit and follow his example. Fox Films buy a considerable interest in the company controlling the Gaumont-British combination.

The British Board of Film Censors is attacked for being indulgent. Attempts are renewed to set up local censorship.

American feature talking films are shown in London with overwhelming success.

Anthony Asquith writes and is co-director of *Shooting Stars.*

E. A. Dupont's *Piccadilly.*

Adrian Brunel's *The Constant Nymph.*

Victor Saville directs *Kitty* for BIP, the first British part-talkie.

1929   The Ostrers acquire Gaumont-British. C. M. Woolf is appointed joint managing-director. Michael Balcon takes charge of production.

Silent films are swept aside by talking films.

Alfred Hitchcock's *Blackmail.*

E. A. Dupont's *Atlantic.*

John Grierson's *Drifters* is acclaimed when shown at a London Film Society meeting, and marks the beginning of the 'documentary' movement in this country.

1930   Sound reproducing equipment installed in all large and most small cinemas.

Several West End theatres permanently converted into cinemas.

The new Ealing Studios opened.

Many British films made, principally as adaptations from stage plays; but the public becomes used to American accents and again begins to veer towards American films.

Victor Saville's *The W Plan.*

1931   Sunday opening of cinemas temporarily halted under the Sunday Observance Act of 1780.

Alexander Korda begins making films in Great Britain.

ACT (Association of Cine-Technicians) formed.

Gracie Fields makes her first film, *Sally in our Alley,* and heads towards great popularity.

1932   Public indignation expressed at the failure of British film-makers to make use of their early advantage with talking films. It is announced that foreign films (almost entirely American) are taking £5 million annually from Great Britain. British films are earning only £0.1 million in the United States and £0.5 in the Commonwealth and elsewhere overseas.

Sunday Entertainment Act regularizes Sunday opening, but on condition that 5 per cent of the takings go into a fund to promote the use of films for entertainment and instruction.

The report of the Commission on Educational Cultural Films, *The Film in National Life,* published.

London Films founded by Alexander Korda.

Walter Forde's *The Rome Express.*

1933   J. Arthur Rank enters cinematograph industry by sponsoring production of religious films.

Oscar Deutsch expands his Odeon circuit.

British Film Institute constituted.

British Board of Film Censors attacked for showing leniency

to American gangster films. The LCC imposes a new category H (for horrific).

Alexander Korda's *The Private Life of Henry VIII* changes the finance houses' attitude to British film production and starts a new phase. Apart from this influence, however, the output of British films has considerably increased (1932, 200 feature films as against 1929, 128).

Victor Saville's *I was a Spy* and *The Good Companions*.

1934 British National Films begin production with J. Arthur Rank as an active participant.

New studios built at Denham for Alexander Korda.

Alfred Hitchcock transfers his services from BIP to Gaumont-British and directs *The Man Who Knew Too Much*.

Robert Flaherty's *Man of Aran*.

Michael Balcon's *Jew Süss*.

Victor Saville's *Evergreen*.

Paul Stein's *Blossom Time*.

1935 The exhibition boom continues. Between 100 and 200 cinemas, many of them large, are being built each year.

John Maxwell decides to make the expansion of his circuit of cinemas his first concern, instead of film production.

C. M. Woolf leaves Gaumont-British to form General Film Distributors with J. Arthur Rank as one of his backers, following the cold-shouldering of the latter's *The Turn of the Tide* (directed by Norman Walker).

J. Arthur Rank becomes chairman of the new Pinewood Studios.

J. L. Baird demonstrates (and CEA discusses) the use of large screen television in cinemas. Opposition encountered from the BBC.

National Film Archive opened.

René Clair's *The Ghost Goes West*.

Alfred Hitchcock's *The Thirty-nine Steps*.

Harold Young's *The Scarlet Pimpernel*.

1936 A *fourth crisis* threatens the industry. It is primarily financial and is attributed in Parliament and elsewhere to gross extravagance.

American interests thwart John Maxwell in his attempt to combine the ABPC and Gaumont-British circuits. Together they would have owned 559 cinemas.

The Odeon circuit contains 143 cinemas. United Artists acquire substantial holding.

The Moyne Committee Report published on the state of the industry.

Opening of the Technicolor Laboratories in London leads to this being known as the year of the 'colour boom'.

Alexander Korda's *Rembrandt* and *Things to Come*.

Robert Stevenson's *Tudor Rose*.

ABPC extend their European markets.

1937   Gaumont-British close down the Shepherd's Bush Studios.

Odeon circuit reaches 250 cinemas and opens the Odeon Cinema in Leicester Square.

George Formby comes up alongside Gracie Fields as the most popular British star.

Alexander Korda's *Fire Over England*.

1938   The (third) Cinematograph Films Act considerably increases quotas. The Cinematograph Films Council is formed.

Cinematograph Exhibitors Association's members, 4,000.

The LCC introduce seat price control for London cinemas.

Alfred Hitchcock's *The Lady Vanishes*.

Victor Saville's *South Riding*.

MGM's *A Yank at Oxford*.

1939   Odeon circuit takes over the Paramount group of cinemas. J. Arthur Rank joins the Odeon board.

Large screen television in use at the Marble Arch Pavilion.

Anthony Asquith's *Pygmalion*.

MGM's *Goodbye Mr Chips*.

Alexander Korda's *The Lion Has Wings*.

All cinemas temporarily closed at the outbreak of war. Government policy reported to be abandoning British studio production during the war and leaving the cinemas entirely dependent on American films. More than half British studio capacity immediately requisitioned for non-cinematograph uses.

The Films Division of the Central Office of Information set up.

1940   British feature-film production falls to fifty-six this year and remains in the region of sixty throughout the war.

The 49th Parallel completed.

Harry Watt's *London Can Take It*.

Humphrey Jennings's *Fires Were Started*.

1941   John Maxwell and Oscar Deutsch die. J. Arthur Rank becomes chairman of Gaumont-British and also of Odeon Cinemas. Warner Brothers acquire substantial holding in ABPC.

British Film Producers' Association founded.

At the peak of enemy bombing, cinemas in London and in some other large towns close at 7 p.m.

Jack Beddington makes British propaganda films more effective. Harry Watt's *Target for Tonight* (August) is seen by fifty million people, including large numbers in North and South America.

Army Film Unit is active in producing training and other films.

Thorold Dickinson's *Gaslight*.

1942 Del Guidice becomes leading impresario in British film industry.

Noël Coward's *In Which We Serve*.

Thorold Dickinson's *The Next of Kin*.

Charles Frend's *The Foreman Went to France*.

Leslie Howard's *The First of the Few*.

Michael Powell's *One of Our Aircraft is Missing*.

Carol Reed's *The Young Mr Pitt*.

1943 C. M. Woolf dies and Leslie Howard is killed by enemy action.

Charles Frend's *San Demetrio, London*.

Leslie Howard's *The Gentle Sex*.

Frank Launder and Sidney Gilliat's *Millions Like Us*.

Harry Watt's *Nine Men*.

1944 Production of British entertainment films begins to break away from Government requirements.

The Rank Organization now owns 619 cinemas and ABPC 442 cinemas. John Davis joins the board of J. Arthur Rank's investment company.

The Palache Committee appointed to examine the degree of monopoly operating in the industry. It recommends the creation of a film finance corporation, particularly to meet the needs of small and other independent producers.

Alexander Korda resumes production in Great Britain with *Perfect Strangers*.

Leslie Arliss's *The Man in Grey*.

Anthony Asquith's *The Way to the Stars*.

David Lean's *Blithe Spirit*.

Sir Laurence Olivier's *Henry V*.

Michael Powell and Emeric Pressburger's *The Life and Death of Colonel Blimp*.

Carol Reed's *The Way Ahead*.

1945 Weekly attendances rise to thirty million (1939, nineteen million).

Total number of cinemas destroyed in this country by enemy action stated to have been 330.

Gabriel Pascal makes *Caesar and Cleopatra* (described as

the most expensive film ever produced in Great Britain).

Leslie Arliss's *The Wicked Lady*.

Compton Bennett's *The Seventh Veil*.

Roy Boulting's *Burma Victory*.

David Lean's *Brief Encounter*.

Michael Powell and Emeric Pressburger's *I Know Where I'm Going*.

1946   The boom continues and weekly attendances rise to thirty-five million.

John Davis appointed managing director of the Rank Organization.

London Films acquire control of the British Lion Film Corporation.

First Royal Film Performance held.

British Film Academy formed.

David Lean's *Great Expectations*.

1947   Dalton Duty imposed on imported films. American companies refuse to pay the 75 per cent *ad valorem* duty and declare an embargo on all film exports to Great Britain. The Government call on British film-makers to produce many more films to fill the gap.

In November the Rank Organization makes its disastrous decision to respond to this appeal and announces a £9 million production programme. Odeon Theatres become the parent company to administer this undertaking. The Odeon and Gaumont-British circuits, although remaining separate, are brought together under the Circuits Management Association (CMA).

Alexander Korda buys the Shepperton studios.

Total number of British feature-films in production stated to be 170.

Association of Specialized Film Producers formed.

First Edinburgh Film Festival.

Carol Reed's *Odd Man Out*.

1948   A new Cinematograph Films Act raises the Exhibitors' Quota from 20 to 45 per cent. The National Film Finance Corporation is set up.

Alexander Korda's British Lion Film Corporation granted a loan of £2 million (later increased to £3 million).

The dispute with Hollywood is settled. An Anglo-American Film Agreement is signed permitting the American companies to take 17 million dollars out of this country each year and allowing them to make investments in Great Britain.

No restraint is placed on the release of the held-up supply of American films which flood this country just when the new British films are being released.

In October, J. Arthur Rank tells his shareholders that the company is considerably in the red and might have to give up production altogether.

Several of the Rank Organization's leading directors join Alexander Korda.

The rebuilt ABPC studios at Elstree are opened.

The Nettlefold Studios at Walton-on-Thames come back into production.

Carol Reed's *The Fallen Idol*.

Sir Laurence Olivier's *Hamlet*.

Powell and Pressburger's *The Red Shoes*.

1949   'The year when things went wrong.'

Box-office returns begin to fall.

Number of people employed in the studios falls from 7,700 to 4,400.

The Rank Organization sells the Shepherd's Bush Studios to the BBC for conversion into television studios.

Lights permitted in cinema façades after ten-year black-out.

Gater Work Party Report on film production costs.

Plant Committee Report on film distribution and exhibition.

Feature films made on the 'independent frame' principle.

Ealing comedies very popular—Henry Cornelius's *Passport to Pimlico*, Robert Hamer's *Kind Hearts and Coronets* and Alexander MacKendrick's *Whisky Galore*.

Carol Reed's *The Third Man*.

1950   The British Film Production Fund established to subsidize British film-makers through the Eady Levy. It is expected to add £3 million annually to the film producers' earnings.

Anglo-American Film Agreement revised.

'Let's Go to the Pictures' campaign opens to check fall in attendances.

Basil Dearden's *The Blue Lamp*.

1951   Second Stage of the Eady Plan. Separate groups formed to deal with the Rank Organization and with ABPC. Group 3 formed to make second-feature films.

The Festival of Britain Telekinema at the South Bank demonstrates three-dimensional films, large-screen television, and stereophonic sound.

Wheare Report on *Children in the Cinema* issued.

Children's Film Foundation formed.

Denham Studios are closed.

Charles Crichton's *The Lavender Hill Mob*.
Alexander MacKendrick's *The Man in the White Suit*.
John Boulting's *The Magic Box*.

1952 Crown Film Unit wound up.
British Board of Film Censors introduces the X category.
The panoramic film successfully established commercially.
David Lean's *The Sound Barrier*.

1953 Two films about the Coronation are shown throughout the world—Rank's *A Queen is Crowned* and AB-Pathe's *Elizabeth is Queen*.
Cinematograph industry organizes a 'Better Business' campaign.
Henry Cornelius's *Genevieve*.
Charles Frend's *The Cruel Sea*.
John Huston's *The African Queen*.

1954 The loss is announced of much of British Lion's share capital, as well as most of the £3 million loan from the National Film Finance Corporation.
David Lean's *Hobson's Choice*.
Betty Box's *Doctor in the House*.

1955 All-industry entertainments tax abolition committee formed.
Sir Laurence Olivier's *Richard III*.
Michael Anderson's *The Dam Busters*.
Carol Reed's *A Kid for Two Farthings*.
Halas and Batchelor's *Animal Farm*.

1956 Rank Organization announces the closure of 79 cinemas.
Sir Michael Balcon sells Ealing Studios to BBC television and enters into a new agreement with MGM.
Alexander MacKendrick's *The Lady Killers*.
Leslie Gilbert's *Reach for the Sky*.
Jack Lee's *A Town Like Alice*.
John Huston's *Moby Dick*.

1957 Attendances at British cinemas are now falling at a rate of 17 per cent annually.
Statisticians estimate that each television licence represents a cumulative loss of approximately one hundred cinema attendances each year.
ABPC announces the closure of sixty-five cinemas.
A new Cinematograph Films Act makes the British Film Production Fund a statutory agency. Its life is extended to 1967, as is also that of the National Film Finance Corporation.
Federation of British Film Makers founded.

The first London Film Festival held in the National Film Theatre.

J. Lee Thompson's *Woman in a Dressing Gown*.

David Lean's *The Bridge on the River Kwai*.

Charlie Chaplin's *The King in New York*.

1958   One-quarter of the country's cinemas being run at a loss.

Film Industry Defence Organization (FIDO) formed.

The National Film Finance Corporation states that only fourteen likely to make a profit out of the thirty-three feature films they have recently helped to finance.

Leslie Norman's *Dunkirk*.

J. Lee Thompson's *Ice Cold in Alex*.

Mark Robson's *The Inn of the Sixth Happiness*.

1959   Attendances continue to fall ($11\frac{1}{2}$ million weekly—less than one-third of a decade ago) but studios are busier than for several years—partly making films for television.

Sir Michael Balcon forms a new group, Bryanston Films.

Basil Dearden's *Sapphire*.

Jack Clayton's *Room at the Top*.

Tony Richardson's *Look Back in Anger*.

Boulting Brothers' *I'm All Right, Jack*.

1960   Number of cinemas still open in Great Britain, 2,819 (Rank, 372, ABPC 266).

The tendency is for films to become longer and to be shown at separate performances.

The Entertainments Duty is abolished.

Karel Reisz's *Saturday Night and Sunday Morning*.

Guy Green's *The Angry Silence*.

Ken Hughes's *The Trials of Oscar Wilde*.

1961   Considerable decline in cinema attendances now reported from the Continent.

J. Lee Thompson's *The Guns of Navarone*.

Tony Richardson's *A Taste of Honey*.

1962   Lord Rank retires.

Proposals made for distributing Eady Money on a new basis.

Complaints are renewed about the circuits' booking influence frustrating creatively adventurous directors and demands are made for the restoration of a third circuit.

Number of British Quota feature films falls to seventy-one.

John Davis puts a realistic budget for a totally British production at £250,000 to £400,000.

David Lean's *Lawrence of Arabia*.

John Schlesinger's *A Kind of Loving*.

CHAPTER ONE

The Inventors

••

THE WONDERFUL NEW MAGIC LANTERN

Victorians liked optical illusions, and resourceful mechanicians devised ingenious and often elaborate toys to entertain them. Some utilized a phenomenon known as persistence of vision, or 'after sensation'. If a series of drawings of, say, a running animal is put inside a slotted drum and then viewed through one of the slots while the cylinder is rotated, the images merge and a solitary figure appears to be moving. The eye holds the impression of one drawing until the impression of the next drawing almost instantly replaces it. Towards the end of the century cinematography was founded on this simple phenomenon of persistence of vision.

In the meantime other technicians recognized that these toys, in spite of all the originality that went into their preparation, had limited possibilities. So they turned their attention to magic lanterns (which go back to the 1600s and perhaps earlier). But all they could do was manipulate the glass slides by levers, gears or frictional devices so as to introduce elementary but actual movements into the pictures on the screen.

Decades passed without anything noteworthy being accomplished and most Western countries could submit lists of men who strove persistently to find a way of animating photographs, but who did not hit on any practicable process and are now virtually forgotten.

The 'break through' began in the late 1880s when an American, George Eastman, of Kodak, substituted sensitized celluloid film for the emulsified glass plates (and transparent papers) then used for negatives. He had not been thinking in terms of cinematography, but of transferring ordinary (but expensive) photography into a popular hobby. 'You press the button. We do the rest.' But his roll of flexible celluloid film made it possible for action photographs to be taken at a rate of 12, 16 or even 20 a second. The hopes of a century of skilled and unskilled inventors were about to be realized.

On June 21, 1889, a British studio photographer, William Friese-Greene, took out a patent which covered several basic principles of cinematography. He envisaged the film going through the projector with an intermittent movement, each frame being held in front of the illuminant for a brief period. A shutter would mask the change-over while the following frame was taking its place, thus allowing the impression of each picture to be retained momentarily in the spectator's eye through 'persistence of vision', until the next picture was flashed on the screen. An illusion of continuous movement would be created.

Friese-Greene's autobiography has been written by Miss Ray Allister, and plaques have been placed on various buildings with which his name was linked. A feature film about his life and works was sponsored, as described in Chapter Twenty, by the British cinematograph industry as their contribution to the 1951 Festival of Britain. Even more recently his name was included in the list of great British inventors, featured at the United Kingdom Pavilion at the Brussels International Exposition of 1958. He was described in the way he liked, as the inventor of cinematography.

His name is little known, however, outside this country. If mentioned at all, it is simply as one of many men whose imagination was stirred by the introduction of the flexible celluloid film, and whose endeavours to invent a practicable cinematograph camera or projector came virtually to naught. Raymond Spottiswoode has expressed the current assessment of Friese-Greene's achievements in an article written for the British Film Academy's *Journal*. 'Friese-Greene,' he said, 'did not originate any of the major ideas of cinematography, though he was much ahead of his time in grasping the possibilities of the motion picture and in working strenuously if lamely towards their accomplishment.'

In two respects he was indubitably a pioneer. He designed one of the first cameras and projectors to use the new film (which he obtained, incidentally, not from George Eastman's company but from a Birmingham manufacturer). Also there can be no question that he did shoot a film in Hyde Park in 1889 showing a man and a boy walking. Whether he succeeded in projecting it, as he claimed, on a screen at 20 Brooke Street, Holborn, is less certain; engineers who have since examined his projector, now a museum piece, have detected deficiencies which, they say, would have prevented the film being shown at the rate of even twelve pictures a second needed to give an illusion of motion.

Friese-Greene died in the Connaught Rooms, in London, on May 5, 1921, at a meeting when British film representatives were discussing the ills afflicting their industry. Lord Beaverbrook, who

1. An historic photograph showing Birt Acres filming the 1895 Derby.

R. W. Paul in his open-air studio at Southgate in 1902.

2. During the First World War Alma Taylor was almost unique among British stars in maintaining her position against the highly publicized American stars. She appears in this Hepworth film (*Cobweb*, 1916) with Henry Edwards and Stewart Rome.

An example of the labelled stills widely distributed in the 1920s. It is from *Fox Farm*, directed by George Pearson in 1922. The players are Ivy Duke and Guy Newall.

RGE CLARK PICTURES L™
NEWALL PRODUCTION
CONTROLLED BY
F STOLL FILM C° L™

FOX FA
BY
WARWICK D

had substantial film interests, was in the chair. A decrepit old man dropped dead while delivering an impassioned speech. After his identity had been established, it was inevitable that his claims should be recalled in the press. Perhaps it was inevitable too that they should not be critically examined. So he inadvertently contrived by the manner of his death to achieve posthumously the recognition and fame that had eluded him.

In the early 1890s Thomas Alva Edison along with his associates invented and manufactured the Kinetoscope. Improving the phonograph (the gramophone) had been Edison's dominant concern. It was the ear rather than the eye that interested him. He gave some thought to ways of combining a gramophone with a projector to show living pictures, but left much of the development to a brilliant British assistant, William Kennedy Laurie Dickson.* They proceeded to design, not as might have been expected, a cinematograph projector, but the Kinetoscope, a cabinet of the peep-show type for films lasting little more than a minute. And so those rows of machines came into being which enabled frequenters of amusement palaces and promenade piers to relish edifying subjects titled *What the Butler Saw, The Night of the Honeymoon,* and *Milady in Her Boudoir*.

Kinetoscope Parlours were first established in New York and their success with a particular clientele led to many others being opened throughout the United States and Europe. By 1893 the machines were being turned out in quantity and a motion picture studio, 'the Black Maria', the first in the world, was set up by the Edison Company to produce more and more Kinetoscope films.

Eventually Edison had to join forces with Thomas Armat, and to make a cinematograph projector, the Vitascope. But they were late (*April 23, 1896*) in projecting films for the first time on a large screen in a place of entertainment—Koster and Bial's Music Hall in New York. By then they had a competitor inside the United States, American Bioscope, on their heels at the Olympia Music Hall, also in New York. It was in Europe, however, that they were left well behind.

The American peep-show machines had been dissected by troubled English, French and German inventors, who had been making less headway than they had sanguinely expected in producing a workable film projector. They found in these machines the solutions to several baffling problems. And they were particularly pleased that the

* The University of California has recently published *The Edison Motion Picture Myth*, which gives 'belated credit to the work done by W. K. L. Dickson'. It is unusual for an American book in recognizing some of Friese-Greene's claims.

C

Edison Company had thought so little of the machines, and of their wider applications, as to be surprisingly negligent in covering them with patents.

THE MEMORABLE WINTER OF 1895-96

The rivalry that has grown up between various countries claiming première place in founding the cinematograph industry has led to comparisons being made between the dates when films were first shown successfully in recognized places of entertainment in capital cities to paying audiences. This is, incidentally, the only satisfactory way in which such comparisons can be made, because the performances were recorded in newspapers and can be verified. Every inventor showed his films to his friends and to others before facing the public, but there is little point in disputing when they did so.

The first to show films commercially were probably the Germans, Max and Emil Skladanowski. This they did in the largest Berlin music hall, the Winter Garden, on *November 1, 1895*. The films for their 'Bioskop' were brief recordings of vaudeville acts. Early in the following year Oskar Messker, whom the Germans regard as the pioneer of cinematography, manufactured projectors incorporating a Maltese Cross mechanism for holding each frame of film briefly at the projector's aperture. In 1897 he built what is claimed as the first studio in which films were made *under artificial light*. And in doing this he might be thought to have inaugurated the practice of making narrative films entirely with studio-built sets, which still characterizes the German cinematograph industry.

Two Frenchmen, Louis and Auguste Lumière, had the distinction of showing films commercially for the first time in Paris (in a café in Boulevard des Capucines on *December 28, 1895*), and in London in a hall in the Regent Street Polytechnic (now occupied by the Cameo-Poly Cinema) on *February 25, 1896*. A point of interest is that, while the sixtieth anniversary of cinematography in the British Isles was honoured in 1956, the French chose 1949, so recognizing Charles Reynaud's beautiful Théâtre Optique at the 1889 Paris World Exhibition. But, while there is appreciation of Reynaud's amazing achievement in using rolls inside the rotating drums in his Praxin-scope containing no fewer than 700 hand-drawn pictures, and incorporating subtly placed mirrors to heighten his effects, nevertheless this was not true cinematography. French historians now accept Louis Lumière as having shown their first moving photographs commercially. He was, incidentally, responsible for the term *cinematograph*.

The Lumières were, by trade, manufacturers of photographic apparatus and materials. The development during the 1890s of photography as a popular pastime brought them as well as George Eastman prosperity and, as patentees of the use of silver bromide emulsion in photography, they benefited materially from royalty payments. Accordingly, they were well placed in the early 1890s to employ able young mechanically-minded scientists to work with them in constructing a practical cinematograph projector. Their patents included the clawing device for moving the film through the projector intermittently but rapidly, frame by frame. Some of Lumière's apprentices rose to be leading men in the French film industry and preserved the Lumière tradition long after the pioneers had themselves faded into the background.

The first British inventor who should be mentioned is Birt Acres (1852-1918), an optical instrument maker, born in Virginia of English parents. Acres constructed a light hand-cranked camera very different from Edison's massive, battery-charged affair. He claimed, apparently with justification, to have been the first manufacturer of portable apparatus for taking cinematograph films in everyday life. He filmed the Oxford and Cambridge boat race as early as the spring of 1895, this being the first time a cinematograph recording was made of a topical news item. He was invited to Germany where he photographed the opening of the Kiel Canal, a military review by the Kaiser, and a charge of Uhlans—all this in 1895 and several months, it should be noted, before the Skladanowskis demonstrated their Bioskop in the Winter Palace.

Like others he encountered more difficulties in devising a projector than a camera, but he made sufficient progress in this year to give a display to the people of Hadley Highstone in Hertfordshire, where his studio was located, and this is commemorated there by a wall plaque. The interest thus aroused led to his being asked to exhibit it during August 1895, before larger audiences in the Assembly Rooms at New Barnet. On January 14, 1896, he demonstrated his camera and projector in London to the Royal Photographic Society, and on July 30th of that year he gave a command performance at Marlborough House to the Prince of Wales, who suggested that the name of his apparatus should be changed from Kineopticon to Cinematoscope.

The man whom the 'veterans' of the British film industry almost invariably mentioned in post-prandial discourses was, however, Robert W. Paul (1869-1943). He too was an instrument maker, his workrooms being in Hatton Garden. On learning that Edison's Kinetoscope was only loosely covered by patents he decided to construct peep-show machines along the same lines. His display of fifteen of his own products at an Earls Court Exhibition in 1895 attracted much attention, and he is said to have been inundated with orders, which presumably he was able to execute because he was already on his way to becoming a wealthy man. However, the real value to him of these contrivances lay simply in the opportunities provided for finding out how to make a workable cinematograph projector.

The relationship between Birt Acres and Robert Paul was not easy. The British Film Institute possesses a copy of an article, written many years later for a photographers' magazine about Paul's contribution to cinematography, on which Acres scribbled such comments as piffle, a lie, and I defy them to prove it. There seems little doubt that Paul did learn much from Acres about the industry, but subsequently he went his own way—successfully from his point of view and acceptably from the point of view of the many showmen groping their way into the new business.

No mention of Friese-Greene was made in this controversy between Great Britain's two pioneers. Perhaps they would have been startled had they known who was going to get the notices in the decades to come.

An odd aspect of the controversy is that neither was aware of the advances being made by European inventors. This may well have been true also of these Continental engineers among themselves. Indeed, the common link between them all seems to have been that each had peered into the workings of Edison's Kinetoscope. The Lumières' first exhibition of their apparatus had been in Lyons on March 22, 1895, and their first performance in Paris, as already mentioned, on December 28, 1895. But when they gave their first display in the Regent Street Polytechnic two months later, Acres expressed astonishment. He had not realized that they had made so much progress. Paul was taken aback too, admitting that 'the Lumière results are at present superior in clearness and steadiness to my own'.

Birt Acres's first display to the Royal Photographic Society (in January) was already past. Paul's first display (in Finsbury Technical College) almost coincided with the Lumières' in the Royal Polytechnic. A period of frenzied effort followed, as each man strove to modify his apparatus according to the lessons he had learned while watching the Lumière projectors in operation. They were both clever engineers and soon British projectors could be claimed to be as good as those made anywhere else.

ROBERT W. PAUL, THE UNIVERSAL SUPPLIER

The Lumière programme received so much approbation that it was transferred to the Empire Music Hall, as a sideshow in the Smoking

Lounge. This stimulated the managements of other central London music halls, notoriously sensitive to their competitors' innovations, to substitute a few minutes of films for one of the lesser supporting acts. Both Birt Acres and Robert Paul were hastily summoned and so far as the latter was concerned the consequences were far reaching.

His own apparatus was considered sufficiently developed for his first commercial show to be held in the Olympia on *March 25, 1896*. The subjects included *Rough Seas at Dover* and *An Indian War Dance*. It was the Alhambra that snapped him up and an early honour came his way when the Prince of Wales (Edward VII) arrived at the theatre to see the film of Persimmon winning the Derby. It was shown on the night of the race—an early indication of Paul's ability as an organizer. His contract with the Alhambra was for two weeks, but his films were so liked that he stayed for four years.

Music halls throughout the country treated the cinematograph as transient and, in modern idiom, as a stunt. Its place in the vaudeville theatres was retained by purveying topical films which were used to bring performances to their end and to disperse audiences. So the cinema first established itself in places of entertainment by substituting for trick cyclists, performing dogs and Asiatic tumblers.

Paul had, however, other associations with the Alhambra besides replenishing its stock of newsreels. His wife was a member of the theatre's ballet and the management, being well disposed towards them, allowed Paul to use the theatre's roof as an open-air studio. There he made many brief story films, with his wife and some theatrical friends in the cast. His first narrative film was *The Soldier's Courtship*. It ran for little more than one minute. The Alhambra itself sometimes showed these story films as well as his news films, and, finding that there was a growing market, he was encouraged to build a small studio at Southgate, where his company continued to produce films for over a decade. The list of his films contains eighty-two titles. Most had a topical character, but some included items from the acts of leading variety stars, such as the conjurors Maskelyne and Devant, and Chirgwin the White-Eyed Kaffir. As the years passed he tended to concentrate more on comedy films.

THE FIRST 'OPUS', QUEEN VICTORIA'S PROCESSION

It was the commercial success of a topical film, however, which led the British film industry to surge forward with a vigour unmatched elsewhere in the world, with the possible exception of France. The event that gave the British industry such a magnificent start was the colourful and spectacular Jubilee procession. Almost all British owners of moving picture cameras came to London for the day, which was gloriously sunny, and contributed various sections of a film record of the occasion. Continental and American cinematographers had never attempted anything on such a scale and were accordingly slower in getting off their mark. In particular the British film-makers were encouraged to think of making films out-of-doors, of news and interest films, which in the course of time became actuality, realist and documentary films. This is the only branch of cinematography in which the British have consistently distinguished themselves. And it can be traced all the way back to Queen Victoria.

In the following months—and years—the film of the procession was shown in every town and village in the country. Although the Lumière programme had already been shown in most large towns during the latter half of 1896, and although films had already been incorporated in a fair number of music hall programmes, most people, and particularly the young, had not seen the wonderful new magic lantern and the animated photographs until this film came to their town. Then they turned out in tens of thousands.

CHAPTER TWO

A Showman's Industry

....

The audiences' attitude to the animated pictures was of amazement at the remarkable new scientific marvel. Having seen it, however, many felt no particular desire to see it again, unless something else as important as the procession came along. By the end of the century some music halls had stopped showing films; and those who retained them must have been in two minds about doing so.

This was less discouraging than it might seem. Patrons of vaudeville were scarcely the most likely people to be entertained by moving pictures—as they had demonstrated by hurrying out when the news film was shown. Support was coming from other quarters—from fairground showmen and from travelling entertainers who toured with small companies of four or five artistes and hired 'one-night stances' in villages and halls. These were the purchasers of the equipment Robert Paul and others were making and of the films they were producing.

Father P. R. Greville, who has taken a beneficent interest in showland folk, recalled some of the men whose services in founding cinema entertainment in this country have not in his view received sufficient recognition. The forerunner was Randall Williams, proprietor of a ghost illusion act. In the spring of 1896 he found himself at the first film *trade* show in Great Britain, held in 'a little basement near Charing Cross'. Chancing his arm he bought several films and changed his entertainment to a Living Picture Exhibition, using electric light from the beginning. Before the end of 1896 some fairground people had gone over entirely to 'biograph shows', while others were showing films as part of their performances.

The decoration of the mobile outfits was often ornate, and the booths could seat up to 800 people. Equipment costing as much as £8,000 was transported, the trailer engine which could pull 35 tons being used to generate the electricity. A brighter picture was thrown than at their competitors' concerts *cum* films in village halls. At some fairs in the early years of this century no fewer than twenty cinematograph presentations were being made simultaneously.

The doormen and ushers at the entrances enjoined the public to walk this way, to see with their own eyes the fabulous wonder of the ages. No expense spared. Roars of laughter. Never a dull moment. So a practice was established among members of the industry for relying on garishly extravagant broadsides, and for eschewing restraint in their announcements. Perhaps they have not really changed very much since.

Apart from these fairground and travelling showmen others early in the business were small-time impresarios, usually concert artistes almost desperately wanting to settle down in one place. They had booked halls to show the Queen Victoria film and were searching for other films with which to repeat their success. However, a surprisingly large number of the pioneers were—as their obituary notices tend to emphasize—working lads not previously connected with show business. In keeping with Victorian and Edwardian determination to get on by working hard, they hired local halls and put on regular Saturday afternoon and evening film shows. Organizations devoted to social reform warmly approved of these ventures which kept kiddies off the streets and provided adults with 'an alternative to the pub'. Some shows did so well that their hopeful sponsors booked the halls for Friday evenings too, and eventually for all other evenings. This enabled them to give up their other jobs and to devote all of their time to running their cinemas—which often involved them in selling the tickets, printing and posting the bills, maintaining order in the audience and acting as deputy operator.

In effect the public halls became the first cinemas. An odd aspect was that many of them were owned by the municipalities, possibly having been built with funds provided in the past by an open-handed local worthy. Changing conditions had turned them into white-elephants; and the lessees were able to convert them into cinemas on condition that the premises remained available for such occasions as school prizegivings and Band-of-Hope gatherings.

THE EARLY FILM PRODUCERS

Some of these pioneers later formed the society of 'Cinema Veterans' and when they held a reunion dinner in the Holborn Restaurant in December 1924 they invited Paul to be chairman. He had been out of the picture industry for a long time and was back at his old business of instrument making and repairing, at which he was also very successful—he left a large sum for scientific research. Possibly as a reaction to the publicity occasioned by Friese-Greene's death three years before in the neighbouring Connaught Rooms, several tributes were paid by the Veterans to Paul as the ever-helpful supplier of their equipment and of their films in the bygone days.

Paul's contribution to the evolution of the British film industry has never been adequately assessed. This can be said, however. He was incontestably the principal figure during its first decade. Essentially he was a mechanical engineer, and he is credited with having made several improvements to projectors, particularly to the 'gate' which stands between the film and the illuminant. By greatly reducing the risk of the film catching fire—as the Frenchman, Léon Gaumont, was to do even more effectively a couple of years afterwards—he made public exhibitions of cinematography more acceptable to the authorities. Building and equipping his studio, making the camera mobile by putting it on a trolley mounted on wheels, devising trick effects, installing artificial lighting so as to be independent of sunlight variations, such were the matters with which Paul was engrossed.

Circumstances required him to become a wholesaler, a film producer and a business man too. As a supplier of projectors and accessories and as a film distributor he was exceptionally able, and it was in these capacities that the Veterans were grateful to him. His contributions to the evolution of the art of cinematography, and even to its practical techniques, were on a lesser plane.

His narrative films that have survived—a list of titles is given in the National Film Archive's catalogue—are commonplace. He had little talent for film directing, and did no more than meet a demand. At first, while the novelty aspect was predominant, his customers wanted to buy all of his films. But they were (or had become) practical showmen and, when they turned more selective and more determined to get what they wanted, the differences between their outlook and his became increasingly apparent. According to some reports he was finding the stresses and the turmoils of the industry irksome by 1904 and was reverting to his scientific instrument making business in Hatton Garden. His company continued to produce and to distribute films, however, until 1910 when an expensive trick film, on which much had been spent, called *The Butterfly,* failed. Then the company went out of existence as an independent organization.

Apart from Paul the best known British film-makers at the turn of the century were members of the 'Brighton School'. They were regarded as sufficiently distinguished for Georges Sadoul to devote a chapter to them in his *Histoire d'Un Art, le Cinema.*

A portrait photographer, Esme Collings, former partner of Friese-Greene, established the school, and Friese-Greene—then living at Brighton—took some minor interest in it. G. A. Smith was another member, and when Princess Margaret opened the National Film Theatre in 1957 he represented the industry's pioneers. He was in his nineties.

The leading member was James Williamson (1855-1933), a chemist who in 1897 turned his hand to film-making. Within a few years he was producing fifty films annually—an impressive figure although, as Rachel Low observed, most were brief and quite undistinguished. His *Two Naughty Boys* series of films was written, produced, developed, printed and sold by himself with comparatively little assistance from anyone else. The boys were his own sons. He acted in the film himself.

How much merit, if any, these productions had is a subject for debate. They would not be awarded many marks at a modern amateur film festival—the absence of a planned scenario, the flimsy story, the reluctance to retake unsatisfactory shots, the boorish acting would be condemned out of hand. The quality of the photography might come in for greater consideration—the 'flicker' at early cinematograph shows originated in the projector not in the film—but the absence of camera movement and the restriction to mid-distance shots would not be liked.

Paul, Smith and Williamson became film-makers almost by chance. They seized an opportunity which more capable show people had not noticed, or at least heeded. The exhibitors who bought their films knew more than they did about entertaining the public, but their outlook was not far removed from that of 'catchpenny' fairground purveyors, and they allowed two Frenchmen to become the predominant figures in this country almost to the same extent as in their native country. They were Léon Gaumont and Charles Pathé, the only two names from the early days of cinematography still familiar to the British public.

Léon Gaumont was an electrical engineer who came into the business early by marketing apparatus devised by Jules Marey and Georges Démeny. He perfected a fireproof projector incorporating the spool boxes in the machine, and on this the fortunes of his company were founded. He opened a London office in the late 1890s in Cecil Court—the industry's first centre and then known as Flicker Alley. The names of the men he engaged as his manager and his assistant manager crop up often, Col. A. C. Bromhead (1877-1963) and Thomas Welsh. They persuaded him to sponsor film-making at Loughborough Junction as well as in France, and so they themselves became more than just distributors of other people's products.

Charles Pathé and his brother Emile were the agents in Paris for Edison's phonograph, and hence benefited from transatlantic connections. While visiting London they bought some of Robert Paul's equipment and, sensing its possibilities, were able by their enterprise and drive to secure financial support far exceeding anything that the British pioneers ever seemed likely to raise. After engaging Ferdinand Zecca as director and building the famous studios at Vincennes, Charles Pathé set up production units in Great Britain, the United States, Italy, Germany, Russia and Japan. By 1908 Pathé Frères were selling twice as many films in the United States as all the American companies combined.

In assessing the merits of the British contribution to cinematography during the early years one fundamental admission must be made. We produced no director of the same stature as the Frenchman, Georges Méliès. As proprietor of a conjuror's sideshow in Paris he had been attracted by the Lumières' first performance. Here, it seemed, was greater magic than he had ever practised. For a brief period he worked with Louis Lumière, but then hived off. In 1897 he built at Montreuil the first film studio in the world to have glass walls and a glass roof, as well as a movable stage on which several different sets could be erected. It was so well designed that it continued in use for thirty years.

Méliès specialized in films of fantasy and, apart from some farcical little sketches, chose his themes from fairy and other imaginative tales. In his *Cinderella,* produced in 1899, he made the first serious attempt to tell a story by film. Even today audiences that have gathered to scoff at early 'primitive' films change their tune when a Méliès' production appears on the screen. They find themselves laughing at it, just as their grandparents (and great-grandparents) did long, long ago.

His great innovation was the use of elaborately painted film sets. His weakness was that he could not get away from them. His outlook was essentially theatrical and this partly explains why, to quote Georges Sadoul, the English music halls immediately absorbed all his output and continued to be his best clients.

Most British producers, including Paul, copied him, sometimes quite effectively. His range was, however, limited and when his satiated audience asked for something fresh he had nothing to offer. In this respect the Brighton School held an advantage because they made their films about real people, set against real backgrounds (usually in the open air). But not only did we lack a man of Méliès's ability, we did not find a Ferdinand Zecca, who understood perhaps better than anyone else the tastes of the uneducated people who composed the audiences in the early cinemas. Zecca went in for the sentimental and sensational potted melodramas to be found in abundance in cheap magazines and novels, and for rowdy farces with lots of elementary fun. Charles Pathé gave him powerful financial support and he responded by making the Pathe company the most important in the world.

French historians praise Zecca's acumen but have little regard for his creative attainments. As Georges Sadoul says, he was mainly instrumental in freeing the cinema from the theatrical prison house in which Méliès had confined it. But his liking for sensational and emotional plots has left its mark on the French cinema, perhaps for all time.

PROGRAMMES TO SUIT ALL TASTES

In spite of the inadequacies the British film-making and film exhibition, London became the principal film distributing centre in the world. Perhaps this reflected London's commercial standing at the beginning of the century—the City simply took this new trading venture in its stride—rather than any exceptional enterprise evinced by the early British film distributors.

Most of the films came from British or French studios, but other European countries contributed their quota, particularly Denmark, Germany and Italy. The United States was bedevilled by litigation (and by threatened litigation) between its leading companies, and made a comparatively minor contribution at this stage. The first films had been short and could almost be described as actuality films. But something more was now called for than shots of people walking in streets, of trains leaving stations, of waves breaking on the shore, or indeed of anything that had come in handy.

Audiences were no longer reacting to the pictures on the screen as if they were being projected from a 'magic' lantern for their instruction and edification. They were becoming engrossed in the action to a much greater degree than at a play in a melodrama house—no proscenium, no curtains, no footlights were interposed between them and the players. The vividness, the visual realism, enabled them to be absorbed as they never could be even when reading a Charles Garvice novel.

Programmes were composed of a mixed bag of seven or eight one-reel films. A considerable improvement in the content of actuality films helped them to retain their place, even after 1906. Themes were being given some preliminary consideration. Shots in travel and nature study films were being selected and in some respects interpreted.

The topicals, shown in music halls after remarkable feats of developing and printing done with primitive equipment in next to no time, were organized by London-based companies and became regular features, changed once or twice a week. (Pathe Gazette began in

1910.) Many of the early topicals had long lives. They eventually found their way to the fairground booths, where they might be shown as 'interest' films a couple of years after the particular event had passed. For more than half a century newsreels formed an indispensable item in every cinema programme and were supplanted only after being taken over by the television services and given greater topicality and indeed immediacy than could possibly be achieved in the cinema.

The first comedies often had no more than one scene and were just episodes lifted from the knock-about 'sketches' then popular in music halls and in concert-party shows. Plots were elementary. If a director chanced on a fresh idea that proved popular, others just copied it. Plagiarism was, as Birt Acres had indignantly protested, accepted as part of the business.

In the course of a few years techniques improved and comedies were expanded to incorporate three or four scenes, suitably linked together. An unsophisticated tale might be told; but the primary concern was with misadventure and catastrophe, which were played for 'belly laughs'. Rachel Low and Roger Manvel commented on the low order of many of the jokes. Infirmity, even blindness, was ridiculed. Marital strife was fun, drunkenness a scream. Physical cruelty was accepted without question, as it still is in American cartoon films. The larks of young scamps were regular stock-in-trade, and, if they led to a man losing his trousers or a woman her skirt, the enjoyment could be ecstatic.

Some directors continued to make comic films in the Méliès manner. They dabbled in double exposures and reversals. They increased or decreased the speed, and interrupted the shooting so that funny men could be conveyed instantaneously from one side of a room to another. Transparent spirits materialized to scare people out of their wits. Grotesque characters found themselves decapitated with their heads grinning at them from across the room. These trick films had their place in the music halls rather than in the cinema, and after 1906 they lost their popularity. People went to the pictures because they were so true to life. Extravaganza was not what they wanted, except as an occasional divertissement.

Few dramatic stories were told in the early days of cinematography. Films that ran only for a few minutes did not allow plots to be developed. That is perhaps why *The Great Train Robbery*, made by Edwin S. Porter in the United States for the Edison Company in 1903, has such an important place in the evolution of cinematography. It ran for about ten minutes, had an original Western-bandit story which was told by means of more than a dozen scenes, neatly joined together. While it was not, as is sometimes said, the first film that told a story, the cinema as a medium of entertainment, as distinct from an ephemeral fairground sideshow, was ushered in by that American film.

CHAPTER THREE

The People's Storyteller

A new class of people was coming into being, picturegoers. At first they were drawn from the untutored and the unenlightened, including the young. They liked the cinema's way of narrating stories. They did not have to read—except occasional subtitles—or even to listen, except almost unconsciously to the background music. Without being called upon to use their imaginations they could watch the incidents being portrayed and identify themselves with one of the characters. It was all so vividly real. They could even fall for the heroine or succumb to the hero's blandishments.

Just as the first comedy films stemmed from music hall sketches, so the first story films had their beginnings in the melodrama houses. Romances had to be brought to the happy fulfilment—or to the pathetic dénouement—without padding and within a few minutes. They were aptly described in the advertisements as 'bits of real life'. The cinema had become the storyteller of the people.

The first picture houses would be known to the trade today as industrial halls. They provided an 'unsophisticated public with low-priced entertainment'. But in 1906 there was a new development, minor in itself but major in consequences. An enterprise of American origin, Hale's Tours, was established in rented shops in most of the large towns. The premises were made up to look like a railway carriage, the spectators gazing through the windows at scenic films.

THE BIJOUS AND THE PICTURE PALACES

Hale's Tours soon lost their novelty, but they heralded the conversion of numerous small shops, as well as roller-skating rinks and garages, into cinemas. These new places of entertainment rarely seated more than 300. They had a continuous programme (changed twice weekly) of nice films, lasting for about seventy-five minutes. Prices of admission were threepence and sixpence.

Their sponsors were local businessmen out to make quick profits. They were better educated and better off than the fairground showmen and travelling entertainers who had steered the industry through its first years. It seemed essential to them (and to their wives) that their picture theatres should be accepted by the middle-classes as respectable. So they chose genteel names such as Bijou, De Luxe, Elite, Gem and Salon, and emphasized the cosiness of the accommodation and the refinements of their clientele.

Not only was everything in the best of taste, it was in the best of odour too, scented disinfectant being sprayed into the air at regular intervals, to the mortification of any fleas that had been brought into the premises. Silent films always needed a background of sound—if for no other reason than to conceal the missing component—and a trio might be engaged to provide mellifluous music. To encourage matrons to patronize the shows, every visitor in the afternoon to the sixpenny portion of the hall was served, entirely free of charge, a refreshing cup of tea and a delectable biscuit.

These cinemas created out of shops did not have a long run, however, although some still survive as news or cartoon theatres. Their seating capacity was too small to cope with the industry's next major development, when the introduction of feature films doubled the length of the shows. Meeting the cost of programmes lasting $2\frac{1}{2}$ hours, or more, was quite beyond their capability. And so, in 1909 and 1910, the first picture palaces came into being. They were larger and conceived in extravagant rather than sedate style, lavishly and even exotically decorated, with spacious vestibules, marble staircases, palm courts and tea lounges (in some cinemas patrons could consume a meal while watching the show). Many became their district's communal centre, especially for the younger generations, in a sense that the owners of local theatres and music halls would have thought impossible.

Although the Bijou cinemas soon became archaic, the local and industrial halls leased by those ambitious working lads could hold large enough audiences for showing the new kind of programme quite economically, especially if padding with third-rate vaudeville turns was discarded. Now their owners followed the example set by the proprietors of the smart new picture palaces. They raised the wherewithal to paint and reseat the halls, so that without gross exaggeration these too could be called palatial.

These halls, as well as the Bijous and the picture palaces, had been financed locally. But big business, always on the alert, had sensed that the cinematograph industry was paying good dividends, and had development possibilities. The first 'circuits', or chains of cinemas, were formed as early as 1907 (Electric Theatres) and 1908 (Biograph Theatres). But the most important of the pre-First World War circuits did not come into being until 1909. It was PCT (Pro-

3. Betty Balfour became the most popular British star of the early 1920s after she had created the character Squibs, a Cockney flower-seller, for George Pearson. Her father was played by Huntly Wright.

Betty Compson, photographed at East Grinstead, in *Woman to Woman*, the most successful British film at the box-offices in this period.

4. It was in 1926 that Alfred Hitchcock first impressed the British public with his murder mystery film, *The Lodger*, featuring Ivor Novello and June.

Walter Forde, who was to become one of G.B.'s leading directors, was for a brief period this country's outstanding comedian. Here he is seen in *Would You Believe It?*, set in a toy store, and released in 1929, just before the 'talkie era'. It broke the box-office record at the Tivoli, in the Strand, with a run of sixteen weeks.

vincial Cinematograph Theatres), whose policy was to open cinemas in all towns with a population of over a quarter of a million. Operations in certain smaller towns were to be undertaken by a subsidiary, Associated Provincial Picture Houses.

When war broke out, and temporarily brought further expansion to an end, there were 109 circuits in Great Britain. They embraced between 15 and 20 per cent of the cinemas, although a considerably higher proportion of the larger halls. The number of cinemas in the country when the war began in 1914 cannot be stated precisely because the records cover many 'marginal' village and other halls where films were shown only occasionally, possibly merely as supporting items in concert programmes. But the total was in the region of 3,000 to 4,000, and the number of people employed by the exhibiting side of the industry (that is to say, excluding those engaged in making or in distributing films) had risen to 75,000.

Distributing films was also on its way to becoming a substantial business. The first travelling showmen had been content to buy some films and to fit them into programmes that they repeated many times. When cinemas came into being programmes had to be changed more often. Companies were formed to operate exchanges where films were resold, second-hand and third-hand, to lesser and lesser cinema proprietors. One of these companies was established by William Jury who was later to the first member of the industry to be knighted. This system could not keep pace, however, with the rapidly increasing number of cinemas, and in 1908 the hiring (or renting) of films for a few days began. This was a development of considerable significance because it was the frequency with which programmes could be changed that enabled the cinema to become the people's storyteller. Col. A. C. Bromhead, of Gaumont, is credited with having made the system more business-like by establishing booking by contract and later exclusive booking at higher rates to particular cinemas.

THE DEVIL'S NEW PLAYHOUSE

Out of interminable wranglings, dissensions and divisions a compact industry was emerging which has in essentials changed little since. Civic and other authorities who had at first been well-disposed towards the cinema, seeing it as a haven for lonely and unhappy people, were having second thoughts. The fairly exacting regulations drawn up for theatres and music halls were not being applied to cinemas (except when performers appeared on the stage), and the same kind of tolerant attitude had been adopted towards picture shows as was customarily taken towards village halls and fairground booths.

D

However, when cinemas in some towns, including London, opened their doors on Sundays, arguing that there was nothing in the regulations to prevent their doing so, they stirred up much opposition, and not merely from the churchgoing sections of the community. The London County Council reproachfully called the cinema proprietors' attention to an old regulation requiring every public place in which music was used as part of an entertainment to be licensed by the Council. The alternative was being treated as a disorderly house.

Cinemas could not do without music, now quite an essential accompaniment for a film show; so perspicaciously they applied for their licences. Stiff conditions were laid down and accepted, but the exhibitors did succeed in their main object, to keep open on Sundays. Other local authorities followed suit. The bye-laws that were drawn up varied widely, and the lack of conformity became confusing and exasperating. But when the industry's leaders complained about 'official interference' they got scant sympathy.

Principally responsible for this rebuff was growing concern about the content of some recent films. In Victorian melodramas the villain respected the heroine's innocence and plotted so that she would marry him. His outlook seemed to be different in the cinema. Most of these productions that have survived and can be seen today are innocuous; but part of the criticism was directed against the lurid posters being displayed outside the cinemas—flaunted before their very eyes, some non-picturegoing critics said—rather than against the films themselves. The demand for Government censorship became insistent.

Many crime and detective films were being produced. Young scallawags when apprehended and brought before the beak realized that, by admitting guilt and pleading that they had 'seen it done at the pictures', they might be exonerated with an expression of hope about coming under better influences in the future. Head teachers took this cue and admonished pupils sufficiently indiscreet to be observed leaving these disreputable haunts. The cinema was taking over the theatre's reputation of a century before, the Devil's Playhouse.

The Western films now being turned out in prodigious quantities in the United States also came in for devastating criticism, alarm being expressed about the possibly harmful effects on boys, and on girls, of playing at cowboys and Indians, and pretending to kill one another. Even greater apprehension was expressed, however, about the perils to which adolescents were exposed when marital problems were unfolded before them. Indeed, it was reported that Latin looseness of morals was establishing itself in the cinema to the extent of showing shameless actors and actresses scantily clad and even naked.

In yet another respect too the cinema was alarming self-elected custodians of the younger generation's moral standards. They were hearing, as such people contrive to do, about 'goings-on' in the back stalls. It is perhaps a diverting thought that many men and women now grandparents did their courting at the pictures. Students of social conditions made no impression with their rejoinders that most of the young people came from cramped 'working-class houses' and could have gone to worse places.

THE FIRST CINEMATOGRAPH FILMS ACT

The cinema trade recognized that restraints were coming and welcomed the (first) Cinematograph Films Act when it became law in January 1910. They called it the Showman's Charter, supposing that, having had an Act of Parliament all to themselves, they were accepted as respectable. This was a delusion.

On some points they had been particularly sensitive on their own accord—for instance, fire risks. Most people in the industry knew how carelessly inflammable film had been handled in the past. Sometimes it had coiled around an operator's feet while he was standing at his projector in a hall filled with children. Disasters had occurred in other countries; it was largely by good fortune that there had been none in Great Britain.

The trade assumed that the Act's provisions for public safety would be applied in this direction, to fireproof projection boxes, location of exits, adequate staffing, better ventilation and the like. It was dismayed to learn that the term 'public safety' could be interpreted to embrace public well-being—and that local authorities, with their new powers, had the right to approve and even to censor programmes.

In such circumstances the various sections of the trade might have been expected to close their ranks. But the schisms went deep. The fundamental issue was simply which of the three main trade groups was to have ascendancy—the producers who made the films, the businessmen (the renters) who marketed them, or the cinema proprietors who showed them. It still troubles relationships, but issues over which there was much squabbling in the past have little meaning today. Many arose out of the distributors' former practice of selling prints outright to exhibitors (and thus losing control of them). Threats of boycotts and counter-boycotts were made on several occasions, and at times carried out, usually ineffectively.

Another cause of resentment in the years after 1906 was the

increasingly large number of foreign films coming into this country. Hence, for instance, the uproar which followed an announcement by Charles Pathé that he would in future hire his films direct to British exhibitors at cut rates and without benefit to intermediaries. The odd thing is that the makers and distributors of British films went around complaining, without realizing that better films were wanted from them.

The days of doing things on the cheap (or, at least, on the very cheap) were passing, although as late as 1912 the average cost to the owners of the Bijou type of cinema of hiring films for a week could be as little as £12, with the average weekly wage bill not much higher.

The first of the three groups to form an association was the film makers. This was in 1907 when the Kinematograph Film Makers' Association (KMA) was created. Its immediate purpose was to resist Charles Pathé in his designs for flooding this country with his films. The original Association of Film Renters followed in 1910. And, after the Cinematograph Trade Protection Society and the Cinematograph Defence League had both had an innings, the Cinematograph Exhibitors' Association (CEA) was constituted in 1912 (It will be noted that the industry has always been divided on the use of *C* or *K*.) Soon afterwards the operators' original trade union was established. It won a minimum wage with an agreed six-day week, and had a register of qualified projectionists accepted by the employers.

The controversy over censorship was settled in typically British fashion. The Government was disinclined to set up a Board of Censors; but it was prepared to be sympathetic if the trade set up a Board, the Censor and his deputies being men in whom the Government (and the Civil Service) had confidence. And so G. A. Radford, a reader of plays for twenty years under the Lord Chamberlain, was appointed the Board's President. (He was succeeded in 1917 by T. P. O'Connor, the journalist.) In spite of some controversies the arrangement can be said to have worked admirably for half a century. The Board's original categories—U for Universal and A for Adults—were generally accepted throughout the industry, and were not altered until the 1950s.

IN THE DOLDRUMS

It would be agreeable at this stage to select for particular mention some outstanding comedy or dramatic films from the earlier crop (pre-1907). But unfortunately, if topical and other actuality films are excluded, there is little left for viewing. As one who has gone through several hoards of very old films, seeking suitable subjects for the National Film Archive, I am perhaps particularly sensitive on this subject. Films that have survived are of little merit. Directors of the Robert Paul era failed to make the transition from amateurism to professionalism. It would seem the British pre-eminence in the opening years of this century had been a matter of quantity not quality.

Little advance can be discerned in the technical and artistic qualities of the British films of 1908 over those of 1903. The British industry's complacency was not duplicated, however, in the United States. In 1909 some of the principal American film-makers agreed to stop bedevilling themselves with internecine disputes about patent rights. Thomas Edison used his authoritative position to bring together the representatives of the leading companies claiming major patents affecting the photographing, developing and printing of motion pictures. They decided to acknowledge each other's claims and to establish a Motion Picture Patents Company. Eight American firms, with Pathé and Méliès of France, formed this Company, which gives incidentally a positive indication of how Americans assessed the contributions made by other countries, including Great Britain, to the development of cinematography.

An attempt was then made to set up a monopoly intended with cool effrontery to be enforced not only in the United States and France but elsewhere including Great Britain. Here, indeed, was a challenge. The attempt failed not because of the sturdiness of British resistance, but because two American companies left out of the consortium fought so determinedly in the law courts as well as in the studios that eventually a truce was declared.

The American industry celebrated its new freedom by leaping forward with furious activity. The British industry, bereft of leadership and inspiration, virtually collapsed (for the first but by no means last time).

CHARLES URBAN'S FACTUAL FILMS

A considerable proportion of the films exported from this country in the Edwardian era were factual films. London was a more conveniently located base than New York from which to dispatch camera units to take scenic shots for travel films. And, as the world's history was still being made in Europe rather than elsewhere, London was perhaps the best jumping-off place for men who might be called upon to photograph a State occasion in Austria, a skirmish in the Balkans, a boxing match in France, or a volcanic eruption in Italy.

The cinema's champions in those far-off days used to dwell on the inestimable importance to posterity of preserving visual accounts of these occurrences. However, no one in the industry felt it his personal responsibility to undertake any of the preserving, and some of us feel a little bitter about this. Having seen the excellent films made from newsreel negatives kept in Paris archives, we are sensitive about having to assemble comparable British films from odd bits of film whose survival was mainly due to chance.

The man with the finest record in Great Britain at this time was actually an American, Charles Urban, and an admirable representative of the transatlantic businessmen who settled in Great Britain in the 1890s and 1900s, before the days of dollar-inferiority.

Charles Urban would not have claimed to be more than an enterprising businessman who took the opportunities that came his way. But his taste was considerably better than that of some people he encountered in the British cinema industry. He had come to London to manage the agency for Edison films. Envisaging greater possibilities he formed his own distributing company, the Warwick Trading Company, and then left it in 1903 to form another trading company under his own name.

He organized and financed the filming of topical and travel items throughout the world, partly by units dispatched on special assignments, but partly also by his local correspondents. Perhaps, however, his outstanding achievement was in sponsoring the production of scientific films. In this his name is linked with that of F. Martin Duncan, later Librarian of the Zoological Society, who made a pioneering series of animal studies for him, but more particularly with that of Percy Smith (1880-1944), who resigned a Board of Education appointment to join him. Percy Smith said that he first conceived the idea of making films after going into a Hale's Tours cinema in the Strand. By using microscopes and speeded-up photography he produced a series of minutely detailed observations of plant life, called *The World Before Your Eyes*. Two of the fifty-four films which he directed before the First World War were widely shown, the speeded-up *Birth of a Flower*, and *Gladioli* which was shot in Kinemacolor. Another British pioneer in making zoological films was Oliver G. Pike, who supplied his films principally to James Williamson and later to Pathé. No fewer than one hundred copies were sold of his film, *Birdland*.

The best remembered British factual film of this period is Herbert G. Ponting's record of the *Scott Antarctic Expedition*. Made in 1911, for Louis Gaumont, it ran for 90 minutes, and was regarded as the brilliant successor to a somewhat nondescript film of Shackleton's Antarctic expedition shot a couple of years before. Another film of the period was Cherry Kearton's account of *Teddy Roosevelt's Big Game Expedition in Africa*. And there was also Charles Urban's own Kinemacolor account of the *1910 Delhi*

Durbar, a film that is almost as vividly remembered as Queen Victoria's Procession was by an older generation.

Cherry Kearton and his brother Richard were probably the best known British producers of actuality films a little later, in the years immediately preceding the First World War. They spent several years travelling in Asia and Africa—and in North and South America—and came back from time to time to their studio at Clapham where they assembled their shots into 'travelogues'—a term which they adopted although it did not originate with them.

CHAPTER FOUR

Hepworth, Barker
and Jupp

··

Towards the end of the Robert Paul era two new directors attracted some notice. One, Walter Haggar, was a former fairground showman whose *The Salmon Poachers* became the best seller (480 prints) of the period. It was a chance success and its popularity was partly due to an unorthodox twist in its plot. Two poachers are caught by the police and the story is sympathetically concerned with their escape from justice.

Haggar made other countryside films which were well received, but he could not be compared as a film producer with Cecil Hepworth, whose *Rescued by Rover*, a chase film, sold 400 copies. A child is stolen from a perambulator by a beggar-woman and traced by the family dog. The cast was composed of Hepworth's wife and daughter and two hired actors. The film has been shown many times in recent years and its precise editing and sense of movement have been praised as showing 'the beginning of modern film technique'.

CAME THE DAWN

Cecil Hepworth (1874-1953) was only five years younger than Robert Paul, but he seems to belong to another age. In his autobiography, *Came the Dawn*, published in 1951, he gave a characteristically modest account of his rôle during the industry's formative years. He was the designer of the projection arc lamp used by Birt Acres at his command performance in Marlborough House. After an early and not particularly happy association with Robert Paul, he branched out on his own and set up a film printing unit. Then he built studios for himself at Walton-on-Thames and, having a greater flair for making pictures than any of his competitors, was soon turning out almost one hundred films a year.

His prospects looked splendid and yet, when the slump began, he gave up his production activities and opened an agency for distributing foreign films in Great Britain. Perhaps this was only too symptomatic of British industry as a whole in the later Edwardian years that ambitious and able young men should choose a soft living by selling foreign goods rather than engage in the arduous and certainly hazardous task of manufacturing. 'Foreign countries had got tired,' Hepworth said in his autobiography, 'of importing English films. Now they were making their own and unloading them on us instead; and the trouble was that many were better than ours.'

The new American tariff, intended to protect the revivified United States cinematograph industry, was taking a heavy toll of British films. Hepworth declared, however, that the consequences were ultimately beneficial. Citing himself as an example he said that seeing American films being shown in this country of better quality than he had ever attained incited him to try again; and in 1911 he directed *Rachel's Sin,* a social drama about a young woman who kills her drunken husband in self-defence, then allows her earlier suitor to take the blame, and to be imprisoned for seven years. Rachel was played by a young actress, Gladys Sylvani. The public liked her very much and she became the first British woman star. Not only was Hepworth encouraged to 'have another go', but so were others. The British industry was emerging from—to quote Rachel Low—'humiliating stagnation'.

RESURGENCE

By 1914, when war was declared, no fewer than thirty studios had been opened in this country. Their location in such districts as Ealing, Elstree, Twickenham and Merton Park shows that the industry was assuming its present shape. Some of the studios were in the north, in Manchester, Sheffield and Glasgow, but these were minor ventures. The industry was growing up around London. It was not breaking away and establishing a separate existence for itself, as was happening in the United States.

In spite of this apparently fine show of activity only three British companies could be said to have made their mark in these last years of the pre-First World War era. The companies are associated with the names of Hepworth, Barker and Jupp; but Rachel Low, in her review of this period, thought it possible to describe seven companies as having reached fair proportions (by the standards of the times). The other four she mentioned were: Cricks and Martin, who specialized in comedy films, often with trick effects; Clarendon, a company that supplied films to Gaumont and failed to live up to a promising beginning; B. and C. (British and Colonial); and Charles Urban's own company which was, however, losing some of its zest.

The three principal companies differed materially in outlook. Hepworth was all for middle-class respectability. His dislike of vulgarity and exaggeration prompted him to produce polite films. He set out 'to make English pictures with all the English countryside for background and with English atmosphere and English idiom throughout'. In particular he directed a series of jolly comedies featuring two fifteen-year-olds, Alma Taylor and Chrissie White, as the Tilly Tomboys. When they grew too old for romping he gave them leading parts in his feature films, and Alma Taylor was for several years the most popular British film actress. Through an associated company Hepworth helped in creating another star, Ivy Close, a former beauty contest winner. His extensive studio at Walton-on-Thames became well known, and was often rented by other companies who made their films there.

Will Barker was a volatile showman with expansive ideas. Having made his name as the quickest producer of topical films, he opened studios at Ealing and produced several spectacular films, the best known being *Sixty Years a Queen*. It is remarkable that the second major British film was, like the first, about Queen Victoria (and that twenty-five years later there was to be a third). Being lengthy it was shown at special performances in hired halls instead of cinemas (which was possibly anticipatory of things to come), and is said to have made a profit of £35,000. Shortly afterwards Barker persuaded Sir Herbert Beerbohm Tree to appear as Wolsey in a film about Henry VIII. His fee of £1,000 for 'five hours' ' work was given wide publicity. Not only did this impress on the public the growing importance of the cinema, but it also gave the cinema a new cachet. Expense was no object.

THE FIRST INTEGRATION

London Films were founded by the one really outstanding man to participate in film-making in this country during the years before the First World War. He was a North of England medical specialist, Dr Ralph Tennyson Jupp, managing director of the principal circuit PCT (Provincial Cinematograph Theatres). Service as a military doctor during the Boer War had ruined his health. During a prolonged period of convalescence in a small seaside town he often visited the local cinema and was disturbed over the poor hygienic conditions, particularly the inadequate ventilation. His idea was that every town with a population of over a quarter of a million people should be provided with a really first-class cinema seating 600 to 800. In 1909 he had created PCT with this aim in mind and became increasingly concerned in the worrying years that followed about the inroads continental feature films and American short films were making into the British market. In 1913 he formed London Films to produce British films, the first instance of 'integration' in this country—that is to say, the combination within one group of the functions of producer, distributor and exhibitor. His studios were at Twickenham. Significantly he turned to the United States not only for directors (Harold Shaw and George Loane Tucker) and for several senior technicians, but also for his principal actress, Edna Flugrath. However, recruits scenting easy money were now pouring in from the London theatre. They included the Shakespearean actor, Henry Ainley, who became as prominent a figure in the cinema as on the stage.

London Films' first production, *The House of Temperley*, was notably successful. At last a British studio was being operated professionally and with adequate financial backing. By contrast Cecil Hepworth was still serving not only as his own director but quite frequently as his own cameraman. That is not the way big businesses are built, and is an early indication of his limitations.

London Films were unique in devoting themselves solely to feature films. During the first years of the British industry's resurgence many more ten-minute and twenty-minute films were produced in this country than longer films. Most of them told adventure and comic stories designed to regale boys, and adults with boys' minds. The dare-devil heroes could have been borrowed from the penny magazines, and the drolls from *Puck, the Jester* and *Chips*, where the fun began with somebody's discomfiture and usually ended in a devastating chase.

The chivalrous Lieutenant Rose (for Clarendon at Croydon) and the courageous Lieutenant Daring (for B. & C. at East Finchley)— the latter played by Percy Moran, described as 'the first British star' —consistently outwitted insidious foreigners plotting against England's well-being. Folly Films made an amateurish film every week at Twickenham featuring a music hall buffoon, Fred Evans, as Pimple. He had previously acted for Cricks and Martin as Charlie Smiler. But the most perfervid patriot would not put him, 'the first British film comic', in the same class as the comedians coming into prominence elsewhere, such as John Bunny and Flora Finch, Eddie Lyons and Lee Moran, and Mr and Mrs Sidney Drew in the United States, or Max Linder in France.

SEARCHING FOR SOMETHING NEW

Some British inventors were still devoting much of their time to the cinematograph, trying particularly to improve the quality of the projection, where the principal weakness was supposed to lie. Cameras were clumsy things to handle but were technically sound and the standard of photography was remarkably good. Edison's desire to make pictures that talked had not been forgotten, and from time to time music hall stars, including Harry Lauder, appeared in singing films. None was successful, partly because operators were unable to synchronize sight with sound.

The variety of hand-tinted films, usually of French origin, shown around 1910 indicates that there was a public demand for coloured animated pictures. And some impressive progress was made by a group of technicians associated with G. A. Smith, of the Brighton School, in developing the two-colour process already mentioned, Kinemacolor. But litigation over patents followed and eventually Kinemacolor was virtually abandoned. Charles Urban's company, which had backed it financially, suffered disheartening losses.

Following Beerbohm Tree's example—and similarly enticed no doubt by high fees—many prominent players of the Edwardian theatre acted for the pictures. This now seems ill-advised. What, one wonders, did audiences in the 'industrial houses' make of Sir Johnston Forbes-Robertson and Sir Frank Benson in potted silent versions of Shakespearean plays? *Hamlet* was produced by Will Barker in twenty-two scenes, all shot in one day, except for the scene showing Ophelia floating in the water. Stock melodramas, *East Lynne, Maria Marten* and *The Lights of London*, would have been more to the taste of the bulk of the picturegoers of those times. But the British film industry—or, at least, a considerable proportion of it—was set on rising socially.

Unlike the American producers, who were creating not only their own stars but also their own scenario-writers, the controllers of the British studios rarely turned to original stories. No longer were they writing scripts on backs of envelopes. Now the preference was for plots of widely-read novels, abridged and adapted for the cinema; or (in the 1912-14 period) from a London stage play, curtailed and presented, mute, by the original cast.

LONDON AS HOLLYWOOD'S RIVAL

Those who believe that but for the First World War London would have been established as the centre of the world's film production make much of the interest shown by American producers after 1912 in London's possibilties. In a widely-publicized move, Florence Turner, at the height of her popularity as a Vitagraph star, deserted the United States and, with Larry Trimble as director, switched her film-making to London. And in May 1914, Edwin S. Porter, director of *The Great Train Robbery*, and Hugh Ford were sent by Adolph Zukor (of Famous Players) to set up a studio in London.

The war brought all these operations, actual and projected, to their end. With the intensification of the fighting in Europe the American film colony in London, including Charles Urban, broke up, and its members retreated to the United States—where most of them vanished into oblivion. It would have been better perhaps if they had stayed in London and risked the bombs. They still had a place here.

The outbreak of the war in August 1914 provides a definite dividing line between cinematography's first two evolutionary phases in Great Britain. By then, as Rachel Low has pointed out, the director had established his authoritative position in the studio. What he said, went. His was the creative mind. Films were being thought out beforehand. Scripts were being more carefully prepared. Cecil Hepworth spoke revealingly about this aspect in his autobiography. He said that a recent request for his views on 'editing silent films' had brought home to him that he had really known 'nothing whatever about editing. None of my films was edited. I had the view that the editing should be done in the original script.'

Cameramen were becoming creatively interested in their jobs and were experimenting—for instance, by photographing from unusual angles. They were moving their cameras about, and were taking close-ups to be interspersed between mid-distance and even long-distance shots (which incidentally enabled film actors to cut down their gesturing).

Only one thing was lacking. Money. The British finance houses still looked askance at the movie business. Consequently managing directors of film-making companies had to work on a shoe-string. They were doing things differently in the United States, and that is why, even if the war had not intervened, London could not have challenged Hollywood. Wall Street was film-minded. The City of London was not.

CHAPTER FIVE

Europe Goes to the War and America Goes to the Pictures

....

While the First World War was in progress American manufacturers established a pre-eminent position in several industries. And in the years that followed the British people found to their concern that the United States were becoming their principal supplier of many things, from automobiles and typewriters to safety razors and some canned foodstuffs.

It was in the entertainment field, however, that the situation became calamitous. The composers of the delightful pre-war vaudeville ditties were swamped by the tuneful outpourings of Tin Pan Alley. The queens of English musical comedy, in their element just before the war, were sent packing by hoydenish Nanettes, Rose Maries, Sunnys and Mercenary Marys. In the music hall, that most English of institutions, top-billing was going to American acts.

The exigency was even worse in the cinema. Before 1914 Dr Jupp and the other leaders of the British film industry had the sympathetic support of their fellow countrymen, in resisting American attempts to supplant them. But by 1918, before the war ended, the public, and particularly the frequenters of the popular halls, had turned against British pictures. They had developed a taste for American films and managers found that to advertise a production as British meant a drop in the box-office takings.

Furthermore, Great Britain had become the most 'film-minded' country in the world, except for the United States itself. During the war the proportion of cinemagoers in the population had risen, partly because picture houses provided the public with an escape from the anxieties, the upsets and the tediums of the war. Few exhibitors, except perhaps owners of self-operated cinemas in out-of-the-way places, had cause in the 1914-18 period to grumble about their earnings. The upward trend continued after the war ended. Going to the cinema had become a national habit.

But virtually all the feature films British picturegoers saw were American. Not only British films, but French, Italian, Danish and other continental films, which had supplied agreeable variety in pre-war programmes, had vanished in the reek of war. Uncle Sam had emerged as the sole provider, and he had created a 'star system' that did much to ensure the continuance of his monopoly.

Newspapers echoed the politicians' fear that this would be injurious to British commercial interests abroad. The Stars and Stripes was being waved in every part of the world, spreading a notion of United States' omnipotence. The benefits that American export industries have derived from this impression are incalculable.

HEPWORTH AND BARKER, WITHOUT JUPP, IN WARTIME

There was little indication of these coming misfortunes, however, during the first years of the war. Indeed, Rachel Low has pointed out that the list of British directors increased to fifty names, and that 500 narrative films were produced during the war years. Most were short, and included many one-reel and two-reel comedies, but feature films were proportionately higher in number than in the 1912-14 period. Some were of only 30 minutes' duration, the intention being to fit them into programmes with longer films. But by 1916 the import of American films into this country was so considerable that the double-feature programme had already put in an appearance.

Of the principal British companies at the beginning of the war, founded by Hepworth, Barker and Jupp, only Hepworth's carried on throughout the four years. At first he had as his second director Larry Trimble, the American who came to this country to make Florence Turner's films. Although her company went out of business, she appeared in some of Hepworth's films herself, until eventually she decided, with Trimble, to make her way back home. Trimble's place was taken by Henry Edwards (1882-1952), and he continued to direct British films—usually in a rather minor capacity—throughout his life. He specialized in tender sentiment, fey rather than mawkish, and often played the hero in his own stories. Alma Taylor and Chrissie White remained the most popular British stars.

In common with the rest Hepworth used adaptations of well-known plays and novels, rarely original stories. Indeed, that list of 500 titles reads like a conglomeration of all the plays which might have been staged by repertory theatres of the day and of all the novels most often borrowed from public libraries. American producers at this time were making far greater use of original plots and were turning to lesser known novels and to current magazine stories.

The most often recalled of Hepworth's wartime films are perhaps those based on Albert Chevalier's *My Old Dutch,* Thomas Hardy's *Far from the Madding Crowd,* Arnold Bennett's *The Great Adventure* and Sir Arthur Pinero's *Sweet Lavender.* Early in the war Tom Bentley made his best Dickens film for Hepworth, *Barnaby Rudge.* Hepworth, who was not lacking in business acumen, built up a fine team of players, including Stewart Rome and Lionelle Howard, and used the film magazines systematically to popularize them. His studios at Walton-on-Thames were well equipped and Rachel Low has paid tribute to his films, 'excellent photographic quality, beautiful exteriors, restrained acting and unsensational stories'.

The largest studios in the country were still, however, those erected by London Films at St. Margarets, Twickenham, where eight sets could be handled simultaneously. This company, with their fine installations, their capable company of directors, technicians and players, their substantial financial backing, and their youthful vigour and enthusiasm, might have been expected to flourish, as did the new American companies, such as Paramount, Fox, Metro and Goldwyn.

This did not happen and the cinema trade was greatly exercised with reports on what was going wrong. As early as 1915 rumours were spreading that London Films were making heavy losses. At first these stories were discredited. Companies being run on a shoe-string are apt to speak unkindly of others with money to spend. By the end of 1916, however, London Films were virtually out of business (at least, for the duration of the war) and the Twickenham Studios were being leased to other companies. By this time several of the smaller studios were regarded as obsolete, and a feature of the war period was the hiring of large studios by their owners to others who optimistically thought they were capable of making better use of them.

The explanation of London Films' decline was the loss of Dr Ralph Jupp's personal drive through recurrent illness. In 1916 he withdrew altogether and two years later disposed of his financial interest in the company, so as to make it easier for new blood to attempt resuscitation. One of his two American directors, Harold Shaw, left him early in the war and his transatlantic team broke up. But its most capable member, George Loane Tucker, stayed on. Rachel Low describes him as a masterly producer with a prodigious capacity for work. In the latter stages he acted as managing director and toiled hard to save something from the wreck. But it was too much for him, and he went home to become one of Hollywood's leading directors.

So the misfortune cannot be laid at Tucker's door. Undoubtedly there had been wastefulness in London Films' studio but, after scanning the titles of the company's films, it might seem that better subjects could have been chosen to appeal to the cinemagoers of the period.

Will Barker was very different in temperament from either Hepworth or Jupp. He was, in fact, a well-to-do commercial traveller. As an amateur photographer he began making films in 1900 with a Lumière camera at Stamford Hill. With his bouncing personality he had many of the characteristics of the showman of the old school. Finding it easy to sell his films he bought the 3½-acre West Lodge estate at Ealing in 1902. Adapting the Lodge itself as his office (as Ealing Studios were to do again much later) he shot his films in the grounds during the hours of sunlight. But in 1907 he built a stage on 'greenhouse principles', and had added two additional stages by the outbreak of the war. Continuing to do well, particularly with elementary crime stories, he boasted that he was always able to finance his ventures by himself.

Apart from *Sixty Years a Queen*, the film with which his name will always be associated is *Jane Shore*, produced in 1915. Impressed by the spectacular qualities of D. W. Griffiths's *Birth of a Nation* he decided to produce a big picture with an immense cast. It was the most ambitious film made in the British Isles until comparatively recent years. Barker transported 5,000 people to Devil's Dyke in Sussex for three days while he shot episodes in the Battle of Marston Moor. He encountered unexpected problems in handling them and his approach to the situation is revealing. He paid the local public houses to close during the three days and, the local authorities having declined to detach members from their police force to maintain order, he dressed up twelve actors as policemen—the pretence being undetected, they played their rôles with a fine show of authority.

Unfortunately *Jane Shore* was a cumbersome piece, incomprehensible in places to people lacking much (or any) knowledge of the Civil War period. Audiences found it boring and laughed at the over-acting. Many recruits from the stage were still unable to grasp that histrionic outbursts, acceptable perhaps to theatre audiences seated some way off and on the other side of the footlights, might seem ridiculous when magnified on the cinema screen. Cecil Hepworth has written entertainingly on this aspect, describing his difficulties in preventing these actors from smothering their faces with make-up.

American producers had perceived that the cinema's greatest asset lay in its capacity for achieving visual realism. An inexperienced

E

tyro behaving 'naturally' and doing precisely what the director told him could give a better interpretation in a film rôle than a practised actress clinging to her customary methods.

The leaders of the Hollywood industry did not think of the cinema as a substitute for the theatre. They wanted members of their audiences to feel that they were taking part in the action. Accordingly, players who showed off their talents disturbed and perhaps shattered this illusion.

American producers also kept their cameramen in check. Mention has already been made of their growing skill, but no whimsical experimenting was permitted—films were to be composed of long- and mid-distance shots blended with a few close-up shots photographed more or less straight on. The camera must never obtrude, because this would make the audience aware that it was looking at a motion picture. Within these limitations, however, Hollywood's cameramen became superbly efficient. Their compositions were imaginative, their lighting was bright and effective, their prints were scintillatingly clear. Perhaps insufficient allowance for their more professional air has been made by those who have tried to explain why American films supplanted British films during the war. Possibly it was the amateurish look of so many British films that audiences found disconcerting.

Like other British producers Barker was taking his stories from well-known novels and plays. Among his later films was a version of Rider Haggard's *She,* with Alice Delysia as the scantily-clad temptress who must be obeyed. The film broke box-office records when shown at the New Gallery Cinema in Regent Street, but was less well received in the 'industrial halls'. By 1918 Barker was conscious of having lost his touch. He retired but although elderly was still full of energy, and went on until the end of the Second World War supervising a Wimbledon factory where millions of prints were developed each year for amateur photographers.

Rachel Low rather chillily remarked that Barker, 'having neither artistic sincerity nor a flair for the kind of showmanship that was to flourish after 1918, had become increasingly out-of-date'. He certainly belonged to the past, but he had done his work well according to his lights. His contemporaries liked him. Indeed Hepworth—in almost every respect his antithesis—described him as 'a rough diamond, but nevertheless a diamond'.

What is puzzling about Barker, and about his cronies such as the gargantuan Bertie Samuelson, who regarded themselves as impenitent, down-to-earth realists, is their obtuseness in not realizing why American films were liked so much more than theirs.

Several anecdotes show that Barker was of much the same timbre as the Zukors, Foxes, Mayers and Laemmeles who were urging the American industry onwards at a fantastic pace. For instance, to make certain of procuring the film rights of the Bombardier Billy Wells-Jack Johnston fight, Barker outsmarted his rivals by promoting the fight himself (and, incidentally, losing £3,000 on it). This man, with more discerning advisers, could surely have made a greater contribution to British cinematography, not perhaps on a high plane but at least on a strictly commercial one, as Zecca had done for Pathé. But it is purposeless to speculate on how the British film-making industry might have fared if it had broken from the London theatre, as the Hollywood industry had broken—almost completely—from the New York theatre (the Biograph Studios in Manhattan, the Edison Studios in the Bronx and the Vitagraph Studios in Brooklyn all closed down during the war); and if, instead of cluttering the London suburbs with minute studios, two or three large studios had been built at places well away from Leicester Square, perhaps at Bristol or Aberdeen.

WORKING TOO HASTILY AND IN TOO SMALL A WAY

Col. Bromhead had ensured that Gaumont were the more active in Great Britain of the two French companies. Their studio at Shepherd's Bush was described as the 'first modern film studio in Great Britain'. It had four sets and in 1915 Gaumont opened even larger studios nearby at Lime Grove. For much of the war they were managed by Thomas Welsh (1871-1950), with George Pearson as chief film director. The latter—whose autobiography, *Flashback*, was published in 1957—became one of the most significant figures in the British film-making industry. The company's achievements during the war were slight—and for this George Pearson puts particular blame on the Government for calling up virtually all their young men. Gaumont of this period are remembered best for a series of films devised and directed by George Pearson about a heroic adventurer, *Ultus*, the man from the dead. Intended for 'the masses', the films originated with a suggestion made by Léon Gaumont while paying one of his periodic visits to this country. Possibly disappointed with the output of his London studios he wanted a British character invented comparable to Fantomas, a current favourite in France. In 1918 Thomas Welsh and George Pearson left Gaumont and founded their own company, all set to engage in the post-war struggle for the glittering prizes ahead.

Pathe did little in Great Britain during the war. They had left an underground studio they had constructed in Great Portland Street and were using the Alexandra Palace Studios of their associate

British producing company, Union Films, whose trade mark was Big Ben. These were requisitioned at the beginning of the war, to Charles Pathé's considerable annoyance, and later were badly damaged by fire. Such irritations made Charles Pathé even more critical than in the past of the British capacity to make films. Still the largest producer of films in the world—he had just had an overwhelming success in the United States where his studios had made *The Exploits of Elaine*—he described the British industry as backward. Its shortcomings were 'due to lack of enterprise. . . . There is no true continuity of effort among the producers. They work too hastily in too small a way.'

YEARS THE LOCUSTS DEVOURED

During the war several young men came to the fore and were thought likely to make their mark. But, except for George Pearson, they did not live up to their early promise. Cecil Hepworth shared George Pearson's view that the withdrawal of virtually all their male staff during the latter stages of the war wrecked their business. And for one reason or another they failed to come back in the American-dominated, intensely competitive, post-war cinematograph industry.

The most remarkable—and depressing—case is that of G. B. Samuelson, a renter from the sturdy and resolute Midlands capital, Birmingham. He had been associated with Barker in producing *Sixty Years a Queen*. Indeed, it was Samuelson who engaged Barker to produce the film and accordingly benefited most from its financial success. George Pearson in his autiobiography writes entertainingly about the young Samuelson. He was only twenty-six years old when he persuaded Pearson to leave the Pathe Studios at Alexandra Palace and to join him at his new studios at Hounslow. 'With his amazing enthusiasm and boundless energy his excitement regarding the venture was infectious.'

They began with Conan Doyle's *A Study in Scarlet*, but on that fateful evening of August 4, 1914, with London almost in a state of pandemonium, he swept everything on one side and spent the entire night in a room at Frascati's planning a film about the coming of the Great War, with actors representing the principal figures. 'He was in dead earnest, and to halt Samuelson when his imagination was alight was as hopeless as to stem Niagara.' A fortnight later the film *The Great European War* was trade-shown to a packed audience of film renters and buyers. Its success was immediate. But almost all other British producers were now on the same track, rushing out films about the war, and the public soon made it very clear to them that this was not at all the kind of entertainment needed in the prevailing trying circumstances.

When his year's contract with Samuelson had ended Pearson wrote to Gaumont seeking employment and he was engaged by Thomas Welsh as chief film director at the new Lime Grove Studio. Pearson says that, although he had been unable to live at Samuelson's frantic pace, and could not fit in with his quick-fire methods and inexhaustible impetuosity, he continued to admire him.

Samuelson, like Barker, did not assess public taste very highly—in 1914 he sponsored a serial about the highwayman, Deadwood Dick. But as the war continued he made his way through Charles Garvice, Ethel M. Dell and Marie Corelli stories to subjects more likely to appeal to middle-class audiences. In the mid-war period he produced adaptations of J. M. Barrie's *The Admirable Crichton*, Stanley Houghton's *Hindle Wakes*, Louise Alcott's *Little Women*, Mrs. Craik's *John Halifax, Gentleman,* Sidney Grundy's *A Pair of Spectacles,* Arnold Bennett's *Milestones* and Edward Knoblock's *My Lady's Dress*. He had prominent stage players in his casts too; yet none of these films is recalled today. He continued making films for several years after the war but without achieving any notable successes. Little more than thirty years ago he was regarded as one of the great hopes of the British film industry. Now most people in the industry, if asked about G. B. Samuelson, shake their heads. They have never heard of him.

B. & C. never recovered from the loss of their managing director, J. B. McDowell, when he went to the war as an official cinematographer. They hired their Walthamstow studios to other companies, one of their tenants being Maurice Elvey, perhaps the most consistently employed of all British directors in the history of the industry.

Others too who were busy during most of the war had by the mid-1920s faded from the scene. They had such little influence on the future of the British film industry that their various productions need not be recalled here. The largest of the companies was Broadwest, the first public film-making company to be registered since Ralph Jupp's London Films. However, their capital was only £50,000 (against London Film's £120,000) and this gives a fair indication of the feebleness of the British response to Hollywood's challenge.

Neptune Films, founded in 1914 by Percy Nash, one of Ralph Jupp's associates, are remembered principally because of their choice of Elstree for their studio.

Several other companies produced pictures in their own minute studios and in other companies' studios, notably Gaumont's at Lime Grove. Perhaps the charge is justified that they were ruined by the Government decision in 1917 to conscript all of their able-bodied young men. But by then the country had been disillusioned by the poor quality of most of the British films being shown in their local cinemas.

'ADAPTED FROM THE STAGE PLAY'

Anxious comments were made in Parliament about the high proportion of American films being shown in British cinemas. The renting companies, exasperated by their financial losses on some of these films, decided to take the matter into their own hands.

Some, such as Walturdaw, tried to help the smaller film-making companies (and some of the larger ones too) by getting their films shown more quickly (or less slowly). A year or more might pass after the completion of a film before it was seen by cinema audiences, and this strained the resources of the companies and their backers.

Others decided to go into production themselves. The best known was the Ideal Film Company, who leased London Films' studio at Twickenham. Whether they understood the American success story might be doubted from their decision to turn to the London theatre even more immoderately then some of the companies whose failures they were criticizing. This is exemplified in the titles of some of their films: Oscar Wilde's *Lady Windermere's Fan,* Arthur Pinero's *The Second Mrs Tanqueray* (with Sir George Alexander and Hilda Moore in the cast), Oliver Goldsmith's *The Vicar of Wakefield* (with Sir John Hare in the cast), Pinero's *The Gay Lord Quex* (directed by Maurice Elvey, with Ben Webster in the cast), *Her Greatest Performance* (with Ellen Terry in the cast), *The Lyons Mail* (with H. B. Irving in the cast), Jerome K. Jerome's *The Passing of the Third Floor Back* (with Sir Johnston Forbes-Robertson in the cast), and Tom Taylor's *Still Waters Run Deep* (with Lady Tree in the cast).

Ideal (of this war period) are best remembered probably for Charles Reade's *Masks and Faces,* produced by Fred Paul in 1917 in aid, with singular appropriateness, of the building fund for the Royal Academy of Dramatic Art. Many of the leading playwrights of the Edwardian era appeared in the prologue, and the cast was stiff with the principal actors and actresses of the day—Sir George Alexander, Sir J. Forbes-Robertson, Irene Vanbrugh, Gladys Cooper, Gerald du Maurier, Matheson Lang, Gertrude Elliot, Lilian Braithwaite, Charles Hawtrey and Ellaline Terriss.

The resentment which some of us feel towards the London theatre because of its considerable but condescending influence on British film-making during these vital years is not shared by everyone with personal memories of the period. Some defend the policy of adapting successful plays for the screen, pointing to its unquestioned advantages. The title is well known and this is useful for publicity and advertising. The book is available for modification by the script writers. The producer and director can watch the piece being acted on the stage and so can form a better impression of incidents to build up for the film (or to cut down). They can assess the suitability of the various actors and actresses from the cast. And so on . . . it is all so much easier and cheaper.

To others, such as myself, it seems that the whole approach, the 'mental set', is wrong, and the final product is an adapted stage play rather than a film.

This is, no doubt, controversial but on one point there is no dispute. Ideal's policy did not succeed, and by 1918 film-making had virtually collapsed in Great Britain. Cecil Hepworth has left an account of the principal men in the industry meeting from time to time and having little to do but to reminisce.

There was no optimism about the future—the prevailing mood during the perilous summer of 1918 could not have encouraged that. Furthermore, it was becoming known that in France Charles Pathé and Léon Gaumont both thought that the Americans had procured such a grip on the industry that they should break up their empires and sell the companies they had established in various countries during the pre-war years.

FILMING THE WAR

Only in one respect could the British cinematograph industry be said to have done well during the war. This was in the production of factual films. The beginning was far from good. In the autumn of 1914 old travel films were revised with new titles, such as Belgrade, home of the heroic Serbs, and Nice, our brave allies' playground. Short films were produced in the course of a few days about Daddy going to the war, a German spy being nabbed, and a Belgian boy outwitting his country's invaders. Amateurish films about the Royal Navy and the Army were rushed out with patriotic titles. Newsreels were in demand and considerable resentment was expressed in the early days of the war about cameramen being denied access to places they wanted to go to. Reports that things were being done differently in France went unheeded, but by January 1915 dismay was being expressed about the better quality of the war films the Germans were sending abroad as propaganda. It was then that the War Office called on the services of several able cameramen, such as Harold Jeapes, who had been associated with Cherry Kearton in assembling a twice-weekly newsreel called the *Whirlpool of War*, Geoffrey Malins, who had been a director at Esher with a small company called Master Films, and J. B. McDowell, already mentioned as the managing director of B. and C.

Originally some of these men worked exclusively for one newsreel company—for instance, Malins for Gaumont—but later photographing the war became a combined operation. This was achieved partly through the Cinematograph Trade Topical Committee which in October 1915 negotiated an agreement with the War Office giving cameramen adequate facilities at the front and, incidentally, diverting their royalties into military charities.

The first films sent home from France and Flanders were unsatisfactory nevertheless, and cinemas were disinclined to show them. They did provide, however, the framework for a film, *Britain Prepared*, which with the active help of Charles Urban was widely shown in the United States and elsewhere overseas. Then the War Office appointed a Cinematograph Committee, the trade being represented by William Jury, described by Rachel Low as a 'renter of the rough old school'. He was later knighted for his services.

By this time cameramen were really being made welcome, and the films they sent home were incorporated not only in newsreels but in longer films distributed without credits either to individual companies or to operators. In February 1917 a further development was made when the Department of Information was formed with a branch assigned to cinematography. The official adoption of films was completed in the summer of 1918—just a few months before the end of the war. This was when the Department of Information became a Ministry, with Lord Beaverbrook at its head. William Jury was appointed Director of its Cinematograph Department.

It is not commonly realized that D. W. Griffith's *Hearts of the World* was made in 1917 by agreement with the War Office Cinematograph Committee, and that later the Ministry engaged another famous Hollywood director, Herbert Brenon, to make a 'great national film'. It has never been seen because the end of the war brought the project to its end, although a considerable sum had been spent by then on its production. Brenon held a press conference before returning to the United States and said that he had found the studios well equipped. He forecast a bright future for British films.

The feature-length film most often recalled is *The Battle of the Somme*, shot in July 1916, principally by Malins and McDowell, and shown within a month throughout the country. It received no fewer than 2,000 bookings. Managers said that the queues were the longest they had ever known. In particular some shots of a tank moving across the battlefield aroused great excitement. The film's authenticity was unquestionable, and scenes of troops being shot down were criticized. Rachel Low quotes a Hammersmith exhibitor as advertising that the film would *not* be shown in his cinema. 'This is a place of amusement, not a chamber of horrors.' Possibly his attitude was more justified than was admitted at the time, because three later films, on the Battles of St. Quentin, Ancre and Arras, received progressively fewer bookings.

The films might seem rudimentary in comparison with those made in the Second World War, and the frequent interjection of sub-titles might be disturbing and irritating. Nevertheless they represented a notable advance in the production of factual films and they kept Great Britain well to the fore. A mass of material was accumulated, notably by the Royal Flying Corps, and some of it was later used, as mentioned in the next chapter, by Bruce Woolfe and others in preparing films about particular battles.

Several series of animated cartoons were distributed during the war years, the first British artists engaged in this work being Lancelot Speed, Anson Dyer, Dudley Buxton and G. E. Studdy. However, their drawings, principally of war subjects, were no more than 'lightning sketches', of a kind well known to music hall audiences of the period. Actual animation of the drawings was rarely attempted, and then only in elementary fashion. The modern cartoon film had its origin in an American series, Bud Fisher's *Mutt and Jeff*, which was not seen in Great Britain until later.

DEARER MOVIES

Within a few months of the outbreak of the war rumours were current about the Chancellor of Exchequer's intention to impose a tax on amusements—theatres, cinemas, football matches and racing. When it was known that the tax on the cheaper admission prices would be small—for instance, just one halfpenny on prices up to 2d —and much heavier on prices never heard of in the cinema business, there was a feeling of relief. The tax was clearly going to bear much more heavily on theatres than cinemas. However, this mood changed, especially later when the Chancellor proposed further increases all round. Now it was said that the tax was really hitting the small proprietor worst, and a demand was made for the tax to be dropped on admission prices up to 6d. The Chancellor revealed, however, that 80 per cent of the revenue brought in by the tax was actually coming from these cheap seats—an indication that a great many more people were going to the popular sections of the cinema than to the expensive sections of the theatre.

The taxation did, however, force cinemas to raise admission prices. The trade in Great Britain had been unable to rid itself of an obsession about the popularity of the cinemas in this country being primarily attributable to its cheapness. (Some perhaps still hold that view.) But Americans were now going to the pictures, not because they were less expensive than the theatre (in some instances they no longer were) but because the public liked the pictures better. The cinema had been brought up from the bargain basement.

Another factor leading to the rise in admission prices was the exhibition of grandiose films—*The Birth of a Nation* had been an early example—in theatres instead of in cinemas, and at theatre prices, not cinema prices. Many cinema owners condemned the practice, but it raised the status of the moving picture industry and encouraged these owners to look beyond threepence and sixpence. The last of the Bijous had to give way to the Majestics, dusty red plush to shiny white marble.

Rising costs were also responsible for the replacement, except in small towns, of twice-nightly shows (three on Saturdays) by continuous performances. Even after 1918 leading exhibitors frowned upon feature films that ran for an hour, or more, and some were still trying to persuade British producers to concentrate on films of only half that length.

Those who objected to showing long films at continuous performances maintained that British people would be most reluctant to look at the second half of a film before the first half. Robert Paul and the other pioneers could never have conceived that audiences would, in fact, do so. Nor would they have supposed that people might prefer to queue in pouring rain for an hour on a Saturday evening, rather than book seats beforehand for the 7 or 7.30 show at the neighbouring repertory theatre or music hall. The casual informality of the cinema apparently outweighed other considerations.

The Government was worried when the American hold on cinema entertainment became increasingly pronounced—chiefly perhaps because of the very large expenditure of dollars needed to bring the films into the country. A tax on imported foreign films—in effect on American films—was proposed as early as 1915, and during the war it was imposed on imported film stock too. These changes made virtually no impression, however, on the flow of American films into British cinemas. In 1917 Sidney Morgan, one of Britain's rising directors, suggested that all exhibitors should be required to show a stated proportion of British-made films, and much was to be heard of this scheme in the years to come. Morgan's proposal was that the quota should be one-third. Even the film-makers were divided on this issue, both Hepworth and Elvey arguing that, if British films could not survive by their own merits, they were better out of the way.

But in 1917 the United States entered the war and the subject was tactfully dropped. It was to come up again.

CHAPTER SIX

The Black November of 1924

....

Much of the bustle (and turmoil) of the Roaring Twenties emanated from the cinematograph industry, but British film-makers contributed little to the vociferation. Their listlessness in 1919 did not occasion much comment as they were known to have experienced many stresses and strains the previous year. But in 1920 considerable doubt was expressed in the *Kinematograph Year Book* about whether the producers were facing up to the post-war world with sufficient realism and determination. They were criticized for buying titles of plays and books, and authors' names. They were relying on 'hack scenarios', and were making cheapness their first consideration. They were not co-operating with one another.

Two of the trade associations (the exhibitors' and the renters') were described as reasonably stable; but the manufacturers' association (the KMA) had 'relapsed into its habitual somnolence, its existence almost forgotten except for the printing and accessories sections'. As it had been the first of the trade associations to be formed (in 1907) this was, indeed, a reflection of the change a dozen years had brought about in the British film industry's complexion.

For another couple of years the studios continued to jog along. Plenty of films of a sort were made, showing virtually no advance in construction, in technique, or in spirit. Reports were published from time to time of various British films being shown in Broadway cinemas, and of others, such as Hepworth's *Alf's Button*, delighting audiences in the Dominions. So the public was unprepared for a disclosure in 1922 that, out of no fewer than 420 British films (of all lengths and descriptions) recently offered for sale in the United States, only six had found buyers.

As if to rub salt in the wound the presentation of 'super' foreign films in major London theatres was under way, notably *The Four Horsemen of the Apocalypse*, which in December 1922 opened a run of 320 performances in the Palace Theatre. In knowledgeable circles, however, even greater interest was taken in a German film

Dubarry (renamed *Passion*) which had put in an appearance at the Scala Theatre. Directed by Ernest Lubitsch, it had Pola Negri in the title part. Few had heard of them in this country, but enterprising Americans had already whisked them away to Hollywood (as they subsequently did with most of the British cinema's promising recruits, particularly its actors).

Italian distributors, hoping to restore the position their country had gained before the war with spectacular films, presented *Theodora* at the Covent Garden Opera House; and then the Germans hired the Albert Hall for three weeks (and subsequently the Scala Theatre for a season) to show *The Nibelungs*. The better informed critics were greatly impressed by these films—particularly by Siegfried's fight with the dragon, which was more ingeniously contrived than anything attempted so far by Hollywood. Various alliances were formed between individuals in the British and German cinematograph industries, but some years passed before they had a marked influence on British production.

A more resolute effort to get British films shown in the United States was made in 1923. Paul Kimberley tried to form a half-million dollar company in Los Angeles to handle Hepworth's truly British films in the United States. But most British film-makers assumed that the only practical solution to their problem was to engage American stars, whose names would attract audiences not only in the United States but also in this country.

In November of this year, 1923, the Prince of Wales attended the inaugural luncheon in the Hotel Victoria of the British National Film League, under the presidency of Col. Bromhead. This body was formed to sponsor British Film Weeks in towns and villages during the coming year, 1924. Unfortunately, in spite of much banging of drums and many declarations of goodwill, the venture ended in disappointment. Insufficient good British films were available for the scheme to succeed. Consequently the inferior quality of the films chosen for some towns during the British Week was sharply criticized. As 1924 was approaching its end there was no denying that most British cinemagoers preferred American films. In November of this British Film Year grim news was published in the press. Not a single foot of negative was being exposed on any studio floor in the country.

The public was appalled. This was worse even than in the black days of 1918.

CECIL HEPWORTH VANQUISHED

There is a tendency nowadays to dismiss the British films of the 1920s collectively as unworthy of mention; and it must be admitted that not one of them is comparable in merit to perhaps a dozen of the great American, German and Russian films of the period. But several had their points and they should not be ignored; and that applies even to some of the films made in the despairing early 1920s.

Not all of the directors who had survived the war gave up without a fight. Alma Taylor was still Cecil Hepworth's leading player and he directed her in an Eden Philpotts's Devonshire story, *The Forest on the Hill*, and then in *Sheba* with a new actor, Ronald Colman, in the cast. Henry Edwards, in charge of his second team, directed Chrissie White in Temple Thurston's *The City of Beautiful Nonsense* and in Philipps Oppenheim's *The Amazing Quest of Mr Ernest Bliss*. Hepworth recruited Gerald Ames to form a third team, and he began by directing as well as acting in *Once Aboard the Lugger*.

It seemed a promising start and in the following year Hepworth had another notable success with the farcical comedy, *Alf's Button*. Leslie Henson was the private with a tunic button made from the melted-down brass of Aladdin's Lamp. According to Hepworth, *Alf's Button* was commercially the most successful film he ever made. As Henry Edwards's version of *The Amazing Quest of Mr Ernest Bliss* also found a place among the top films of 1921, Hepworth had good reason for feeling optimistic and for getting expansionist notions.

His two stages at Walton-on-Thames were inadequate both in number and in size. Having estimated that six stages would meet his needs, he acquired additional ground. Then he decided to generate his own electrical power, and this proved a costly venture. Indeed, in later years he described it as his worst blunder. But, he added, 'we were making good money with good films all this time, and we might have won through if the national post-war boom had continued'. This last point, about the economic depression which afflicted this country during the early 1920s, is sometimes missed by those who assume that conditions after the First World War resembled those after the Second World War.

Hepworth had intended to float a public company to provide the capital for his developments, but his cautious financial advisers told him to wait until the trade recession (of 1921) was over. This proved to be another (and probably much worse) mistake, because the trade recession continued and eventually he had to launch the company when the money market was apathetic. The proposed capital was £250,000, and the flotation was 'very badly under-subscribed'. The City of London was still convinced that the reckless spending of money in Hollywood would end in disaster, and it was quite content to let American bankers take the inevitable consequences of their imprudence.

Before Hepworth went bankrupt in 1924 his company made several other feature films, including Harry Edwards's *Lily in the Alley,* and Hepworth's own *Comin' Thro' the Rye.* The former was a courageous effort as it had no sub-titles, but picturegoers found it puzzling.

Hepworth had been associated with Col. Bromhead in floating the British Film Week venture, and *Comin' Thro' the Rye* was to have been his contribution. It was a remake of one of his 1916 productions. But many difficulties were encountered, and the leading man contracted typhoid fever when two-thirds of the film was made. In consequence, *Comin' Thro' the Rye* was not ready in time—although perhaps this did not do the Film Week any particular harm, because eventually the film had a lukewarm reception.

Hepworth was most unfortunate in the receiver appointed for his company, and he gives in his autobiography a distressing account of his difficulties with the obtuse man. The aspect which is infuriating to us today is his decision to dispose of Hepworth's complete stock of films, including negatives, so that 'a chemical could be recovered to make aircraft wing dope'. Hepworth had to stand impotently aside watching twenty-four years' creative work being utterly destroyed. A copy of *Coming Thro' the Rye* was all that was saved. Fortuitously it was in the United States at the time.

In the creative sense Hepworth never mattered again. He was given a post by Paul Kimberley, once his studio manager, now back in this country and in charge of the British unit of an American concern, National Screen Services, making advertising trailers. He earned his living for the rest of his working years in a relatively minor position. His studios were taken over by others, and the place has now become very valuable because of building developments ('a $1\frac{1}{4}$ million new town', the press said, 'on the $10\frac{1}{2}$-acre site').

It is tragic that the only feature film by which his talent can be assessed, *Comin' Thro' the Rye,* was perhaps his worst film. Like so many remakes it had none of the freshness of the original. Iris Barry in her book, *Let's go to the Pictures,* written in the mid-twenties, described it as 'most awful and unendurable'.

Although attractively photographed against the old English garden background of which he was so fond, it was slow-moving and packed with wordy sub-titles. Hepworth had clung to his middle-class respectability, and had so diluted the dramatic content of this as well of his other films that they became insipid. He had disliked the vulgar brashness of American films, but did not understand that they had other qualities which made them popular. And, while the dreadful misfortune which befell him is deplored, it was apparent by 1924 that he was incapable of standing up to the American challenge. British films were in need of a new champion.

GEORGE PEARSON AND THE BETTY
BALFOUR COMEDIES

Another British film-maker, George Pearson, has also described his studio experiences during the 1920s. This is in his autobiography, *Flashback*. After working with Pathe and Samuelson he joined Gaumont's London studios and came under T. A. Welsh. At the end of 1917 they left Lime Grove to form their own company, Welsh-Pearson, although Gaumont continued to distribute their films. With a capital of £6,000, they converted a disused school at Harlesden into a studio, and later opened another studio at Craven Park. Pearson's province was the studio floor. The rest was Welsh's.

George Pearson might not have had Hepworth's flair for cinematography but he had a better understanding of public taste. His stories were specially written for the cinema because, he said, adaptations of plays and novels required the use of innumerable sub-titles while unfolding the plot. He created a stock company of players more attuned to the post-war than to the pre-war world. It is noteworthy that three young women, all of whom became popular in British films during the decade, appeared in his 1919 and 1920 films, Betty Balfour, Mabel Poulton and Annette Benson.

During the early 1920s Welsh-Pearson could afford only one expensive set for each film. After Tom Bentley had directed *The Old Curiosity Shop* for them, with Mabel Poulton as the devoted Little Nell, they realized they had two potential stars in Betty Balfour and Mabel Poulton. As they could not produce more than one film at a time they released Mabel Poulton to a French company.

In 1920 they made *Nothing Else Matters*. A most successful trade show in the Alhambra led to its being hailed by sections of the press as the first great film produced in this country. Undoubtedly it was the outstanding British film of the year. The story was written by Pearson himself in association with Hugh E. Wright, who in turn played the principal rôle, that of an ambitious actor disposed to blame his failures on everyone but himself. Eventually he realizes that his wife's love is everything—nothing else matters.

This was the film in which Betty Balfour, although in a relatively minor part, came to the fore, and during the next few years Welsh-Pearson were linked in the public mind with her considerable popularity. While they were searching for a suitable story Eliot Stannard, the scenario writer, told them of a music hall sketch about the escapades of a Cockney firebrand called Squibs. It was typical of Pearson that the company bought the name and the character, but created a new story. They turned her into a Piccadilly flower-seller in love with a young policeman. After they had cast her as Pett Ridge's *Mord Em'ly* and as J. J. Bell's Christina in *Wee MacGregor's Sweetheart*, they metamorphosed her into Squibs again, and eventually produced a series about her adventures. She also appeared in *Love, Life and Laughter,* loosely based on Marie Lloyd's career, which Pearson described as the film which gave him most happiness in the making.

Betty Balfour's films were jolly, unpretentious affairs aimed at the less fastidious sections of the British public. The best evidence of her acceptability is perhaps that she was cast in more films during the 1920s (although not for Welsh-Pearson in the later years) than any other British star.

Probably the most important of Pearson's other productions of the period were *Reveille,* an episodic film about people to whom the war had brought great misfortune (its première at the Palace Theatre was attended by the Prince of Wales), and an adaptation of John Buchan's *Huntingtower* with Sir Harry Lauder in its cast. Then in common with other British companies Welsh-Pearson had, to quote Pearson's own words, to 'slow down'.

DISASTER AT COVENT GARDEN

In 1918 Sir Oswald Stoll, one of the leading figures in the vaudeville world, entered the film business. Shocked by the British industry's ineptitude and convinced of cinematography's potentialities, he established well-equipped studios first at Richmond and then at Cricklewood, where things were to be done better. They had not only his active personal support but his considerable financial support too.

Yet the history of this venture is one of almost unrelieved disappointment and when in the middle 1920s his vexed shareholders began to protest with a vigour that became the talk of the industry, Sir Oswald must have reflected bitterly on the various adages about keeping to your own trade.

The Cricklewood studios were in almost continuous use throughout these years, and many directors worked for him there. His first production in 1919, was *Comradeship*, directed by Maurice Elvey and with Lily Elsie and Gerald Ames in the cast. His last was Sinclair Hill's *The Price of Divorce*, made as a silent film and then altered for release as a sound film. His best films were probably the Guy Newall-Ivy Duke 'society dramas'. *Duke's Son,* produced in

5. The first British talkie, *Blackmail*, directed by Alfred Hitchcock for B.I.P. in 1929, has a prominent place in the history of the British cinematograph industry. Its stars were John Longden, Donald Calthrop and Anny Ondra.

Four years later Alexander Korda directed *The Private Life of Henry VIII*, which occupies an even more important place. In this scene Charles Laughton is accompanied by Binnie Barnes and by Robert Donat.

6. Almost as important, because of its influence on G.B.'s policy, was Walter Forde's *Rome Express* (1933). The players here are Elliot Makeham, Cedric Hardwicke and the continental actor, Conrad Veidt.

In this year Victor Saville made an excellent version of *The Good Companions* and set Jessie Matthews on her way to become the most popular actress ever to appear in British musical films. The film had a 'star cast'. In this scene she is accompanied by A. V. Bascomb and John Gielgud.

1920, was praised by the critics, one of whom said it was 'a model of what a British film should be', and as a film 'that would leave American buyers convinced of England's ability to deliver the goods'.

His greatest failure was probably the astonishing *The Prodigal Son*, which had its première in the Covent Garden Opera House in 1923. The title gave a wrong impression that the film told a Bible story. In fact its characters were Norsemen living in Iceland during the Middle Ages, and they were played by Stewart Rome, Henry Victor and Colette Brettell. The trade found the film tedious, heavy and gloomy—'never rising to the dignity of tragedy and never relieved anywhere by a single gleam of humour'. Consisting of 'long series of incidents explained by a wealth of sub-titles', it was in two parts, of eight and nine reels. The total running time was three hours. Subsequently attempts were made to persuade the public that it supplied what was in effect a double-feature programme.

Disaster also befell J. Stuart Blackton. Still vice-president of the Vitagraph Company, the most capable in a professional sense of all American companies in the pre-war years, he returned to Great Britain, the country of his birth, and directed a version of H. G. Wells's *Kipps*, which did very well for Stoll and, incidentally, made George K. Arthur a star.

J. Stuart Blackton's real purpose in coming to London was probably, however, to produce spectacular films in natural colour. Vitagraph's decline had left him at a loose end. He wanted to get back into big business and believed he had found the way through a colour system, the Prizma Process. The scepticism of his Hollywood associates led him to turn to England where minds were less prejudiced—and production costs were less high. So, with Stoll's blessing, he went ahead with a costume piece, *The Glorious Adventure*, his star being none other than Lady Diana Manners.

But the film, when presented with a great flourish at Covent Garden, did not impress the critics. Prizma was just a two-colour system, and the results were 'anything but natural'. The story was weak and the scenario badly constructed. Americans, when they saw the film, were even less impressed.

Undismayed and with fine determination Blackton returned to the attack and made *The Virgin Queen*, refusing to agree that a two-colour process could not possibly give natural effects. He engaged the Hollywood actor, Carlyle Blackwell, to support Lady Diana. However, the reviewers found that her acting 'still left something to be desired'. Crowds came to see the film during its fortnight's run in the Empire music hall, but these were perhaps the only crowds that ever went to the film.

F

It was understandable that many people should be greatly disturbed by some aspects of the transatlantic films now sweeping almost all others from this country's cinemas. They resented their disregard of certain generally-accepted social standards, their superficiality, their provocativeness.

Where their thinking went astray was in not discerning the qualities which had made these American films popular—their quickness of action, their exciting plots, their boosted glamour, and their natural (as distinct from theatrical) style of acting.

The best known of the companies founded to make *good* English films was perhaps Minerva Films. The membership of its directorate shows the extent to which its inspiration came from the London theatre—R. F. Power, Aubrey Smith, A. A. Milne, Nigel Playfair, Leslie Howard and Adrian Brunel. It would be interesting to know how many of them had ever sat through a show in an industrial hall in, say, Burnley. The company's activities were restricted to two-reel comedies—an incidental reminder of the extent to which short films continued to be produced by the studios until well into the 1930s, when 'double-feature' programmes cut the 'shorts' down to newsreels, cartoons and possibly some 'interest' films.

Minerva's comedies were to be 'funny without being vulgar'. A. A. Milne wrote the first stories and Adrian Brunel, until then a scenario writer, was director. However, picturegoers did not take to Minerva's 'better' films—even with such players as Aubrey Smith and Leslie Howard in their casts—and eventually the venture was abandoned. Brunel's comment in his autobiography, *Nice Work,* was that a few people lost sums they could not afford, but nobody was ruined. A couple of years later George A. Cooper was no more successful with a second attempt along these lines, undertaken by a company called Quality Films.

Perhaps the British studios' only noteworthy achievement in the early 1920s was in nurturing several actors who later went to Hollywood where they became stars (and then were used to increase the popularity of American films in this country). George K. Arthur and Ronald Colman have already been mentioned. Others were Clive Brook, Ralph Forbes, Percy Marmont and Victor MacLaglen, who was first seen as a fighting gambler in *The Call of the Road,* written and directed by A. E. Coleby. Ivor Novello too, who began his cinema career in 1920 supporting Matheson Lang and Hilda Bayley in Harley Knowles's production of *Carnival,* had a spell in Hollywood.

Some have questioned the statement about things having become so bad in the British industry during November 1924 that not a foot of film was shot in any of the studios. But the references in the trade press can be given and few would be inclined to dispute that British studios could scarcely have been more desolate than in that black month.

CHAPTER SEVEN

Getting to Grips with Hollywood

••

NEW MEN TAKE OVER

Jack Graham Cutts (1886-1958) was commended in the trade press as 'a realist with no illusions who kept the showman's angle instead of experimenting with strange angles'. This was said in 1922, when he made the critic's choice of the year, *The Wonderful Lie*. It was based on a novel by I. A. R. Wylie, about a farmer, crippled and embittered by an accident, who is jealous when his fiancée marries his brother. Later his peace of mind is restored and he forms a deep affection for their child. Sentimental stories of this kind were very popular with the post-war generation—and for some time after, as is indicated by the remake of the film as one of the early talkies.

The film was produced by a new company, referred to later, called Graham-Wilcox Productions and had a young Irishman, Herbert Wilcox, as producer. It established Lillian Hall-Davies as a star. She was the most consistently popular British film actress through the 1920s—on the Continent as well as in this country.

Graham Cutts's particular importance at this moment in British cinematography came from his influence on three young men, Michael Balcon, Victor Saville and Alfred Hitchcock. They were associated in making *Woman to Woman*, the only outstandingly successful film, as judged by box-office standards, produced in Great Britain during the first eight years after the war. *Woman to Woman* has a place in the history of the British cinematograph industry. Its wide distribution in the United States as well as in this country did much to restore our self-respect by demonstrating that British studios could still make films that would be popular both in this country and abroad.

The story was simple but had, as the trade would say, a 'strong emotional pull'. A British officer is wounded in France in 1917. He loses his memory and forgets the French dancer who bears him a child. Years later they meet again, and the past comes back to him. His wife is understandably resentful but, after the dancer's death, takes the son into her home. Perhaps all this seems familiar because the film has been remade twice, in 1929 as an early talkie and in 1946. Presumably it was good cinematic material in any age.

The original film, shown in 1924, sometimes gets a mention in American histories of the silver screen, although it might be described as American because of the use made of the star in advertising it. She was Betty Compson, once the vivacious girl-friend in the Lee Moran-Eddie Lyons comedies. During the intervening dozen years she had become one of Hollywood's leading actresses and had developed an 'alluring personality'. She was not the first American star engaged by a British company in these post-war years so as to make a film more acceptable to overseas markets—others included Norma Talmadge, Mae Marsh, Betty Blythe and Dorothy Gish—but she was probably the first who still had a place in the top rank. Hollywood was accustomed to speak cynically about the British habit of grasping at 'falling stars'. Betty Compson was worth the £1,000 a week that Michael Balcon was reported to have paid her to come to London.

Michael Balcon was a Birmingham renter, still in his middle twenties. He acted as producer of *Woman to Woman*, along with Victor Saville and John Freedman, the more experienced Graham Cutts being director as well as their guide and friend. The film cost between £30,000 and £40,000, raised from C. M. Woolf, then a city man taking an interest in film renting, and from other friends, including a Birmingham metal merchant, Oscar Deutsch.

Victor Saville too was a Birmingham man and only slightly older than Michael Balcon. In their first joint London venture they had devised advertising films, and it was the shrewd Graham Cutts who advised them that entertainment films were a better line. *Woman to Woman* was the result.

The film was produced in the Islington studios, opened by Paramount in an unsuccessful enterprise for making films in Great Britain. (Other American companies made similar attempts, and their directors' inability to turn out good films in this country was attributed by Hollywood primarily to the laziness and incompetence of their British employees.) Among the staff still working at Islington was a young engineer turned artist and now chief of the Art Title department. This was Alfred Hitchcock, and it was Graham Cutts who promoted him to script writer and assistant director of *Woman to Woman*. It was an important film too for the leading man, Clive

Brook, who received offers to go to Hollywood, where he became one of the foremost stars.

Apart from Balcon, Saville and Hitchcock, the only British director who established a lasting reputation during the 1920s was Herbert Wilcox. Born in Cork in 1892 he entered the film industry at the end of the war, and in 1920, with his brother Charles and with Graham Cutts, founded the company called Graham-Wilcox Productions. They pursued the policy of importing Hollywood stars with great thoroughness. Perhaps Wilcox did not establish himself so quickly as some of the other young men just mentioned; but in 1926 the *Kinematograph Weekly* said, 'Herbert Wilcox has shown that he is a far better director than many of us realized and his handling of the plot (of *The Only Way*), both as regards script and direction, is sincere, assured and smooth'. In 1927 he joined the British and Dominions Film Corporation, and he has remained one of the best-known—as well as one of the most independent—of British directors.

The partnership between Balcon and Saville broke up. Balcon, with 'the optimism of youth and youth's belief in itself', formed Gainsborough Pictures. keeping Graham Cutts as co-director. They linked up with the Gaumont Company, still under the Bromheads (Reginald Bromhead had joined his brother in 1923) and later merged with it, Balcon taking charge of production for both companies. Gainsborough acquired the Islington studios and these became his headquarters for several years, including the rest of what is now known as the silent era.

The recovery of the British cinematograph industry was slow, and these young men had failures in store as well as successes. The reputation of British films continued to rest during these mid-1920s, as explained later, with the directors of factual films. Indeed, the only feature film from the period still revived is *The Lodger*, directed by Alfred Hitchcock after a spell in German studios. It was produced in 1927 by Michael Balcon.

The critics were becoming exasperated by our continued inability to make films acceptable to American audiences. Iris Barry—later of the Films Section of the New York Museum of the Modern Arts—complained in her *Let's Go to the Pictures* that 'British companies still go on making pictures in the same dreary tradition—clean pictures with smudgy, dull photography, solid all-British heroines and impossible plots'. And soon afterwards C. A. Lejeune, of the *Observer*, was saying that the 'British cinema has been handicapped in every way—with bad brains, shortage of money, lack of confidence, injudicious flattery, misdirected talent and unfortunate legislation'.

Perhaps such harsh words were not entirely warranted. 'Jaydee' Williams, the creator of the large Elstree studios, pointed out that the film industry differed in one fundamental respect from all other production industries. Even if the number of cinemas in the world were doubled or even trebled, it did not follow that any additional films would be needed. An annual output of 400 might still be sufficient. The increased demand could be met simply by having additional copies printed. And Hollywood was quite capable, and hopeful, of providing the lot. The number of cinemas in Great Britain was the largest outside the United States, and Americans with their keen commercial sense were in no way concerned about keeping the British studios alive.

Hollywood had all the advantages because, with the cost of its films covered by bookings in the United States, these films could be —as a matter of tactics—released to British cinemas at quite un-economic prices. They represented the surplus or additional profit. Showing cheap American films was an attractive proposition for British cinema-owners too, and this accounted for their disinclination to go out of their way to help British film producers. The latter, finding it virtually impossible to get their films shown in the United States, had a valid excuse for their inability to make these films pay.

THE BATTLE OF THE QUOTA

The collapse of the British film-making industry was discussed by the House of Lords as early as 1925, and the debate prompted the Federation of British Industries to intervene with proposals for adopting a quota system, first spoken about in 1917, and for setting up a Corporation that would make advances to British film pro-ducers and even make films on its own accord. The Corporation would derive its funds from licences and from taxes levied on any British exhibitors who still preferred to show foreign films.

These suggestions seem to have taken the trade by surprise. The exhibitors and the renters were prospering. It was only the producers who were in trouble. But the Federation of British Industries pointed out that great harm was being done to British trading interests abroad by the monopoly which had been established for American films; and it insisted that positive steps be taken to redress the situation.

Whether the public, with its taste for American films, appreciated what was happening and had strong feelings about the wrongs being done to British film-makers is debatable. But an American company inadvertently chose this moment to be incredibly gauche. One of its representatives had a bright idea for 'exploiting' a new film. When the first copy of *The Phantom of the Opera* was landed at the quay-side he induced a body of Territorials, in uniform, to form a guard of honour and to escort it to the company's office in Wardour Street. The following day, when photographs of the incident appeared in the press, the protests were so loud and so prolonged that the Cinema-tograph Exhibitors' Association acted quickly—questions about the affair were being asked in Parliament—and demanded that the film be withdrawn. Feeling continued to run so high that the ban was not raised until November 1928—three years after the incident occurred.

With feeling running so strongly against American domination it might have been expected that British cinema proprietors would have gone out of their way to give British film-makers a helping hand—by, for instance, accepting this quota proposal, at least in principle. But they knew that their audiences had by now formed a marked preference for American films. So, they reasoned, if they showed more British films, they were likely to do less business—not a pleasing thought. Even less pleasing, however, was the fear that, as insufficient British films—good or mediocre—were being made to meet the needs of *all* the cinemas in the country, the production of many quickly-turned-out films of inferior quality ('quickies', they were called) would be encouraged. This may account for the voting when the CEA took a referendum on a scheme which its own Council had devised. Its members turned down the proposal by a small majority. The Council reaffirmed its conviction that the scheme was necessary and passed the whole problem of 'securing a place in the sun for the British film' over to a joint trade committee. This could not increase the chances of arriving at an agreed policy, because the renters, with their American affiliations, were the least likely group to be sympathetic.

Reports on discussions at the meetings of the joint committee were closely studied in Hollywood. American producers realized that influential British opinion was set on bringing to an end the state of affairs which had prevailed since the war. Much interest was taken in the proceedings also in the Commonwealth, where the American domination of the cinema had been causing even greater worry than at home.

When it became plain that the members of the trade would never solve the problem voluntarily the way was open for Government action. A (second) Cinematograph Films Bill was drafted by the Board of Trade and discussed in both Houses during 1927. It insti-tuted, in spite of determined opposition by Lancastrian and other exhibitors, a quota of five per cent for the first year. The legislation covered ten years, ample time, so it was argued, for the industry to find its feet. If it failed to do so during that decade it deserved—and the Government said so—no further support.

The measure was immediately effective and at the end of the first few months of its application the *Kinematograph Year Book* commented that 'the trade should admit that the Government had done for them what they had tried in vain to do for themselves'. George Pearson mentioned his own case by way of example. He had been strongly opposed to the quota scheme, believing it would promote the production of inferior films. When the Bill was enacted in December 1927, his own company, Welsh-Pearson, was virtually out of action. But within little more than a year they had no fewer than three separate units at work.

The Act also restricted block and blind booking. This was a system, enforced almost entirely by American interests, which had contributed materially in ensuring that American films had a wide showing in British cinemas. Films were hired to cinemas in blocks, or packets, containing perhaps a couple of very attractive films, certain to do well at box-offices, several 'programme films' of no particular merit but capable of doing average business, and one or two films that had disappointed their producers and were described in the trade press as 'doubtful propositions'. An even worse aspect was that the cinema owner had to book these groups of films in advance, without having seen them—perhaps some had not even left the studio floors—and eighteen months might pass before they became available for showing in his cinema.

These tough American business methods were partly responsible for forcing cinema owners to combine for their general protection, and for leading to a continuous extension of the circuit system. In the period just prior to the outbreak of the First World War 6 per cent of the cinemas in Great Britain belonged to large companies (large being defined as owning, at least, ten cinemas). In 1920 the PCT group—Jupp's original creation—increased their capital to over £3 million and became the owners, with subsidiaries, of sixty-eight cinemas. By 1927 their acquisitions had grown and they owned eighty-five cinemas, with more under construction.

In that year there were twenty-three circuits in the country having ten or more cinemas, the second largest being the Gaumont-British Picture Corporation with twenty-one cinemas. Altogether, however, these circuits controlled no more than 13 per cent of the cinemas in the country. Presumably they could bargain more effectively with the American film-renting companies, and could cut down their costs by doing their booking centrally. But in 1927 the rest, the 87 per cent of the cinemas in this country, were still owned by small, local companies, and the going was hard.

PEP, when they reported in 1952 on the *British Film Industry*, thought that the passing of the Act had been of such importance that—'coupled with the formation of the large-scale film combines which it largely inspired and with the introduction of the sound film'—the year 1927 marked the real dividing line in British film history. The period 1927 to 1930 was described as the watershed between 'medieval and modern' cinematography in Great Britain.

CHAPTER EIGHT

Breaking Out from Isolation

In 1922 there had been a widespread fear that attendances were about to fall, and the proprietors of the country's 4,000 picture houses pressed for the withdrawal of the 'iniquitous' entertainment tax. Various Chancellors of the Exchequer, beginning with Philip Snowden in 1924, made reductions, but the trade had to wait almost forty years for the 'total abolition' they were seeking.

The exhibitors' confidence had been restored by 1924 and with the easing of building restrictions the erection of 'super-cinemas' began. A point to be emphasized is that the majority of these Babylonian halls were sponsored by locally-financed companies and not by circuits. The pioneers, those enterprising young men of twenty years before, now enjoying the prosperity and ease to which their earlier efforts entitled them, were sometimes associated with these ventures. But very often the companies were founded by local businessmen. Perhaps they had been dabbling in the cinema trade since the days of the Bijous. Others were newcomers who had listened to wondrous tales about the picture business's profits. Knowing litttle about the undertaking in which they were investing their money they relied on the ability and the diligence of underpaid managers to earn them their dividends. Some years later, when perhaps one of the circuits came along with an attractive takeover proposal, they accepted with alacrity—to the gratification of their shareholders and often to the mortification of their manager.

During the mid- and late-1920s the cinema industry secured a substantial footing in the heart of London theatreland. Stage people found this juxtaposition embarrassing. They had retained their disdainful attitude to film-making, while participating in its activities to the benefit of their incomes.

The first super-cinema planned for central London was the Tivoli in the Strand. It was to replace the famous Victorian music hall. Construction, which should have begun in 1921, was held up for a considerable time by the London licensing authority. The cinema was acquired by PCT in 1928 and remained in the possession of that company's various successors until its demolition in 1958 shortly before the Strand widening.

The New Gallery in Regent Street was the West End's largest pre-1914 cinema, but it was comparatively small in size. Reconstructed in the mid-1920s, it too has ceased to be a commercial picture palace. The Capitol, the next super-cinema, was located in Haymarket. Opened in 1924, it was rebuilt as the Gaumont which has recently been replaced by the Haymarket Odeon. The Astoria in Charing Cross Road followed in 1927, and the Regal (now the Odeon) at Marble Arch in 1928.

The two cinemas which probably excited London filmgoers most at the time were the Plaza in Lower Regent Street (1926) and the Empire (1928). The latter, which replaced another famous music hall, was the first cinema to be built in Leicester Square, and it too has recently been rebuilt. Possibly William Shakespeare has since looked disapprovingly from his statue in the gardens as other buildings in this theatrical centre have been converted into cinemas, although he might conceivably have been unhappy earlier about some of the shows presented in the years before the cinema took over.

The Plaza, which usually showed Paramount films, and the Empire, which was associated with Metro-Goldwyn-Mayer, made this impression not only because of their luxurious seating arrangements but also because of their flashy but brilliant orchestral music. They had 'prologue presentations' with troupes of chorus girls prancing about the stage, mechanically and meaninglessly, to the delight of the under-sophisticated and the over-sophisticated members of their audiences.

A FRESH OUTLOOK ON THE CONTINENT

In the early-1920s the leaders of the cinematograph industry in other Western European countries had taken no less well than the British to the American inroads. Salesmen pushed American wares persistently, and American film stars' faces appeared almost as often in continental journals as they did in British newspapers. Foreign studios, attempting to keep up with the Americans, were handicapped even more than the British by lack of technical facilities. They could not afford, for instance, the immense Kleig lights which enabled Americans to achieve such brilliant photography and, in consequence, their own pictures had a misty and even muddy look. Cinéastes could see through the gloom and relish the skill with which the camera had been used. But to the public the films just looked blurry.

Later, after the introduction of sound films, the Americans encountered language difficulties in countries where English was not spoken; but adapting a silent film for, say, the Italian market was an easy matter. Apart from cutting out scenes unacceptable to local tastes little had to be done except prepare a new set of sub-title cards in the Italian language—the kind of work, in fact, on which Alfred Hitchcock was engaged at the Paramount's Islington Studio at the beginning of his career.

Some countries well represented on British screens before the war were almost completely crowded out by American films. The Italians tried unsuccessfully to regain lost markets by making spectacular films. They then fell back on mediocre costume and social melodramas which were presumably liked in their own country but were of no interest to British cinemagoers. They ceased to have any place in this country until after the Second World War. Sweden and Denmark were proud of their three distinguished directors, Victor Seastrom, Mauritz Stiller and Carl Dreyer, but they chose subjects that were too sombre for British tastes, and they too lost their place in the British cinemas.

During the first half of the war Germany had been supplied through Sweden with many films from the United States. (It still surprises British people that Charlie Chaplin and Mary Pickford became familiar figures to German as well as British cinemagoers during the course of this war.) But after the Americans became combatants the Germans were cut off, and had perforce to expand their existing industry.

Ufa were established towards the end of 1917; to regain prestige after her defeat a year later, Germany decided to develop a film industry of international significance. With Government support the Ufa studios at Neubabelsburg, Berlin, were supplied with equipment such as no other European country possessed, or seemed likely to possess. As early as 1919 the Germans presented a film, Robert Wiene's *The Cabinet of Dr Caligari,* which excited film-makers elsewhere, if not the general cinema-going public. In the years which followed directors such as E. A. Dupont, Fritz Lang, Ernst Lubitsch and F. W. Murnau, greatly influenced the way in which the camera is employed in cinematography. In the hands of their skilful photographers the camera became, as critics of American techniques observed, much more than a recording instrument. The camera participated in the acting and, by focusing on a tightening of the lips or the withdrawal of a hand, and photographing the players from unusual but significant angles, it contributed materially not only in telling the story but in 'creating the atmosphere'.

Film acting took on a new look, avoiding both the overplaying

associated in the past with recruits from the theatre, and the under-
playing favoured by American directors as they strove after greater
realism. Such actors as Emil Jannings, Conrad Veidt and Werner
Krauss were much more penetrating in their portrayal of the
characters in the story. By comparison the actors in American
(and British) films were stock figures. German films were never
popular with British audiences. The treatment was heavy-handed,
the movement was slow, and the glitter to which American films had
accustomed their devotees was missing. American producers were,
however, tremendously impressed by these Teutonic achievements.
Erich Pommer was among the German directors persuaded to go to
Hollywood, and the German influence on American films became
very marked in 1926 and 1927. By this time too a fairly close bond
had been established between British and German studios. Michael
Balcon went for a time to Germany, and Alfred Hitchcock directed
his first feature film, *The Pleasure Garden*, in Munich in 1926.
However, a couple of years were to pass before the Germans made
their first descent on British studios.

The French cinematograph industry, as it had been created by
Pathé and Gaumont, wilted and occupied a much less prominent
place than formerly. It received even less Governmental aid than
the British industry in its efforts to get back in the ring. During
the war, however, intellectuals began to take an interest in the cinema
(which would not be claimed so soon for the United States or for
Great Britain) and Louis Delluc is said to have been the first critic,
in 1917, to write about films seriously. The small pre-war studios
were still in use and were leased by companies formed to make
perhaps just one particular film. Individualism triumphed, and
eventually several directors came to the fore—René Clair, Jean
Epstein, Jacques Feyder, Abel Gance and Jean Renoir. Unlike
German directors, who continued to shut themselves up in their
studio sets and preferred to build a street of wood and plaster rather
than to go out-of-doors, the French went into the open air. Their
productions were artistic without seeming to strive, as the Germans
did, after aesthetic effects.

ESCAPING FROM SELF-ENFORCED ISOLATION

Long after Hollywood had come under the spell of German directors and technicians British film-makers went on, as a contemporary
writer said, turning out passé American formula pictures to the best
of their limited financial resources and to the best of their limited
capacity.

In spite of the many new super-picture palaces, the British cinematograph industry had not yet established a creditable position among the various branches of public entertainment. Although many more people were going to the movies, this was the Roaring Twenties, and more were going to the theatres too, and to the music halls and to the dance halls. Certainly the masses, as the trade called them, were going to the cinema, but statistics showing that half the population went to the pictures every week were misleading. Some people went three and four times a week; others not from one year's end to another.

To older generations the cinematograph was still something that had emerged from the showgrounds and had somehow contrived to acquire a measure of respectability. But to youngsters from all social grades who were school pupils in the First World War period, going to the pictures had become part of their way of living. Their attitude remained uncritical, except that they knew what they liked. A few were being elevated, however, to the ranks of cinéastes. An afternoon at the pictures meant more to them than spending some hours imaginatively rushing about with cowboys, revelling in uproarious comedy, or being emotionally submerged in not fully comprehended romances.

By the mid-1920s there was a fairly substantial body of cinemagoers in this country, isolated perhaps from one another, who were outspokenly dissatisfied with the programmes being presented at their local cinemas. Some objected to the banal treatment of the stories, having been shocked by the mishandling of one or two of their favourite novels in the course of adaptation for the screen. Some realized that the photography and the cutting were pedestrian, and convinced themselves that cinematography was a lively new art whose potentialities were not being adequately explored. Some wanted to make experimental films such as they read about in a new quarterly magazine, *Close Up*. This English periodical was printed and published on the Continent, most of the unusual films mentioned in it having been seen and reviewed in Berlin.

These rebellious cinemagoers' first move was made at Cambridge in 1924 when a Kinema Club was formed. Its founder chairman was Cedric Belfrage, later film critic to the *Sunday Express*. Although the society arranged lecture meetings and film shows, it would probably be treated today as an amateur ciné club. In the opening announcement the Club's sponsors declared their intention of making a film about Cambridge life—the sort of statement, in fact, that has since been made hopefully by many people in many walks of life over many years.

The formation of the London Film Society in the summer of 1925 made a considerable impression and has been mentioned in the reminiscences of several people associated with the industry. Its first Council included Iris Barry (film critic), Sidney Bernstein (film exhibitor), Hugh Miller (film actor), Walter Mycroft (later of Elstree but at that time a film critic), Adrian Brunel (film director) and Ivor Montagu, generally spoken of as the prime mover. Miss J. M. Harvey, a concert agent, was secretary.

George Pearson has written about the visit paid to him by Ivor Montagu, saying that he wanted to start a society that would enable British film-makers and the public, to see the progress made by the *avant garde* in Russia, Germany, France and Middle Europe. Pearson regarded it as a splendid project, but wondered where they would find a suitable cinema. Then Ivor Montagu 'startled the film world by securing the best-known cinema theatre in the West End, the New Gallery in Regent Street, for a Sunday afternoon once a month'. George Pearson became one of the thirty Founder Members —who included Roger Fry, Julian Huxley, Augustus John, Ellen Terry, Anthony Asquith, J. B. Haldane, Bernard Shaw and H. G. Wells. He comments in his *Flashback* on the crowds that packed the New Gallery at every performance, and on the inspiration which for many years the Film Society gave our 'isolated British film industry'.

Adrian Brunel says that the original membership was drawn from the *beau monde* of Bohemia, as well as some of the more adventurous members of society and official circles. 'Chelseaites and Bloomsburians were in evidence, younger men in beards and young women in home-spun cloaks.' They were ridiculed in sections of the press, and libel actions were threatened when it was alleged that certain members had a political motive for wanting to show Russian films.

The Society flourished and attracted a large membership. The film critics of the *Observer* and the *Sunday Times* gave considerable space to its performances, and this made cinéastes in other parts of the country resentful because they had no opportunity of seeing the exciting new films being made abroad.

The Society reached its peak in the 1929 period when it moved to an even larger cinema, the Tivoli, in the Strand. This inspired the formation of film societies in some other large cities, but already by the mid-1930s the London Society's best days were behind it. The war was not the only factor which contributed to its end in 1939. The principal cause was probably the steadily growing number of cinemas specializing in showing continental films. Not only did they siphon off the Society's members but they booked the films the Society would have liked to show. This partly explains why the later development of the film society movement took place in other

7. The star who always attracted the public came from the Lancashire
music halls, Gracie Fields. In her film about depression on
Clydeside, *Shipyard Sally*, she was supported by Hay Petrie.
It was directed by Monty Banks.

A pleasant if undistinguished film by Norman Walker, *Turn of
the Tide* (featuring Geraldine Fitzgerald), did more to shape the
pattern of the British industry than any other film because it brought
Arthur Rank into the business.

8. A notable success was achieved by Anthony Asquith in 1938 with *Pygmalion*. Leslie Howard is using small marbles to improve Wendy Hiller's diction.

M.G.M. made three outstanding films in London shortly before the war. Sam Wood's *Goodbye Mr Chips* is recalled with particular affection, because of the moving performances of its leading players, Robert Donat and Greer Garson.

parts of the country where cinemas of this kind are fewer in number.

In the early 1920s several cinemas, such as the Marble Arch Pavilion, had been willing to show 'unusual' films occasionally. According to Paul Rotha the first London cinema to announce that it would confine itself to continental films was the Embassy, situated near the present Holborn Underground Station. To most people, however, the cinema particularly associated with the adoption of this policy was the Shaftesbury Avenue Pavilion, situated near the present Columbia Theatre.

It has been owned by the Davis Brothers, whose circuit was absorbed by Gaumont-British in 1927. Being small and situated near larger Gaumont-British cinemas its future in the combine was uncertain, and Stuart Davis persuaded Reginald Bromhead to adopt the policy of the Cameo Cinema in New York, by showing foreign and other 'unusual films', including revivals. So they turned the Shaftesbury Avenue Pavilion into the 'Home of International Film Art'.

In the summer of 1929 the Davises' contract with Gaumont-British came to its end and the latter decided to convert the Shaftesbury Avenue Pavilion into London's first newsreel cinema. But the way had been prepared for Elsie Cohen, with her considerable experience of film-making in Europe, to take over the Academy Cinema in Oxford Street, and to show continental films there. Stuart Davis allowed the supporters of this new cinema to use the Shaftesbury Avenue Pavilion mailing list. It contained no fewer than 12,500 names. Cinematography in Great Britain was, indeed, escaping from its self-enforced isolation.

GREAT BRITAIN'S LEAD WITH ACTUALITY FILMS

In one respect British film-making had continued to do well even during these doleful early-1920s. And when in 1926 Iris Barry wrote *Let's Go to the Pictures,* she could claim that 'England is still unbeaten in making documentary films'. This early use of the term documentary referred, incidentally, to actuality films, as they had evolved from the 'interest' films of former decades (rather than to the more social-conscious 'documentary' films of the 1930s).

The man responsible for Great Britain having this distinction was Harry Bruce Woolfe. His early inspiration had been derived from Urban's nature study films. He was thinking about making similar films himself. The war intervened and it was not until 1920 that he founded British Instructional Films in a disused Army hut at Elstree. In 1921 he engaged Percy Smith, and inaugurated

G

the 'Secrets of Nature series. Oliver G. Pike and Charles Head also served as members of his team.

His experiences during the war had left their mark on Bruce Woolfe and during the next few years he produced several films, such as *The Battle of Jutland, Armageddon, Zeebrugge, Ypres* and *The Battle of the Falkland Islands,* incorporating authentic pictorial records from the fighting services, with contemporary scenes shot in the studio, and—as was inevitable—a good many sub-titles. Walter Summers directed some of the later and more ambitious films for him.

The trade had shown no more interest in his war films than in his nature films, and he was greatly indebted to (Sir) Gordon Craig who founded a company, New Era Films, specifically to distribute good but unwanted feature and short films.

Mary Field, a university historian, joined Bruce Woolfe in 1926 and began by improving the cutting of the 'Secrets of Nature' films, which had not in this respect advanced much beyond the pre-war 'interest' films. She also cut the long explanatory titles employed in these pre-'talkie' days. Later, in 1940, when Bruce Woolfe's twenty-one years as a film-maker were being celebrated, many tributes were paid to his courage, determination and integrity. As Mary Field said, his films were 'always good, well-made jobs, with nothing skimped, nothing done carelessly'. On the same occasion John Grierson commented on the beauty of his productions which 'strove less to be dramatic at all costs than either American or German films, and were more continuous, patient, analytic and in the best sense observant'.

So it came about that Great Britain's reputation for making quality films stood so high in a decade in which such magnificent feature films were being made abroad in this genre as Flaherty's *Nanook* (1920) and *Moana* (1926), Cavalcanti's *Rien Que les Heures* (1926), and Rutmann's *Berlin* (1927), besides others (greatly cut by renters to increase their 'box-office appeal'), such as Schoedsack and Cooper's *Grass* and *Chang.*

CHAPTER NINE

The Last of the Silent Years

....

BENEFITING FROM THE CINEMATOGRAPH FILMS ACT

Silent films were forgotten overnight in the furore that followed the all-conquering sweep of the 'talkies' in 1929. Many people in the trade became so obsessed about them that they disparaged their own earlier productions. They dismissed them as clumsy gropings towards something better.

They were being less than fair to themselves. The silent films of the second half of the 1920s were considerably in advance of those of the first half. They had got away from what Ernest Lindgren has described as the post-war 'dream world of plenty, luxury and easy achievement'. Some British feature films of this period can stand up quite well to critical analysis.

By 1928 the mood of the industry had swung from self-pity to self-criticism. Indeed, there seems to have been a fairly general acceptance of some opinions expressed by George Pearson to an assembly of British film directors. He said that in 1927 British studios had turned out fifty-two films. Not more than half a dozen were outstandingly good. Another half a dozen had been so bad that they had not been given a trade show. Half of all the British films made in that year were not fit to be shown in first-class halls.

In the discussion that followed the screen-writers came in for rough handling. They, it appeared, were principally to blame. They could not hold a candle to Hollywood's talented scribes, who composed scenarios in which something was happening all the time, who used short sequences to ensure that the films never went slowly, who told stories without excessive reliance on sub-titles.

The significance of these criticisms was that, as British film-makers were now benefiting from the protection provided by the Cinematograph Films Act, they must make better films. Their confidence was, in fact, sufficiently restored for them to produce no fewer than ninety feature films during the following year, 1928.

The new finance procured by the industry enabled several British studios to extend their premises, to buy new equipment and to improve administration. Those mentioned in the trade press of 1928 included the 'enormous BIP studios at Elstree and the Whitehall Studios, almost completed, nearby. Gaumont's greatly enlarged studios were at Shepherd's Bush, and British Instructional's new studios were at Welwyn. Others were the 'reawakened' studios at Cricklewood, Twickenham (St Margarets), Beaconsfield and Walthamstow. 'Producers can now,' the trade press said, 'go to the city with a business-like proposition, which is a notable advance upon that obtaining in former years.'

George Pearson did not particularize about the six 1927 films he thought of outstanding merit, but only one is on the list of British films frequently revived at the National Film Theatre and by the many film societies of today. This was Alfred Hitchcock's *The Lodger*. Produced by Michael Balcon for Gainsborough it was based on a novel by Mrs. Belloc Lowdnes. Set in a London terrorized by a fiendish murderer of golden-haired girls, it had as leading players Ivor Novello, June and Malcolm Keen. Reviewers described it as the most polished and most imaginative British production they had ever seen. There were few sub-titles, the story being told pictorially. The *Kinematograph Weekly* commented on 'the expectation that was keyed to the highest pitch, making the audience forget that the Lodger would not possibly be the Avenger by all the rules of the novel'. Viewed today the film clearly demonstrates the influence of German producers on Alfred Hitchcock at this stage in his career.

The only 1928 film which is sometimes revived probably owes some of its durability to the fact that it was the first film made by Anthony Asquith, son of the former Prime Minister. In this venture he was associated with A. V. Bramble. It told a dramatic triangle story tinged with kindly satiric humour, with Donald Calthrop, Annette Benson and Brian Aherne all playing unsympathetic characters. The plot was set in a film studio background. Although *Shooting Stars* was not an outstanding box-office success it provides another example of the attempt being made to raise the standard of British films.

Another film of 1927-28 which is often recalled, but which is rarely if ever seen today, is Adrian Brunel's *The Constant Nymph*, based on Margaret Kennedy's book about the strange Sanger home in the Austrian Tyrol. Its cast included Ivor Novello, Frances Doble and Mabel Poulton (in her best part as Tessa). It was regarded at the time as a further demonstration of what the new policy in the British cinematograph industry might achieve.

Most memories of it are, however, now confused with those of another version of the story made in the early days of the sound film.

Victor Saville established his position as one of the country's leading directors with a most polished film, made at Elstree (where the German influence was now strong), about a ballet dancer, *Tesha*, who was unorthodox in gratifying her desire to have children. The name part was taken by Maria Corda—better known in those days than her husband—and the German cameraman, Werner Brands, was responsible for some quite brilliant photography. But, although Jameson Thomas and Paul Cavanagh were in the cast, the film was too continental in treatment for British tastes. Nevertheless the critics and the cinéastes appreciated it as a production of quite exceptional promise; but this was perhaps not much consolation to the film's financial backers when they were told that it had been made before its time.

The public was now talking about Elstree as the British Hollywood. Great interest was taken in BIP's first productions, especially in *Moulin Rouge* (there have been several films of this name), a spectacular theatrical film made in the American manner by the outstanding German director, E. A. Dupont. Two Hollywood comedians, Syd Chaplin (Charlie's brother) and Monty Banks came to Elstree to make comedies, although the most successful British comedy of the year was Walter Forde's *tour de force, Wait and See*. He wrote it, directed it and played in it. Forde made several feature comedies during the late 1920s in which he appeared as a Harold Lloydish character. In the concluding year of the 'silent era', 1929, his last comedy film of this kind, *Would You Believe It?*, had the record run for a British film at the Tivoli of sixteen weeks.

The fact that the British industry had produced some very good films in 1927 and 1928 could not hide the lamentably large number of bad films that had been made. Exhibitors were outspoken about the failure to benefit properly from the Cinematograph Films Act. For instance, P. L. Mannoch asserted in the *Kinematograph Weekly* that 'half the British directors who have made films this year should never be allowed in the studios again'. It was pointed out that none of the leading newspaper critics had included even one British production in their list of the dozen best films of 1928, and this is, incidentally, an interesting indication that newspaper criticism of films was now being taken seriously, and that the platitudinous clichés, used even today in reports on music hall shows, were being discarded.

The *Kinematograph Weekly* was often outspoken in its editorial columns. 'Thanks largely to mismanagement and to the appointment of unfit persons to boards of directors we have seen the failure of one company after another. They had been floated with high hopes, with much confidence in the spoon-feeding of the Quota Bill and with little executive competence. Few good British films were made; many commonplace. Very few were fit for world distribution.' And again: 'The year has been one of heart-searching and the trade has not been seen in its best light. Several annual reports of companies formed to make easy money and to take advantage of opportunities presented by the Quota clauses have revealed a disastrous condition of affairs. Support from the City has been much less than in the previous couple of years and there was plenty of justification for the coldness shown to the film companies.'

During the 1920s there was one aspect of the cinematograph industry which continued to exercise the public. This was censorship. The Roaring Twenties were not only raucous. They were 'saucy' in a curiously adolescent fashion. American films came in particularly for criticism, but British films were by no means exempt. Keeping the party clean was quite a task for the British Board of Film Censors, under 'Tay Pay' O'Connor. (He died in 1929 and was succeeded by the Rt. Hon. Edward Shortt.) The Board came under fire from members of the trade, simple and ingenuous men, who supposed that no objection could be taken to an orgy provided the story could be said to have been derived from the Old Testament. It came under fire also, however, from the members of self-appointed social reform organizations for not using scissors on lingering kisses.

Educational and welfare bodies in various towns, including Glasgow, were so incensed by the indulgence shown by the official censors that they tried to institute censorship by their local authorities. These 'campaigns of calumny organized by sectarians from the pulpit and magisterial bench' were successfully resisted. At the end of the decade most fair-minded people agreed that the censors had carried out their duties most resourcefully during these difficult 'twenties.

THE DIVIDING LINE

How the British silent film would have fared in 1929 had it not been swept aside in the 'talkie' revolution is impossible to say, although there are indications that the answer would have been, 'not very well'. E. A. Dupont was now in charge at Elstree and, with Alfred Junge as art director and Werner Brands responsible for the photography, he set out to make the most spectacular film attempted up to then in Great Britain, *Piccadilly*. The star was the American cabaret dancer, Gilda Grey. Anna May Wong was also brought in from Hollywood. Jameson Thomas was the principal actor, and among those in supporting parts were Charles Laughton and Cyril Richard.

Henrik Galeen, director of the superb *The Student of Prague*, had been put in charge of a murder mystery based on Hitchen's *After the Verdict*, Olga Tschechowa and Warwick Ward coming from Germany to lead the cast. Hall Caine's *The Manxman* was being re-made with Anny Ondra, from Czechoslovakia, somewhat oddly chosen for the principal rôle. Mady Christians was to star in Anthony Asquith's third film, *The Runaway Princess*. Certainly the Teutonic influence on British films in the last days of the silent film would appear to have been irresistible. But it was in Hollywood too.

Some directors, aware of the enthusiastic reception given to sound films in the United States, suspected that they were on the wrong track and tried to introduce snatches of dialogue into their productions. Perhaps the best-known of the British part-talkies was Victor Saville's *Kitty*, based on Warwick Deeping's novel about a wartime marriage. It was another Elstree production and had John Stuart and Estelle Brody in the cast.

The swift advance made by the early American sound films stunned European producers, particularly the Germans who realized that a language barrier was being set up against their films. But in June, joy spread throughout the British studios when BIP presented Hitchcock's brilliant *Blackmail*. English voices sounded so much nicer (at least to English ears) than American voices that great opportunities were discerned in the offing. So that month, June 1929, marks a division in the history of the British cinema. Some might say that it is really the only dividing line that matters. All films, in their opinion, can be put simply into one of two categories, pre-talkies and talkies.

JOHN MAXWELL, THE OSTRERS AND C. M. WOOLF

Although the new Cinematograph Films Act had a disappointingly slight effect on the quality (as distinct from the quantity) of British films, it brought about immense changes in the structure of the industry. The two vertical combines (embracing production, distribution and exhibition) which still hold the dominating position were shaped during these years. An incidental point is that one absorbed the Gaumont interests in this country and the other the Pathe interests.

Associated British Cinemas were incorporated at the beginning of 1928 with a capital of £1 million. The chairman and driving force was John Maxwell (1874-1941), a Glasgow solicitor who had owned cinemas since 1912. He became chairman of Wardour Films, which he built up into one of the leading British renting companies, and in 1927 merged the (British) Pathe company with the American company First National. It was his acquisition of the Elstree studios, however, that attracted notice.

They had been opened in 1926 by J. D. Williams with Herbert Wilcox as director-in-chief. The studio's early history was chequered, and after litigation John Maxwell virtually took over J. D. Williams's project. (Williams subsequently became a prominent Hollywood figure.) With so many undertakings coming under his direction John Maxwell formed a new production company, British International Pictures, and it was as BIP that his studio enterprises were known for a decade. Five years later, as noted in the PEP report, when the Associated British Picture Corporation (ABPC) was formed as a holding company to take over the capital of British International Pictures, British Instructional Films, Wardour Films, Pathe Pictures and the original Associated British Cinemas company, the circuit had 147 cinemas.

John Maxwell thought it wiser to concentrate on films acceptable to Central Europe, which could be marketed through Germany. If the United States also took the films so much the better. If they declined it did not matter very much—hence his policy in employing E. A. Dupont and other Germans at Elstree. He announced that BIP would make up to twenty films annually, at an approximate cost of £50,000 each. In fact, from the beginning of 1928 to the introduction of the 'talkies', no fewer than 24 feature films were produced at Elstree.

This was, indeed, a challenge to the Gaumont group. After the war Col. A. C. Bromhead and his chartered accountant brother, Reginald, bought out the French holdings in the (British) Gaumont company and during the 1920s they controlled its interests in production, distribution and exhibiting. In February 1929, Ralph Jupp's PCT circuit became part of the group, raising the total number of cinemas in the Gaumont-British circuit to 287.

The principal directors now were, besides the Bromhead brothers, two other brothers, Isidore and Mark Ostrer. Wealthy woolbrokers and merchant bankers of Polish origin, they had taken an interest in the cinema trade in 1926 when they acquired one of the smaller circuits. Alan Wood in his book about the Rank Organization has described Isidore Ostrer as 'a cultured Jew with a mission, an idealist with many and varied interests'. Among his other purchases were a Sunday newspaper (*The Referee*), Baird Television, Bush Radio and the Luxembourg Radio Station.

Within six months of this new grouping being established the

Bromheads resigned, but not before they had procured from Isidore Ostrer an assurance that the company would remain in British hands and would not become a subsidiary of an American company. (William Fox's Corporation were proposing to build a cinema near the Trocadero to seat 6,000 people, and were thought to have their eyes on the Gaumont circuit.)

The Ostrers thus obtained control of the largest chain of cinemas in Great Britain, two important distributing companies (Ideal Films and W. and F. Films), the Gaumont Studios at Shepherd's Bush, and Michael Balcon's Gainsborough Studios. The Ostrers were disturbed about the poor standing of British-made films and, finding their studios short of technicians, created their own training school. Mark was dogged in his attempts to get their films shown abroad, and one of his proudest moments came in the early 1930s. When visiting New York he found no fewer than three of their films showing in central cinemas.

When the Ostrers obtained possession of the W. and F. renting company they brought that company's owner, C. M. Woolf, into their camp, and in the reorganization following the Bromheads' retirement he became joint managing director. Charles Moss Woolf is spoken of in Alan Wood's book as 'an extremely able Jew: dynamic, highly temperamental and often quarrelsome'. Wood also quoted an estimate of C. M. Woolf's character made by his lawyer. 'He had an endearing quality of explosive excitability, tremendous if merciless fairness, surprising reasonableness when one put up with his irascibility, and immense popularity with the exhibitors with whom he had to deal.'

C. M. Woolf had been a fur merchant in the City. In the early 1920s he was persuaded to buy shares in a film renting company and had given some attention to the distribution of American films in this country. He became a well-known figure in Wardour Street, showing a greater willingness than some to support British films. He was described by Adrian Brunel as 'a courageous backer with a faith in British films at a time when it was most needed'. Among the ventures he had helped to finance was Michael Balcon's profitable apprentice effort, *Woman to Woman*. And it was this film which first brought him into contact with another of Balcon's backers, Oscar Deutsch, the Birmingham metal merchant who later founded the Odeon circuit.

The silent era ended in Great Britain with the industry conscious that two big combines were emerging and that two able and determined men were in charge of them, John Maxwell and C. M. Woolf. It also had an uncomfortable feeling that they were going to clash.

CHAPTER TEN

The First of the 'Talkies'

THE MISSING ELEMENT

During the 1920s the sound film came into being in the same order-less fashion as the silent film thirty years before, with knowledgeable men confidently asserting that the new-fangled contrivance offered no commercial advantages. Talking films would be no more than a craze of the moment. Then in a matter of months a swarm of inventors broke through, blazoning their far-from-mutually-exclusive patents. The inevitable discord, law suits and international disputations all come in their train, but eventually a general amnesty —or something approximating to it—was painfully negotiated.

As long ago as 1889 Thomas Alva Edison had attempted to syn-chronize moving pictures of people with recordings of their speech. Subsequently many others in different countries had followed his example, but with indifferent success. In this country, for instance, systems linking film with gramophone records had been adopted by entertainment proprietors in 1899 and again in 1912, with music hall turns as subjects. But projector operators were unable to match the movements of the performer's lips precisely with the words they were singing. And the faint, tinny, almost imperceptible voice seemed grotesquely out of keeping with the vocalist's immense picture of the screen.

The desirability and, indeed, necessity for providing silent films with some kind of background of meaningful sound had been dis-cerned from the beginning. The Lumières had not only musical accompaniments for their films, but 'sound effects off'. And so every cinema show throughout the 'silent age' had a pianist to thump his way hour after hour through a routine of sheet music—*In the Shadows, Rendezvous, Hearts and Flowers, Dreaming, Song of Autumn, Nights of Gladness*, and other intermezzos and waltzes, with marches and other brisk items introduced to provide the atmo-sphere for the comedy chase or the newsreel. Some artistes tried to suit their accompaniment even more closely to the incidents being depicted on the screen, and after 1912 were able to turn to volumes of 'mood themes for the cinema' on sale at the music shops. A few years later D. W. Griffith had an orchestral score prepared for use when *The Birth of a Nation* was being shown.

Comparatively few members of the audience heeded the pianist's efforts, but they were immediately disturbed if he stopped playing, partly perhaps because of the distractions which assailed their ears— mechanical noises emanating from the projection box or the ventilators; and human noises such as the coughing, munching, chattering, shoving and seat-banging occasioned by the members of the audience themselves. But they missed the music too.

During the 1920s trios and larger orchestras established themselves in cinematograph entertainment. In super-cinemas they could be over twenty strong, and they might be allotted a quarter of an hour's interlude to play one or two of their party pieces. They might be given even longer on 'popular' nights, usually Fridays, when they led the audience in thirty minutes' robust singing of some of the innumerable chorus songs with which the Roaring Twenties were regaling themselves. Often the choruses included the 'theme song' from the following week's feature film. Not only were scores now being provided for all major films—scores which orchestra leaders, at the height of their glory, accepted or dismissed as the whim took them—but songs were being written around film titles, and sometimes these became popular in their own right. Indeed, several have survived although the films for which they were written have been almost forgotten.

During the late 1920s massive organs were installed in the larger cinemas, fitted with rows of ivory keys and arrays of stops, pistons, levers and pedals. The organist could make a cinema reverberate with his accompaniment to a film as well as with an astonishing variety of sound effects. Although his original duty had been to take over from the orchestra during its intervals of rest and relaxation, many musicians feared that this egocentric soloist was destined to supplant them. They could not conceive that soon some irresponsible inventors were going to bundle out the lot of them, leaving these grotesque monoliths, almost stone-like in appearance, survivors from a fantastic past.

LONDON'S FIRST COMMERCIAL SOUND FILMS

Great Britain contributed less to the invention and development of talking films than is sometimes supposed, but there are grounds for claiming that the first commercial showings of talking films were in this country. Also there is no question about Sir Ambrose Fleming having been the first scientist to announce (1904) the invention of the thermionic valve from which most later inventions sprang.

The valve was applied principally to telephony and to telegraphy, little importance being attached to the work of an American, Elias Reed, who found in 1913 how to record sound on film. Patents affecting various modifications and adaptations of thermionic valves were taken out in most industrial countries, but notably by an American, Dr Lee De Forest. His work was chiefly concerned with wireless broadcasting—hence the title of his biography, *Father of Radio.*

De Forest was particularly active in 1920, a year in broadcasting comparable to 1895 in cinematography. However, he had the vision in the midst of the hurly-burly to found a company, Phonofilms, to make talking pictures. Indeed, he disposed of some of his earlier patents to the Bell Telephone Laboratories, and began to give most of his time to these new possibilities. Unfortunately he continued to use gramophone discs because they were acoustically better than sound on film, while a former associate, Theodore Case, was taking out further patents for recording sound on film.

De Forest moved from the turbulence of New York to London and leased a studio at Clapham Junction where he produced several short sound films in which such well-known players as Owen Nares and Malcolm Keen participated. (One which has survived consists of scenes from Dickens's *Bleak House.*)

By living in London during the first years of the talking film he has left an impression in some quarters that he was an Englishman. But, while this is clearly unfounded, it does seem true that the first sound films to be shown regularly in public cinemas were made in this country. This explains why elderly people sometimes write to the press asserting, quite correctly, that they saw a sound film in a British cinema as early as 1926 or 1927.

There was considerable scepticism up to 1927 (and even 1928) about the commercial value of talking pictures. Indeed, as long ago as 1923, some young scientists had demonstrated in Germany their Tri-Ergan system of recording sound on film. Ufa had snapped up the process and then failed to profit by it.

Every schoolboy knows (or used to know) how in April 1926 Sam Warner persuaded his three brothers in New York to adopt the Bell Laboratories' system, using immense gramophone records, now owned jointly by Western Electric and the American Telephone and Telegraph Company. Risking their whole future on this venture they leased a New York theatre, in which for a year they presented with mixed success various short musical films as well as silent feature films to which a synchronized musical accompaniment had been added.

The doubts which continued to be entertained about the commercial future of sound films changed overnight in October 1927, when Al Jolson spoke as well as sang in the film, *The Jazz Singer*. Furthermore, Fox-Movietone were now at Warners' heels, and were already using the sound-on-film process which eventually supplanted Vitaphone's discs.

By 1928 the Germans had at last sensed the commercial value of the Tri-Ergan process. The Tobis company (Ton-Bild-Syndikat A.G.) was formed to develop its applications and showed the first German sound film in January 1929. But litigation over rights, initiated by William Fox, followed at once. Tobis and Klang Films (founded by AEG and Siemens) came together to resist the American challenge and eventually won the lawsuit, but only after Central Europe had been prevented for a considerable time from heralding with the rest of the world the early American talkies.

Warner's *The Singing Fool*, the first major sound feature film, was presented in London during the autumn of 1928, the cinema chosen being the recently-opened Regal (now Odeon) at Marble Arch. Nothing comparable to the public's unquenchable desire to see and to hear Al Jolson croon to his Sonny Boy had been encountered before (or since). The queues that formed at John Maxwell's cinemas in the larger towns, when the film was shown during the first months of 1929, are still remembered for their prodigious lengths.

Cinema proprietors were delighted with the bigger audiences the talkies were bringing; but meeting the vastly increased costs was less pleasurable. Not only had they to pay heavy instalments on new equipment, and for such incidentals as wiring the hall, but they had to pay much more for the films themselves. Renters no longer supplied them with films for a simple hiring charge—'at a flat rate'. They now wanted a percentage of the box-office takings and with a stipulated minimum.

When more sound films became available, and exhibitors had greater bargaining power, they strove to break free of these sharing terms; but the renters still held the stronger position. Accordingly, cinema running costs had to be reduced and it was then that the managers turned out their orchestras, brushing aside the pleas of the more discriminating members of their audience for the retention of, at least, some silent films. The cinemas were becoming completely mechanized.

FROM *BLACKMAIL* TO *HENRY THE EIGHTH*

The British film industry experienced such mixed fortunes during the 1930s that, instead of treating the decade as a whole, it is best to distinguish between three phases. The first lies between two out-standing successes, *Blackmail* and *Henry the Eighth*—that is to say, it runs from mid-1929 to 1933. No one called on to select the dozen most momentous British films would omit Alfred Hitchcock's *Blackmail*. Even if the qualifications were altered so that the selections were based on quality rather than importance, *Blackmail* might still retain a place. The scenario—written originally for a silent film—is tidy, the characters are clearly etched, the symbolism is used discreetly, and the sequences are dextrously assembled. Modern audiences might titter at Anny Ondra's child-like innocence and at Cyril Richard's transcendent villainy. But Donald Calthrop's sauve blackmailer is still sinister. By sparing use of dialogue, Hitchcock set an example which few directors followed in this first stage of the 'all-talking' period—some have learned better since—and by substituting Joan Barry's mellifluous voice for Anny Ondra's mid-European twittering, he applied 'dubbing' right at the beginning of the sound film era, although the substitution was done on the spot, Joan Barry speaking into the microphone while Anny Ondra mouthed the words.

Another 1929 Elstree production which attracted considerable attention was E. A. Dupont's *Atlantic*. Employing the Titanic theme, about the reactions of a luxury liner's passengers to sudden catastrophe, he produced the film at Elstree with three casts, speaking English, French and German. It was not outstandingly successful in this country, the dialogue in particular being found stilted; but it was one of the first sound films shown in those European countries where the dispute over patent rights was holding up the presentation of talking films. Few people in this country realize that *Atlantic* is classed elsewhere as one of the great early talkies, along with *Sous les Toits de Paris* and *The Blue Angel*. This is what H. H. Wollenberg says about it in his *Fifty Years of German Films*—'language, music, natural sounds were blended with cinematic unity with the work of the camera and actors. This British film was undoubtedly a milestone in the history of European cinema and made a tremendous impression in Germany.' Which might mean, of course, that a film can be made in three languages, but the version in the director's own language is the one which counts.

The number of feature films produced in this country increased steadily: 1926, 26; 1929, 128; 1933, 200. But by then questions were again being asked in Parliament about the state of film-making in Great Britain, and the newspapers were once more asking, what's wrong with British films.

In 1930 the trade press had been very pleased with the level of production achieved by British studios and had observed that, if the quality had been so good in 1926, the 'Quota Act' would never have been needed. Particularly gratifying, they had said, was breaking down the American barrier against British films. The same note was struck again in 1931, but this time perhaps with less certitude. Maybe the barrier had been only temporarily breached. The transatlantic market was drying up. By contrast, American films were becoming more popular than ever in this country. The shrill and raucous intonation which had made some voices unacceptable in 1930 disturbed few people a year or two later; and by contrast some English voices had become unpopular—a change in public attitude of considerably greater social significance than has so far been recognized.

OTHER YEARS AND OTHER LOCUSTS

History was repeating itself. The opportunities with which the British film-making industry had been presented by the introduction of sound films were being lost. Nobody seemed to be getting anywhere. American films had more speed, more action, more gloss. The characters in them were real people (or at least tried to look as if they were). English films, even when processed in three languages, had made little impact on the continent. They were not doing much more business in the United States with their original versions in English.

Almost all of the principal British films of this period were taken from the London theatre and played by theatrical casts. (The most notable exceptions were Alfred Hitchcock's thriller *Murder* and Victor Saville's *The W Plan*, a spy story taken from a newspaper serial.) These films are rarely revived today, except for a few extracts containing some cinematic feature. For instance, Alfred Hitchcock's version of John Galsworthy's *The Skin Game* is notable because of a brilliant study of the antagonism between the aggressive industrial boss, Hornblower (played by Edmund Gwenn) and his sensitive opponent (played by C. V. France). Victor Saville's *Hindle Wakes* is probably recalled because of Belle Chrystall's acting. But again the point can be made that the scenes during a Wakes Week at Blackpool and Llandudno have a marked documentary quality.

They might be contrasted with Cecil Lewis's production of Bernard Shaw's *How He Lied to Her Husband*. The film was given much advance publicity during its production, a great deal being made of the personal attention it was receiving from its distinguished author. His deistic insistence on every movement, every word, being just right was interpreted as guaranteeing that the film would be devastatingly funny. But when it was given a special première in the Carlton Theatre, it was found merely boring. It must have been one of the worst failures (although not necessarily in a financial sense) in the history of the British film industry

The filmed play which aroused most controversy was, however, an adaptation of St John Ervine's *The First Mrs Fraser*, which had had a long theatrical run. Henry Ainley, romantic lead in films fifteen years before, appeared in it, although the critics now thought him prone to overact. The aspect which caused most discussion was the introduction of a lavishly presented cabaret scene with Billy Cotton and his Band. This was done, so the public was told, to make the film more to the liking of cinemagoers. The reputable author was brought into the argument to affirm agreement that the interpolation was a good idea. Inevitably the film became just a photographed play, full of literary dialogue and empty of live conversation.

Anthony Asquith's *Tell England* was worth more notice. Based on Ernest Raymond's novel about the tragic Gallipoli campaign, it described the young British officer's attitude to the First World War with a sympathy perhaps never equalled in any other film, not excepting even *Journey's End*. Geoffrey Barkas, who had taken a leading part in making *The Battle of the Somme,* was associated with Asquith in directing the film. When viewed today the presentation as well as the acting seem almost amateurish, yet the film's authenticity gives it a merit lacking in other films of this period, when the British cinematograph industry was once again falling behind in the race.

The view that the disappointments and failures experienced by British film-makers were attributable, at least to quite a considerable extent, to the dominance achieved by representatives of the London theatre, is not shared by everyone with personal memories of the studios in the early 1930s.

One screenwriter for whom I have much respect read the first script for this book and commented that 'it was easy to criticize producers for lack of initiative, and for filming stories of well-known plays rather than others written specifically for the screen. It is, however, even easier to find the reason for their doing so. The policy made for success. Throughout film history many box-office hits have been based on theatre shows.'

The question has been debated frequently and opinions are unlikely to be changed now. Perhaps insufficient emphasis has been laid, however, on the difference between the two media. In a play the story is told primarily by words, in a film by pictures. A filmed play usually warrants its description as a 'talkie'. Plays and films are designed to appeal to different audiences, and there are few reasons for supposing that a play which has been well received by a Shaftesbury Avenue stalls audience will be as acceptable to picture-goers in a North of England industrial town. Cicely Courtneidge in her frank way has described (in her autobiography) how stage people looked at film-making in these difficult years. 'There was no financial risk for us to underwrite in films, and one picture, which took, say, eight weeks to make, earned us more money than a year's run in the theatre. . . . When we received our first pay packet for our first film we thought they had made a mistake and added too many noughts.'

Some producers, with an eye on the industrial north, made 'cheap budget', farcical comedies with music hall and concert party comics, such as Leslie Fuller, Ernie Lotinga, Sandy Powell and Jerry Verno. They overacted monstrously and relied on old wheezes and gags instead of on new situations with unexpected twists. But their public supported them loyally and their inexpensive films often showed substantial profits.

Several musicals produced at this time were little more than rehashes of stage shows. Jack Buchanan had come home from Hollywood with a fine cinema reputation. Now he made *That's a Good Girl*, based on his 1928 show. To see this film today beside the American *42nd Street*—they are contemporaneous—is to be confronted with what went wrong with British films. The Jack Buchanan film is slapdash in every way. In Hollywood he had had to be strictly professional.

This may partly explain too why the best British musicals of the period were based on German films. The first was *Sunshine Susie*, directed by Victor Saville. Renate Muller came to this country to play her original part, and had Owen Nares and Jack Hulbert to support her. Lilian Harvey and Conrad Veidt also repeated their rôles in *Congress Dances*, made by Pommer and Charell, who had been responsible for the first film. Another remake of a German film *Tell Me Tonight*, in which Jan Kiepura and Magda Sneider (quite unknown then to the British public) sang beside the Swiss lakes, had a remarkable success in this country in spite of little advance publicity. It also helped the case of British advocates of a divorce between the theatre and the cinema (and who were accustomed to being reminded that both *Sunshine Susie* and *Congress Dances* had, in fact, been produced on the Berlin stage). *Tell Me Tonight* was made in the open air.

J. C. Trewin has commented on the 'triumphant blare' with which in 1930 the cinema conquered the provinces. He spoke of the great reduction in the number of touring companies to be seen on the platforms of Crewe Station on Sundays. In their place had come immense numbers of the tin boxes in which films were circulated

H

each week. Cinemas did the theatrical profession much harm at this period when the economic depression was at its height. Perhaps actors and actresses could be excused for sensing retribution in the grip the members of their profession were securing on the film studios.

GOING TO THE PICTURES ON SUNDAYS

Although many actors, authors, directors, stage technicians and other people of the theatre made a bee-line for the film studios, theatre proprietors were less well placed during these dark days. Some of the new theatres, such as the Carlton, the Dominion and the Leicester Square, were permanently converted into cinemas. The Alhambra and Daly's were pulled down and cinemas built on their sites. The Pavilion became a cinema. So for a short time did the Palladium itself.

Some theatrical interests, rather pointlessly resentful about film theatres opening on Sundays (while 'live' theatres could not), openly supported certain organizations in seeking out new ways of enforcing obsolete provisions in the Sunday Observance Act of 1780. At this stage they met with some success and compelled the cinemas to close; but after a while the Government realized that public opinion could not be flouted. A short Bill was approved giving English local authorities the right to license Sunday opening: and in 1932 the Sunday Entertainments Act was adopted. It included a vigorously-contested provision that 5 per cent of the industry's Sunday takings were to go into a fund 'to promote the development of the film as a means of entertainment and instruction'. A new body, the British Film Institute, was to derive its income from the fund. This reflects the general awareness that the cinema was having an immense influence on the people of this country and the feeling that the influence was not altogether for the good. The Institute itself is referred to later.

The trade's support for Sunday opening of cinemas has never been unanimous. That Sunday cinemas provide a commendable social amenity in large towns with floating populations was recognized. Their importance in keeping young people off the streets was appreciated, as well as in providing a place to which friendless people could go on Sunday evenings. Indeed, all this was demonstrated by the large attendances that Sunday shows did, in fact, attract. In many cinemas the Sunday's box-office takings were second only to Saturday's.

However, takings on Mondays and Tuesdays tended to fall, one possible explanation being that a fair proportion of the public would have gone to the pictures on these nights if they had not spent their money on Sunday. It must be admitted that another explanation of some trade members' hostility to Sunday opening might have originated in an understandable dislike of having to work at weekends.

Then there was a practical objection based on the difficulty of getting suitable films to show on Sundays. Those in tin boxes, which J. C. Trewin noticed circulating throughout the country between late Saturday night and early Monday morning, could not be transported in a moment. Their collection, reallocation and distribution principally by the Film Transport undertaking had become one of the industry's outstanding feats of organization. But the practice which grew up of showing old films on Sundays for a single-day's run was unavoidable. Sunday audiences, which tend to come from the more youthful and less accomplished adult members of Society, have displayed a strong preference for the Westerner's flashing fists and the gangster's eviscerating tommy gun. Cinemas are now open on Sunday in most parts of the country, but they sometimes show programmes that are scarcely suitable material for entertainment on the Sabbath.

The cinema was becoming tougher, and censorship continued to be a major issue. Liverpool decided that children should never be allowed to see 'A' films, even if accompanied by an adult. Manchester tried to substitute classifications of their own for those of the British Board of Film Censors. The Government was again pressed to set up a state censorship; and again it declined to do so. The new chairman of the Board, the legalistic Rt. Hon. Edward Shortt, found himself in a difficult position. He appealed to producers to keep off sordid subjects, and particularly those in which lawlessness was glorified. At this moment, however, when those who had admired T. P. O'Connor's common sense attitude in the past were preparing to defend the censor again, Mr Shortt decided to be logical in applying a principle in circumstances never intended. This was in refusing a certificate to *Outward Bound* because it dealt with after-life. It was based on a current and well-known stage play, and local authorities throughout the country followed the London County Council's lead in authorizing the film's showing in their district. Many regret—particularly in the light of happenings in recent years —that this loophole was opened.

Informed American opinion had also become concerned about the possible harm being done by their gangster films. Mindful of the contribution the cinema had made during the 1920s to spreading the presumption of American omnipotence, it was worried—and with good reason—about what these new films might be doing.

But the needs of business came first and the American film industry pushed ahead, with its eye focused particularly on the English-speaking markets. It wanted, as was said at the time, 'every cent it could get from Great Britain—because of the reduced value of sterling and because of its own economic pressure'.

CHAPTER ELEVEN

The Second Phase in the 'Thirties

••

The second of the three phases into which the 1930s has been divided covers the years 1933 to 1936. It began with splendid triumphs and the production of some of the finest films made in this country. It ended in disillusion and dispute. New names come into the story—Arthur Rank, Oscar Deutsch, Alexander Korda. These have, in fact, been described as Korda's years, because his reputation and influence were immense just then.

This is misleading, however, and it can be argued that the phase really began earlier, in 1932, with Michael Balcon's *The Rome Express*. Directed by Walter Forde in the greatly enlarged studios at Shepherd's Bush this film was hailed by C. A. Lejeune as the best full-length British film ever produced. It did much to re-establish British values during some bad moments towards the end of that year. It was an exciting cinema melodrama played as the title suggests on the Rome Express by an international cast including Conrad Veidt, Esther Ralston and Gordon Harker.

MICHAEL BALCON'S FILMS FOR GAUMONT-BRITISH

Three of Michael Balcon's 1933 productions reached an equally high standard, and all were directed by Victor Saville. *I Was a Spy* was set in Flanders in 1915 during the Occupation, with a German officer trapping a spy who turns out to be the girl with whom he has fallen in love. By his masterful portrayal of this officer Conrad Veidt established a permanent place for himself in British studios. Madeleine Carroll was the girl, Herbert Marshall her fellow spy.

Although *Friday the 13th* was described by some critics as a charade put on by a cast of familiar character actors, this episodic film, woven around the passengers on an ill-starred bus journey, is often recalled, and it is interesting to record the names of these character actors—Jessie Matthews, Sonnie Hale, Gordon Harker,

Edmund Gwenn, Max Miller, Robertson Hare, Emlyn Williams, Frank Lawton, Elizabeth Allan and Ralph Richardson.

J. B. Priestley's *The Good Companions* is perhaps the best remembered of this group of films. It was the first talking film seen at a gala performance by King George V and Queen Mary. Described as the outstanding example of the English picaresque on the screen it fitted admirably with the mood of the British people, as they adapted themselves to the long depression and groped about in their search for a way to recovery. The leading parts were vivaciously played by Jessie Matthews as Susie Dean and amiably by Edmund Gwenn as Jess Oakroyd. Jollifant was portrayed by John Gielgud and Miss Trant by Mary Glynn.

In 1934 Alfred Hitchcock, who had left Elstree for Shepherd's Bush, directed *The Man Who Knew Too Much*, and from then until 1939 he made at least one thriller a year for Michael Balcon. *The Man Who Knew Too Much* was about a couple, played by Edna Best and Herbert Marshall, who had their child, the juvenile Nova Pilbeam, stolen from them. Alistair Cooke said that Hitchcock directed the film with his 'familiar mastery of a slow ominous tempo, passages of breathless tantalizing cutting, and some psychological detail which advances him in the path previously trodden by Fritz Lang'. The frequency with which Hitchcock was likened in the 1930s to Lang now surprises us. Resemblances were there, no doubt, for those who sought them, but Hitchcock's approach was light and often amusing while Lang's was invariably heavy-fisted.

Michael Balcon's outstanding productions in 1935 and 1936 were probably two more by Hitchcock, at last being accepted as the British master of mystery melodramas. One of these films, loosely based on John Buchan's *The 39 Steps,* is fondly remembered partly because the principal parts were most delightfully played by Robert Donat and Madeleine Carroll. Although the film has been much praised to the detriment of its 1959 successor, it was criticized by John Buchan's admirers who could not accept the deviations from the plot. Hitchcock replied to them by saying simply that the original book had been altered to suit the cinema—but critics, such as Alistair Cooke, persisted in saying that the original story had not been digested—'Hitchcock sees his way clearly round bits of business, never round incidents'. His film in the following year, *Secret Agent*, was perhaps one of his lesser achievements. Its relatively lukewarm reception by the press now brought Alistair Cooke to his defence—'Hitchcock is still underrated. He is no Fritz Lang but in the photoplay he stands for our self respect.' The film was based on Somerset Maugham's novel *Ashenden*. 'Hitchcock has strained it,' Ian Coster said, 'through the sieve of his individual mind and has subtracted the meat to make a stimulating broth of his own concoction.'

In 1934 Michael Balcon embarked on a campaign to put the British musical on its feet, and in the account of his first twenty-five years in pictures he could with justification describe this period as 'the golden age of musicals', which he added really meant the age of 'the enchanting Jessie Matthews'. It began with an adaptation of the Rogers and Hart-C. B. Cochran show *Evergreen*, with Jessie Matthews in her stage part. Even today the film is notable, if only because of Jessie Matthews's superb dancing. The following year she sang and danced her way through Victor Saville's *First a Girl*. Conceived in the light-hearted style of continental musical films, produced in simple fashion with a good story and a few jolly tunes, it inaugurated a series of films (written for the cinema), all featuring Jessie Matthews. They were almost as popular in the United States as in this country—and that cannot be said of any other musical films exported from Great Britain.

Michael Balcon also produced in this period *Tudor Rose*, still among the best historical films ever made in this country. It was directed by Robert Stevenson, a former President of the Cambridge Union and Editor of *Granta*. It delved into the intrigues which led to the execution of Lady Jane Grey, exquisitely played by maturing Nova Pilbeam. Cedric Hardwicke was the Earl of Warwick, others in the cast being John Mills, Sybil Thorndike and Gwen Ffrangcon-Davies. Stephen Watts put it among the best half a dozen films ever made in Great Britain. He found it beautiful, moving and completely intelligent. C. A. Lejeune too regarded it as a picture in a hundred, set out in extremely simple fashion and played extremely quietly, with no one having the bad taste to exaggerate his portrait.

Michael Balcon produced other films in this second phase of the 1930s including *Jew Süss*, which cost £100,000, 'probably a record for those days'; *The Iron Duke* and three other films featuring George Arliss; *Rhodes*, with Walter Huston in the name part, and Viertel's 'weeping success', *Little Friend*. He brought stars from Hollywood such as Richard Dix and Richard Arlen. But there were losses as well as profits and on February 26, 1937, the closing down of the Shepherd's Bush studios was announced. The purpose of the closure was to enable Gaumont-British 'to develop the company's prosperous theatre interest'. Production was not to be abandoned altogether, as some films would still be made by Gainsborough at Islington and by GFD at Pinewood. But it meant that Michael Balcon's Gaumont-British period had come to its end. A 'funeral' lunch was held, and, as Michael Balcon's story says, it 'combined genuine regret and sympathy with something of the hectic unreality that had touched that era of British film production and had invested it with glamour as well as failure'. From March 1929, with the introduction of the sound film, to March 1936, Gaumont-British under Michael Balcon's leadership had produced no fewer than 133 feature films, an average of sixteen a year.

Mention should be made here of another Gaumont-British film of the period. It is Flaherty's *Man of Aran,* which took three years to make and was released in 1934. Made in the documentary tradition it was criticized for being fictional in parts. Set in the islands off Galway its theme was, as described by Paul Rotha, 'man fighting sea and rock'. Rotha paid a tribute to the opportunities given by Gaumont-British to several young directors and technicians to work with Flaherty for some months. The film is one of the best-remembered British films of the 'thirties.

'THE KEY FILM IN THE HISTORY OF BRITISH CINEMATOGRAPHY'

Alexander Korda (1893-1956), originally a Hungarian journalist, built studios in Budapest, worked for the Sascha company in Vienna, and directed spectacular films in Berlin for Ufa. He was responsible in the period 1926-30 for a dozen Paramount films made in Hollywood (including *The Private Life of Helen of Troy,* which featured his wife, Maria Corda). With the introduction of sound films his career in Hollywood ended, but he persuaded Paramount to sponsor two films to be made in Paris. One of them was Raimu's entrancing *Marius.*

Ideal, perceiving that he was capable of making cheap as well as good films, brought him to London in 1931 to direct two smart frothy films, *Service for Ladies* and *Wedding Rehearsal.* Critics were delighted and the films did very well, particularly in the 'better-class halls'. So the way was prepared for the founding of London Films—a title that had been used before, as incidentally had the introductory sequence showing Big Ben. Part of the British and Dominion Studios at Elstree were hired, and there on a single stage Korda, now joined by his brothers Vincent and Zoltan, directed *The Private Life of Henry VIII.*

The intention had been for London Films to make cheap Quota films; but Korda put his own money into *Henry VIII,* so that the film could be more worthy of its subject. And, as Ian Dalrymple wrote in his British Film Academy appreciation of Korda, it has been hailed ever since as the key film in the history of British cinematography. In the next twenty-five years, Dalrymple said, 'Korda dreamed-up, created, promoted, financed, directed, produced or otherwise fostered some hundred films; mostly of high standard, some of them of the highest, some of them commercial failures, one or two of them disastrous: yet the majority of them successes, *and at least eighteen of them top winners for the box-office.*'

Why was *Henry VIII* so popular, and not only in this country but in other parts of the world? *Henry VIII* is a legendary character known presumably to everybody because of his eccentric fancy for acquiring six wives legally. Charles Laughton treated him as a figure of fun—as Emil Jannings had done a few years before in Lubitsch's *Anne Boleyn*—and that too is how people have come to think of *Henry VIII*. The more pleasing of the six wives were charmingly portrayed by Merle Oberon, Wendy Barrie and Binnie Barnes; and, if the court and other scenes are unimpressive by present-day standards, they were found thoroughly satisfying at the time. The film aroused disapproval in educational circles. Charles R. Beard was speaking for many teachers when he remarked that it might be 'good entertainment but feeble history, bad psychology and worse archaeology'. Paul Rotha was less concerned with this aspect— 'Laughton's King may not be the Tudor stallion which pleases all tastes, but its tremendous display of emotions cannot be denied, whether achieved by fair means or foul'.

There was much conjecturing about the cost of making the film. This was not above £58,000. The earnings were over £500,000, and the film was reported recently to be bringing in £10,000 a year from revivals. These figures were much to the liking of the City finance houses. For a couple of years their feelings towards the cinematograph industry had been turning chilly because, although British cinemas were making fine profits, British films were not.

Now the money bags were prised open. The Prudential Assurance Company became Korda's principal backer, and work was put in hand to build for him at Denham, at a cost of more than a million pounds, the finest studios in the world. Korda, who shared Sam Goldwyn's confidence that a good film will always find a market, hoped and believed that Denham would become the international film-maker's Mecca. In the meantime he went on making films at Elstree and elsewhere in other companies' studios.

Almost without exception Korda's films are well known to the present public because they have been frequently televised—an indication in itself of their entertainment value. Comparatively few viewers realize, however, that some of them were made a long time ago, and it might be of interest to place a few in chronological order.

Korda's second major film was *Catherine the Great*, featuring the German actress, Elisabeth Bergner, and directed by her husband

Paul Czinner. Although the film had many splendid qualities the choice of the subject itself was probably ill-advised. Henry VIII was a well-known character to mid- and east-Europeans (such as Korda himself), but Catherine the Great was not even a name to most British and incidentally American people.

Not discouraged, however, by this disappointment, Korda made another spectacular costume film about another private life, this time Don Juan's. The script was written by Frederick Lonsdale and the title part was played by Douglas Fairbanks (senior). In spite of the introduction of some most attractive young actresses in the supporting cast, including Merle Oberon, the film was a failure and Korda's reputation slumped—and this before his immense studio at Denham was opened.

He was being criticized as a man whose reputation rested on one picture, 'a lucky break', and the suggestion was made that the success of even this picture was attributable more to Charles Laughton than to Alexander Korda. In 1935 C. A. Lejeune came to the defence of 'this unaccountable entrepeneur', whose advent in this country had certainly been to its benefit. He is, she said, neither a dilettante nor a highbrow, but a shrewd practical film-maker, an inveterate showman and a brilliant gambler. 'His weakness is that he plays a lone hand. His final authority is unshared and undeputed.'

Nothing could get this courageous, energetic and imaginative man down, and he came back with another outstanding success, an adaptation of Baroness Orczy's *The Scarlet Pimpernel.* Directed by Harold Young it had Leslie Howard, Merle Oberon and Raymond Massey in its cast. Alistair Cooke described it as a smooth melodrama, eased by Korda's liking for gracious landscapes, and with a story exactly as long as its suspense.

Still working in the British and Dominions Studio at Elstree and at Isleworth—Denham was not ready—he produced several other widely distributed films, the best remembered of which is probably Zoltan Korda's *Sanders of the River.* Based on some of Edgar Wallace's stories it had Leslie Banks and Nina Mae McKinney in the cast. But Paul Robeson was in it too and his singing holds the film in the memory.

Next came another of the films with which Korda's name will always be associated. Its director was Cameron Menzies. A particular aspect of H. G. Wells's prophetic book (*The Shape of*) *Things to Come* has been forgotten. Serialized in one of the most widely circulating Sunday newspapers it compelled the British people in the early 1930s to face for the first time the probability that another world war was coming soon. They were still deluding themselves that the war to end all wars had accomplished its purpose. Hence there was great curiosity to see the film, and this was followed by considerable astonishment at some of the effects achieved by Ned Mann and photographed by George Perinal.

Ned Mann's inventive talents were applied by Korda in another film based on an H. G. Wells's book, *The Man Who Could Work Miracles*. It was directed by Lothar Mendes and featured a British actor who had become a Hollywood star, Roland Young. Views expressed about its merits were very divergent too. John Marks thought that words plus tricks do not make a talkie, and that the film was like nine out of every ten British films—it went wrong in the dialogue. But Paul Dehn said he would feel an active and overwhelming anger if the picture were not attended by the success it so valiantly deserved. Graham Greene was far from convinced. He dismissed it as an orgy of trick photography. It suffered, he said, 'from the slowness, vulgarity and overemphasis of Korda productions'. Korda never lacked his critics.

Not all of Korda's productions were of a spectacular character. Perhaps the most warmly remembered of his films set among contemporary people was directed by the up-and-coming Carol Reed. Based on J. B. Priestley's play *Laburnum Grove*, it had a brilliant interpretation by Edmund Gwenn in the part of the douce middle-aged householder who really was the international crook he jokingly declared himself to be. This time Graham Greene was greatly pleased. 'Here at last,' he said, 'is an English film one can reasonably praise. The camera has gone behind the dialogue. Suburbia insinuates itself in every shot.' Revived since on several occasions it stands up well when compared with much later and more expensively made films.

Rembrandt is certain to be included in any list drawn up of Korda's best films. Most critics would put it among the first three, and it is probably the finest biographical film ever made in any country. Many would also say that Charles Laughton's portrayal of the Dutch painter was his greatest rôle—in exposition, in appearance and, especially, in voice. The dialogue had lyrical qualities rarely encountered in the cinema and Laughton was superb in putting them into effect. The period was brilliantly recaptured and the settings —themselves in keeping with the subject—are still impressive. Unfortunately the film did not do particularly well at the box-office, sections of the public apparently finding it deficient in story-value and suspense.

CINEMAS MAKE MORE PROFITS THAN FILMS DO

Delineating the period covered by this second phase is difficult because the other large group, headed by John Maxwell, carried on with its policy steadily throughout 1932 and 1933. There was no clear-cut division. The studios at Elstree and Welwyn made films according to budget. Costs were controlled in a business-like way, and the extravagance with which some studios were often charged was not to be found at Elstree.

John Maxwell made an outstanding contribution in establishing the modern British film industry. Indeed, the view is held in many quarters that his calm and stabilizing influence in the late 1920s and early 1930s enabled the industry to survive the vicissitudes which assailed it. In the late 1930s, when the situation had again turned desperate, he came to the rescue, as is mentioned in Chapter Thirteen, by financing Erich Pommer's Mayflower Picture Corporation.

His British International Studios at Elstree and Welwyn were in fact almost unique by being consistently busy throughout the 1930s. Walter Mycroft—who as film critic of the *Evening Standard* had been one of the founders of the London Film Society—was put in charge of the Elstree Studios in 1928. He was directly responsible to John Maxwell and his authority was so considerable that he was nicknamed the 'Czar of all the Rushes'.

Elstree set the pace in the early days of the talkies, not only with *Blackmail* and *Atlantic*, but with other films calling for considerable technical ingenuity. Perhaps the best remembered is a version of *The Informer*, directed by the German, Dr Arthur Robison, with the continental stars Lars Hansen and Lya de Putti at the head of the cast in this most Irish of plays. Lya de Putti was quite incapable of speaking any English and her voice had to be 'dubbed' throughout. The long tracking shot which opened the film is still mentioned in textbooks on film technique.

Walter Mycroft is most often recalled today for his commercial successes, and this is perhaps responsible for his achievements sometimes being overlooked when accounts are given of films not specifically aimed at the 'popular markets'. There can be no doubt, however, that the policy at Elstree must have been influenced by the remarkable earnings in 1931 of a low-budget farce, *My Wife's Family*. Subsequently a number of other pictures characterized by 'down-to-earth, slapstick clowning' were made at Elstree, and this led some film critics to cold-shoulder BIP films in general.

An interesting contrast is provided by the cool reception given to Elstree's *Blossom Time* and by the much warmer approbation which a German film (subsequently redirected by Anthony Asquith for Gaumont-British) received. The latter was *The Unfinished Symphony*, and it was chosen to open the Curzon Cinema in Mayfair. Both films were romances based on episodes in Franz Schubert's life.

Recently Lord Harewood stated that his interest in music had been stimulated by Richard Tauber's singing in *Blossom Time*.

Although economic considerations influenced BIP's promotion schedules, expensive films were made at Elstree as well as in the Korda and Gaumont-British studios. There were, for instance, *The Red Wagon*, based on Lady Eleanor Smith's circus novel, in which the principal rôles were taken by players from other countries, Charles Bickford, Raquel Torres and Greta Nissen; Frederick Zelnik's *Dubarry* with Gitta Alpar and Arthur Margetson in the cast; *Royal Cavalcade,* a pageant of the years 1910 and 1935, made on the occasion of King George V's Silver Jubilee, with scenes recreated in the matter of Will Barker's *Sixty Years a Queen,* Paul Stein's version of *La Boheme*, with Gertrude Lawrence and Douglas Fairbanks, junior, in the principal parts; and *McGlusky the Rover,* based on A. G. Hales's novel, with Jack Doyle as McGlusky. Whether all these films would stand up to modern criticism is doubtful, but the particulars now available certainly suggest that they were, at least, interesting. Indeed, Will Hay's first film, adapted from Pinero's *The Magistrate*, and directed by Tom Bentley, with young John Mills as the mischievous scamp, was very well received when revived in 1959 at the National Film Theatre. It too was made at Elstree.

BIP's Elstree Studios have been called the School for British Film Makers, because of the large number of men and women who received their early training there, and later made their mark in the industry. It was at Elstree, for instance, that the revolutionary changes in technique brought about by the talkies had to be assimilated by the writers of the scripts (then known as scenarios), Frank Launder, for instance, had gone to Elstree to devise captions for silent films. Others who obtained early training in BIP's Scenario Department include Rodney Ackland, Leslie Arliss, Jack Davies, Sidney Gilliat, J. Lee Thompson, Dudley Leslie and T. J. Morrison. Ronald Neame and Jack Cardiff are among those who were once camera operators with BIP; Leslie Norman and Charles Frend began their careers in the cutting rooms at Elstree.

Although the Elstree and Welwyn Studios continued to be kept busy throughout this period, John Maxwell and his colleagues were increasingly aware that, while their cinemas were unquestionably profitable ventures, some of their films were not. This led the Associated British Picture Corporation to announce in 1936 (and before Gaumont-British had come to a similar decision) that they would reduce the amount of film-making in their studios and concentrate on building up their cinemas.

It was at this time that Simon Rowson gave a most disturbing report to the trade on the circulation of British films in the United States. He estimated that over £5 million pounds were leaving this country annually to pay for the foreign films (almost entirely American) shown here, while only £0·1 million was coming back from the United States and £0·5 million from other countries overseas.

THE TURN OF THE TIDE

Before discussing the changes which were made—or proposed—during this period in the ownership and control of the British cinematograph industry, one other film must be mentioned, *The Turn of the Tide*. It would not be included in a list of great British pictures, but it probably did more to shape the future development of the British cinematograph industry than perhaps any other film (not excluding even *The Private Life of Henry VIII*).

In 1933 a new personage, quite unknown to the trade, J. Arthur Rank began to take an interest in films. Within the next eight years he acquired control of two of the three principal circuits of cinemas in Great Britain, the Ostrers' Gaumonts and Oscar Deutsch's Odeons, as well as the studios at Denham, Pinewood, Shepherd's Bush and Elstree (Amalgamated).

The films which brought him into the industry were short and had religious themes. He was guided by the Rev. Benjamin Gregory, editor of the *Methodist Times*. After commissioning various companies to make these films, he founded British National Films late in 1934 along with another very rich person, Lady Yule. The intention was to make more religious films (he had several subjects in mind, including *The Pilgrim's Progress*). But instead of doing so British National produced *The Turn of the Tide*, a simple feature film about family antagonisms in a Yorkshire fishing village. It was ably directed by Norman Lee and presented a new star, Geraldine Fitzgerald. *The Turn of the Tide* was liked by the critics, who appreciated its humanity and its sincerity. Arthur Rank was delighted, because the film's theme, although not religious, had high moral tone.

A short while after the film's release he inquired how many cinemas were showing the film, and the answer was 'disappointingly few'. Seeking an explanation he ascertained that a handful of Wardour Street men who booked films for cinema circuits had decided that many audiences would not care for *The Turn of the Tide*. They had presumably substituted a second-feature American film for it. Being a most capable businessman himself he wanted to know how the distributing company handling the film had dealt with this cold shouldering of his film; and he was not favourably impressed by the answer to his question.

Alan Wood in his book on *Mr Rank* says that religion is the key to his whole career. Confronted with this displeasing situation he decided that the film business 'had got into the hands of the wrong people', and made up his mind to get it into his own instead.

CONFLICT AT THE TOP

Gaumont-British's decision to follow ABPC's example by concentrating on circuit building precipitated an incident late in 1936 and a threatened lawsuit. Even now Wardour Street does not fully understand the various developments and implications.

John Maxwell gave the press the quite sensational news that the two major groups—Gaumont-British and ABPC—were combining forces. He would join Gaumont-British's board of directors immediately and procure control later through the acquisition of voting shares. The first actually happened. The second did not. One possible explanation is that two American companies used their combined financial interest in Gaumont-British to prevent this powerful British group coming into being. Had it been effectively established it would have been strong enough to break the American hold on the British cinematograph industry.

In the absence of any book or even series of articles telling the John Maxwell story we can only surmise what happened, and what would have happened if the two groups had come together.

In May 1935, C. M. Woolf had resigned his directorship in Gaumont-British and had formed a renting company of his own, General Film Distributors. When Arthur Rank asked for the name of the most capable man to advise him on film distribution he was told about C. M. Woolf and he sought his help. Then in the course of sorting out of interests with some of his business associates, including Lady Yule, Arthur Rank became chairman of Pinewood, the magnificent new studios in Buckinghamshire, only a few miles from Alexander Korda's Denham Studios. He invited C. M. Woolf to join his board and Richard Norton, whose British and Dominions Studios near Elstree had been turned down, to be managing director.

That a business association could ever have been effected between Rank and Woolf would seem improbable. But, to quote Alan Wood, 'a strange friendship with real affection grew up between the two men. To this day Rank still wears the watch which Woolf left him in his will when he died in 1942'.

Before Arthur Rank's name became well known to the trade another industrialist was becoming very prominent. He was Oscar

Deutsch, the Birmingham metal merchant who had backed Michael Balcon at the beginning of his career and had made various minor investments in the cinema business in the following years. In 1933 he formed Odeon Theatres. His policy was to build palatial new cinemas, named Odeon, which would always show first-class programmes. This he saw as an application of the 'brand selling' that had become common practice in many branches of commerce.

Each new Odeon was floated as a separate company, local shopkeepers who would benefit from having an Odeon nearby being encouraged to invest in the new venture. Oscar Deutsch raised the rest of the finance from larger undertakings, such as insurance companies. So effectively did he carry out his scheme that by 1936 his circuit had become the fourth largest in the country, with 142 cinemas.

Nevertheless, this was insufficient to ensure a regular supply of the 'right sort of film'. The two large circuits owned between them 559 cinemas (or 17 per cent of the cinema seats in the country) and other circuits had been growing besides Odeon. There were, in fact, seven medium-sized circuits, including the Odeon, each with more than ten cinemas; and they, along with the two large circuits, controlled one-third of the country's seating capacity and—what was even more important—one-half of the first-run cinemas.

In his endeavours to get 'quality' films for the Odeons, Oscar Deutsch tried to procure sources of supply from various producing and renting companies. But even the American company, United Artists, with which he entered into a close financial arrangement, had to safeguard its wider interests so as to let other groups and individual cinemas hire its films too. United Artists liked having a certain market of 142 cinemas for their films; but they needed a much larger total than that.

The principal weakness in Oscar Deutsch's plan was his inability to ensure that week in and week out better films really would be shown at the Odeons than at the Gaumonts, the Regals and the other cinemas he was challenging. The British public, and particularly the women, had become discriminating film 'shoppers'. They read the movie gossip in their newspapers. They bought astonishing quantities of fan magazines. If they had to choose for their evening's entertainment between seeing a particular film or relaxing in luxurious surroundings they chose the film.

TWO HUNDRED FILMS A YEAR

It would not be suggested that insufficient films were being produced in Great Britain. More would have been welcomed, no doubt, but

9. The British film most widely shown in the United States since *Henry VIII* was Noël Coward's *In Which We Serve*, made in the dark days of 1942.

The film which depicted the munitions workers most accurately was *Millions Like Us*, made in 1943 by Launder and Gilliatt. The foreman in this scene is Eric Portman. The girls are Anne Crawford and Patricia Roc.

10. One of the last of the memorable British war films was Anthony
Asquith's *The Way to the Stars* (1945), set on an airfield. Here are
Michael Redgrave, Trevor Howard and John Mills.

Towards the end of the war some of the British studios reverted
to the production of costume melodramas. In Leslie Arliss's
The Wicked Lady Margaret Lockwood was a society girl who turned
highwayman. James Mason was not a good influence in her life.

the steady rate of 200 feature films being maintained each year was reasonably satisfactory.

The three principal sources, Gaumont-British (with Gains-borough), Associated British Picture Corporation, formerly BIP (with Pathe) and London Films have been mentioned. There were many others.

Two American companies still had production subsidiaries in the London district: Warner Brothers with studios at Teddington, and Twentieth Century-Fox with studios at Wembley. Besides these there were, to quote the Klingender and Legg survey, 'a large and fluctuating number of independent English producers renting through the two major and the independent English renters, and/or producing quota films for the Americans'.

Some of the leading women stars were appearing in films which could be described as independently made, although their sponsors' liking for freedom of action did not necessarily preclude arranging beforehand with one of the large companies for the films' distribution. They included Gracie Fields, Anna Neagle and Elisabeth Bergner.

Gracie Fields's films were now taking more money at box-offices throughout this country than those of any other star, American or British. She had made her first film performance several years before in *Sally in Our Alley* (based on the play *The Likes of 'Er*), directed by Maurice Elvey. Her popularity on the screen had grown rapidly and in most years after 1934 she had been in two films annually. Some were written by J. B. Priestley, such as *Sing as We Go,* which was located in Bolton and Blackpool. Describing her as 'the unique professional amateur', *World Film News* observed that 'she is not an actress but a single personality act, a mill girl who has made good but is still a mill girl'. There were critics, however, who found her films bogus—for instance, Paul Rotha: 'If this is to be the way of putting England on the screen, then stay in your studios, producers, and leave England to the makers of documentary films.' However, America had not yet taken to Gracie as a living artiste and few people outside Great Britain and parts of the Commonwealth saw her films at this period.

Anna Neagle had advanced from relatively minor parts in Jack Buchanan's films; and in 1933 she played the lead in Noël Coward's *Bitter Sweet.* This she followed with *Nell Gwynn, Limelight* and other pictures directed by her husband, Herbert Wilcox. He is one of the few men whose name runs throughout the story of British cinematography, from the early 'twenties to the late 'fifties. As C. A. Lejeune remarked, 'he is a director who believes in simple statements and no beating about the bush'.

I

Turning over the pages of film periodicals of a quarter of a century ago brings back memories of many other British films of these times: Paul Czinner's production of *As You Like It*, with Elizabeth Bergner as a rather skittish Rosalind; Seymour Hicks's splendid version of *A Christmas Carol*, with Oscar Asche as the Spirit of Christmas; Maurice Chevalier in a film directed by Kurt Bernhardt in English and in French, *The Beloved Vagabond*, with Betty Stockfeld and Margaret Lockwood in the cast; and Douglas Fairbanks, junior, in an adaptation of Jeffrey Farnol's *The Amateur Gentleman*.

There are hundreds more to choose from; but the disturbing fact remains that fewer than half a dozen are worthy of recall as being of really superior quality, or as having made a major contribution to the development of cinematography. They may be revived today for sentimental reasons or for studying the style of a particular director or player; but they were not notable productions in themselves.

With few exceptions they do not bear comparison with many excellent Hollywood productions of this vintage period. When it is recalled too that this was one of the most brilliant moments in the French cinema, and that German films, although not much liked in this country, were being widely shown throughout the Continent, there can be little surprise that first John Maxwell and then Isidore Ostrer decided that the game in this country was not worth the candle, and that their business was to show films rather than to make them.

'THE FILM IN NATIONAL LIFE'

Early in the 1930s a Commission on Educational and Cultural Films was set up, and in its report, *The Film in National Life*, a recommendation was made for establishing an Institute 'to promote the development of the film as a means of entertainment and instruction'. It was to be financed from the fund created by the percentage deducted from the Sunday takings of all cinemas open on that day in England and Wales, as required by the new Sunday Performances Act.

Some ten objectives were mentioned for the proposed Institute. They included influencing public opinion to appreciate the value of films as entertainment and instruction; 'advising' educational institutions and other organizations; acting as a means of liaison between the trade (producers, distributors and exhibitors) and cultural and educational interests; and maintaining a national repository of films of permanent value.

The Institute was established in the late summer of 1933 in an office building near the crossing of Oxford Street and Tottenham Court Road—near but 'not too near' Wardour Street. J. W. Brown of the British Institute of Adult Education was appointed Director (at first, Manager) and Reginald V. Crow, a past President of the CEA, secretary.

The authors of *The Film in National Life* had not performed any notable feat of percipience in advocating the wider showing of foreign films and the revival of meritorious old films. Indeed, they were rather behind the times. The Shaftesbury Avenue Pavilion and its successors (such as the Academy Cinema and the Curzon) had been showing foreign films since 1927. And before the Institute was formed a Federation of British Film Societies had come into being with a dozen members, some such as Glasgow, Edinburgh and Newcastle being, like London, of considerable size. Whether the Institute should show films to the public—as was done in New York by the Museum of Modern Art—was keenly debated but the discussions were essentially academic as, until the National Film Theatre was opened in the early 1950s, the Institute lacked the necessary facilities.

Committed to sending a monthly bulletin to its members setting out the titles of recommended films, the Institute was confronted with a most difficult problem—how with its limited staff to review all the films being trade-shown in London and then to arrive at recommendations.

There were other problems ahead for the Institute. Schools throughout the country were keenly interested in the use of films in the classroom. Indeed, Glasgow Education Authority was about to take the lead by installing a projector in every one of its schools. Both Gaumont-British and the Associated British Picture Corporation (through Pathe) were being most enterprising not only in manufacturing and supplying equipment for educational bodies but in producing instructional films. Finding that the Institute had virtually nothing to contribute the companies and the schools tended to by-pass it.

In two respects, however, the Institute was successful from the outset. The National Film Archive was set up in 1935, and as a repository of worthwhile British and other films has done notable work for which posterity will be grateful. And the quarterly magazine, *Sight and Sound,* contrived to be not only informative but readable.

In 1936 the Institute almost came to an early end through a lawsuit, affecting its Governors, which made headlines in the popular press. Its reputation fell and, when the third Annual General Meeting was reported in the newspapers, acid comments were made.

World Film News scoffed at the annual report in which 'the same old wordy claims about education and culture have been trotted out, and the same old wordy claims have been made as to the value of the work done . . . , the fact being that the Institute has become a source of ridicule and distrust'.

It was at this disastrous moment that the Governors selected Oliver Bell as director. Several knowledgeable men associated with the industry had been invited to fill the post, and all had declined. Apart from having sat on one or two committees dealing with aspects of cinematography, notably with religious films, Oliver Bell knew little about films. Yet, during the next dozen years, he completely changed the Institute's outlook and status. In particular he established much healthier relations with the trade, and fostered the film society movement in England and Wales. The Institute subsequently became a body of quite considerable influence in the industry.

CHAPTER TWELVE

Speculative Financing

....

NO DIVIDENDS

The bankruptcy of three small companies fairly early in 1936 went unheeded. But it was the first sign that a major crisis would develop in the middle of this decade (as had happened in the middle of each of the century's three earlier decades).

For the first months of 1936 'sucker money', as *World Film News* called it, was still being poured into British productions. Indeed, according to that outspoken periodical, film-making expanded throughout most of the year 'with tremendous violence to the tune of £24 million'—and notwithstanding the new centres at Denham (120,000 square feet) and Pinewood (73,000 square feet) now coming into full production; and the 'Amalgamated' Studios at Elstree (130,000 square feet). The older studios at Elstree, Shepperton, Teddington and elsewhere were also fully occupied.

In 1928 the stage area in British studios had been 105,000 square feet. By 1938 it was to be seven times as large, 778,000 square feet, far more, in fact, than was needed. At this moment in their history British producing companies had sufficient resources in the studios to turn out a feature film every day of the year. In 1936 they actually made 220—as against their forecast of 200. Exhibitors had shown no enthusiasm when given this estimate. 'How many of them will be good?' they asked.

'The riddle is how to make art and business run side by side,' S. G. Rayment, editor of the *Kinematograph Weekly,* commented. 'We have, or can buy, all the talent we need, stars, directors, cameramen, artists, writers. What we cannot buy is the higher direction, the big organizing and co-ordinating brain which America has evolved and which we have not—the peculiar assembly of qualities in one man : vision, courage, power, probity, infinite patience, fierce drive, commercial shrewdness, artistic perception and sensitiveness, with a flair for showmanship over all.'

It was *World Film News*, however, that blew the gaff. In an article published at the beginning of 1937, much discussed in the City (and later published as a brochure), it said, 'banks, insurance companies investment trusts, even motor manufacturers have been falling over each other in their eagerness to join in the Gold Rush and to stake a claim. Yet, in spite of the torrent of money in which British producing companies have revelled, few have paid a dividend since 1932 . . . and, as most of them have been formed since 1932, that means most have never paid a dividend at all.'

Besides emphasizing that the boom was based almost entirely on expectation with few concrete results, the report directed attention to a particularly unsatisfactory aspect. The expansion was being financed not by increasing capital but by raising loans. *World Film News* even forecast that the Official Receiver would become the star in one expensive new film about to go into production; and it was not far off the mark.

The British Film Institute's journal *Sight and Sound* thought that at the root of the trouble were not only highly speculative financing but 'inefficient production methods, sharp trading practices and monopolistic tendencies'. Instances were given of films which had been hurriedly planned, publicized, begun and never finished; of films which had taken months longer in production than was scheduled; of American stars being engaged at salaries far exceeding their current box-office value and being paid those salaries although summoned to London before a suitable script or even story had been provided for them.

An editorial in the *Daily Telegraph* provoked, however, a sharp retort from Alexander Korda. His view was that when the film industry makes money it is in millions of pounds; 'and so, obviously, when we lose, it must be in millions'. The City did not find this one of his more comforting pronouncements.

As John Maxwell and Isidore Ostrer well knew, investors who put their money into the exhibiting side of the industry had not done badly. Many had, in fact, done very well and were still feeling optimistic. There were still opportunities ahead. Simon Rowson, the industry's statistician, maintained that 'for every two eligible persons who go to the cinema in a week in Great Britain there are three who do not'. In Great Britain there was a cinema for each 8,000 members of the population aged 15 and over. But the corresponding figure for the United States was 6,200. So there was still scope for more business.

QUOTA QUICKIES

Rowson traced the crisis back to the quota requirements of 1928, and in particular attributed it to the American companies' disregard for the reciprocity understanding they had then entered into, that one British film would be released in the United States for every fifteen or twenty American films released in Great Britain. This understanding had never been put in writing, however, and was essentially a gentlemen's agreement.

Only two American companies, Warner Brothers and Twentieth-Century Fox, had set up and maintained production subsidiaries of any size in Great Britain to fulfil their quota requirements. The other six large American companies were content to employ British independent producers to make films for them on 'tight terms'. Among these films were those humiliating 'quota quickies' produced at trifling cost, perhaps without any intention of ever being shown to the public. Allegations were made about quota requirements being met by screening films in a few cinemas at 10 o'clock in the morning, when the cleaners were carrying out their manifold duties, or by giving them a run through each day for a brief period at the opening of certain cinemas while the audience was very small. The only good thing to say about most of these films is that scarcely anyone ever saw them, and so they did the reputation of British film-making little harm. But others found their way into a fair number of cinemas because exhibitors as well as renters had to meet quota requirements; and some of them did do a great deal of harm.

THE GERMAN INVASION

The films that caused the greatest amount of mischief, however, were the very expensive ones intended for wide circulation without the least prospect of making a return to their backers. Particularly exasperating to British directors was the extent to which these films were directed by Germans recently arrived in this country.

Korda's achievements were still used to charm companies and individuals who, in these years of depression, were looking far and wide for good investments. The profits made by *The Private Life of Henry VIII* were already becoming legendary, and people unacquainted with the industry supposed that his flair for making successful films was in some way linked with his mid-European background.

All that was needed, they believed, was to discover another Korda; and after 1934, as if by miraculous chance, German and Austrian producers, stars and technicians began to descend on this country almost in their multitudes. Either directly or indirectly they were refugees from the Hitler régime. Probably to their surprise as well as gratification they were welcomed here by people with money to spend. Some lists published in trade periodicals giving the names of the émigrés who had found employment in British studios were astonishingly long.

It was on the whole a most mistaken policy. Most of these men were able; some were brilliant. But their work had a Germanic flavour. Unlike Korda, who had spent several years in Hollywood, they had a decidedly mid-European approach which was remarkably dissimilar from the British. Even masterly films, such as Erich Pommer's *Farewell Again*, did not make much of an impression at British (or overseas) box-offices. And there were the inevitable adventurers, less able than they claimed.

Rightly or wrongly the diminutive Max Schach was picked on for particular criticism, and the failure in 1936 of his expensive and over-publicized *The Marriage of Corbal* was another indication of the boom's rapidly approaching end.

A NEW CINEMATOGRAPH FILMS ACT

Such was the background to the *Daily Telegraph*'s attack on British film finance, that 'the real objects of the Cinematograph Films Act of 1927 have not been realized. More films have been made, but the industry has not been put on a sound financial basis and the quality of British films has not been materially improved.'

The trade fell back on the argument it had used for a dozen years. 'The producers cannot compete successfully against pictures of equal quality made by the United States with four times the market to sell them in.'

'Cinema entertainments,' so it was maintained, 'differ in one important respect from theatre, concert and other entertainments. This is in "duplicability". Production costs are incurred only once in cinematography. Subsequent performance costs in picture houses are just a bagatelle in comparison with those in theatres and concert halls. The more often a film is shown the more money it earns, and this revenue becomes available for advertising it in export markets and for making other films. The United States, with its 14,500 cinemas, could for a time afford to give its films away in Great Britain or elsewhere in order to wreck native production. Furthermore it had the resources to lure away stars, directors and technicians by doubling their wages. And it had done this over many years to the British cinematograph industry's considerable impairment (as well as to the industries of other European countries).'

The Government appointed the Moyne Committee to recommend what new legislation would be required when the ten-year period ended in 1938. And in due course this Committee proposed that the industry should be placed under a small and active permanent Film Commission which would *administer* (not advise on) the new Act. In particular it would supervise the application of a test of 'quality' which all British films would have to pass. But this recommendation was set aside when the Act became effective in April 1938, an Advisory Films Council being substituted for the proposed Commission. It had twenty-one members, ten representatives of various trade interest and eleven independent of the trade.

After much wrangling in and out of Parliament (the three trade groups were deadlocked as they had ten years before) the Moyne Committee's view was accepted that steadily increasing protection must be treated as a *sine qua non*. Quotas were continued for long films (over 3,000 feet) and for short films. They were to rise progressively. The renters' quota was to advance from 15 per cent to 30 per cent in 1946 for long films, and for exhibitors from 12½ per cent to 25 per cent. Separate quotas were introduced for short films. To encourage the production of expensive films a system of double and even treble quotas was devised, based on labour costs.

To prevent foreign exploiters avoiding their legal obligations by turning out cheap 'quickies', films with a labour cost under £7,500 would not qualify for quota. This struck many critics as inadequate. Nevertheless the new Act immediately brought about an important development. Realizing that the Government was prepared to get really tough this time in a way Americans understood, several United States companies decided to take film-making in Great Britain seriously. Metro-Goldwyn-Mayer were early in the field, Michael Balcon, now dissociated from Gaumont-British, becoming their British production manager; Victor Saville terminated a brief rapport with Korda to become their producer-director. MGM's plan was to make four expensive feature films, probably at Denham, and then take particular note of the progress they made in British, American and overseas markets.

Radio appointed Herbert Wilcox as their British chief and announced that they too would make four films, each to cost £150,000. At Pinewood 20th Century-Fox also chose to go ahead with four films, but with an American, Robert Kane, at the head of their enterprise. Warner Brothers extended the rebuilt studios at Teddington and said that they would make fifteen films in the first year. Not all would be expensive films, but four would be taken from their Hollywood schedule. Not to be outdone Adolph Zukor told the press during a visit to this country that Paramount would make films once again in Great Britain.

So an entirely novel situation was created. The large British-owned groups held to their decision that they would concentrate on their cinema circuits rather than on film-production. They had made up their minds and the provisions in the new Act did not persuade them to change their policy. Associated British Picture Corporation took over Union Cinemas and brought their total number of halls up to almost 500. Gaumont-British continued building and their total reached the 350 mark. Oscar Deutsch went full out for expansion and by constructing new Odeons as well as by buying cinemas from other companies raised his total to 250.

CHAPTER THIRTEEN

The End of the Party:
The Late 'Thirties

ONE OF THE FEW VINTAGE YEARS

The last of the three phases into which the decade has been divided covers 1937, 1938 and 1939, each year having had its own individual character. The slump had become worse during 1936 and some of the films then in production were completed only after desperate appeals to backers for further loans to save something from the wreck.

In spite of this most discouraging send-off 1937 was to be one of the few vintage years for British films, and several of the productions are well known today, either through frequent revivals in cinemas or through their use on television.

One film dominates 1937 and it is among the most successful films commercially ever made in this country. This was Herbert Wilcox's *Victoria the Great*. Its remarkable popularity not only in the United States but in European countries—it had the quite exceptional honour for a British film of being acclaimed at the Venice Festival—no doubt prompted Radio to put Wilcox in charge of their new British production activities. The film was shown in Oscar Deutsch's Odeons almost immediately after completion, and this was important in itself because other companies followed suit by cutting the interval between the completion of films and their release to the cinemas. In the days of silent films the interval was often eighteen months and more.

Much of *Victoria the Great*'s success can be attributed to Herbert Wilcox's remarkable sense of timing. The film made its appearance in the cinemas at an opportune moment when, with threats of war in the air, there was general concern over the country's loss of prestige. It was not conceived as a portrait of the age—James Agate said it resembled Jane Austen's works in giving no notion whatever of the England over which Victoria ruled. It was essentially episodic, with its story focused on the Prince Consort, cleverly if not particularly accurately portrayed by Anton Walbrook. The film provided, as Alan Page remarked, refined entertainment. 'Anna Neagle never allowed her Victoria to waver from her determination to be good.' This was, of course, as Herbert Wilcox intended. He has consistently said that he does not make films for sophisticated audiences.

There is no doubt about *Victoria the Great* being the outstanding production of 1937. But who could select the runner-up from *Wings of the Morning, The Edge of the World, Storm in a Teacup, Sabotage, Young and Innocent, Fire Over England, The Ghost Goes West, Love From a Stranger,* or *Elephant Boy*? And there were also the box-office successes, such as the Jessie Matthews, Gracie Fields and George Formby films. But at the time everybody in the trade realized that, after these films had been shown in the cinemas, little was coming up to take their place. The party had been grand, but it was nearly over.

Perhaps the film which made the greatest impression was *Wings of the Morning,* directed by Harold Schuster for 20th Century-Fox. It had an attractive title, *Wings of the Morning,* although this really had little significance since it was just the name of a racehorse. The involved and almost naïve story was about a horse winning the Derby after his gypsy owner had died; but it was charmingly interpreted by an international cast including Annabella, Henry Fonda, Leslie Banks and Stewart Rome, with John McCormack and Steve Donoghue as 'guest artistes'. It was the first British feature made in Technicolor and its success was to a considerable extent attributable to the beautifully mellow effects achieved. America realized with surprise that the soft British light was better for exteriors than the harsh brightness of Californian sunshine. Frank S. Nugent described the film in the *New York Times* as 'a visual delight; as a colour venture it is the best chromatically we have seen'.

Alfred Hitchcock's *Sabotage* seemed to C. A. Lejeune the cleverest film made in this country 'since the silent days'. In it he revealed to the full his flair for creating and maintaining suspense. The plot had its grim moments. A boy, unaware that he is carrying an infernal machine, is delayed and in consequence blows up himself and other passengers in a bus. Although some critics said Hitchcock always used the same plot and general construction, and that this item of unpleasantness was simply one of his twists, others noted that he was getting cleverer and cleverer—more detached, more calculating, more cold-blooded. His people were still real Londoners, however, and not 'incidental attachments to an ingenious and thrilling script'. C. A. Lejeune said that he was unlikely to direct 'a film with a social message', or 'a starkly honest film', because he believed the first purpose of the screen is to endue its customers with pleasure.

Sabotage was an ambitious film with foreign stars, Oscar Homolka and Sylvia Sidney. Before the year was out Hitchcock had almost completed another film, *Young and Innocent*, a homely and fairly plausible little murder story with the heroine and hero, Nova Pilbeam and Derrick de Marney, chasing the criminal and being chased by the police. This was lighter fare and contained a good measure of humour—a gesture perhaps to his public. Alan Page's assessment of Hitchcock's standing at the end of 1937 was that his pictures were 'earning more prestige for British studios than all the spectacular historical pageants produced in the last few years'.

'QUALITY AND THE BIG TIME'

Alexander Korda was very much in the news during 1937. He was responsible for several outstanding productions, the best remembered probably being René Clair's *The Ghost Goes West*. Describing the astonishing experiences of an American millionaire, Eugene Palette, who bought a Scottish baronial castle for erection way back home and found to his great satisfaction that a ghost, played by Robert Donat, went along with the castle, the film was shown throughout the world and was one of Korda's greatest international successes.

Like Herbert Wilcox he was conscious of the country's disquiet about the political situation in Europe and about our loss of face. He turned, however, to Queen Elizabeth instead of to Queen Victoria and engaged an American director, William K. Howard. The film was *Fire Over England*, a story of Armada times written by A. E. W. Mason. It was superbly presented with a cast which included Laurence Olivier, Vivien Leigh, Leslie Banks and Raymond Massey. Flora Robson's portrayal of Queen Elizabeth was possibly very sound but it did not appeal to some audiences. Graham Greene remarked rather cruelly that she had played Queen Elizabeth as if she were headmistress of Cheltenham Ladies' College. The critics also questioned the wisdom of going on making English costume films in the hope that *Henry VIII*'s successor was hovering around the corner. It was perhaps fair comment by the *New York Times* that the British, in order to make an epic film about their glorious past, called on a Hungarian as impresario (Korda), a German as producer (Pommer), and an American as director (Howard).

The choice of *Knight Without Armour* might be regarded as an error. For this film Korda engaged the French director, Jacques Feyder, who confessed to the press after the film had been completed that he had found Korda altogether incomprehensible. Marlene Dietrich, who was brought to this country to take a leading rôle, might look back with satisfaction on the startling way in which she set London agog with her flaunting appearances among theatre audiences; but the critics did not speak well of her performance in the film. It is, indeed, impossible to discern why Korda saw in James Hilton's story of revolutionary 1917 St Petersburg material for the kind of film the British public wanted at this moment. And he did not improve things by dressing up the Russian Revolution to look, as the critics said, like a Drury Lane musical.

It was for another reason, however, that 1937 was his unhappiest year. He had brought that erratic genius Von Sternberg to this country to direct a highly spectacular film version of the Robert Graves's best-selling novel, *I Claudius*. A 'star-studded' cast was engaged, and five scriptwriters—two British, one American, one German and one Hungarian—were put to work on the scenario. A visit paid to Rome was much publicized. Its purpose was to get the details correct and to make suitable purchases, such as real bronze bedsteads, real pieces of sculpture and real mosaics. An unhappy venture, the production was abandoned after tens of thousands of pounds had been spent. Those who had seen the early 'rushes' said that it was going to be Charles Laughton's best film.

Korda was being warmly criticized in Parliament, the press and elsewhere as the begetter of the financial crises that were upsetting the industry. But *World Film News* now pleaded his cause. It said that John Maxwell of the Associated British Picture Corporation, with his capacity for waiting, his organization, his long-term policies and his realistic sense of business values, might denote the British industry's stability; but Korda, though less successful on the business side, denoted the industry's reputation.

'When he came to this country,' it observed, 'he represented the new cinema that was to come to England and the light of a great promise shone round his Hungarian head. Today his friends are on the defensive and, with them, that rich version of the British cinema for which he stood. The fear now is that, in the drive for economy, a premium might be put on to canny mind and the petty project. For all his faults and errors Korda represents the one thing that is most precious to the British cinema. *He represents quality and the big time.*'

Two unusual films released in 1937 are often recalled. Robert Flaherty's *Elephant Boy* was based on Kipling's *Toomai of the Elephants*, but it was not one of Flaherty's better films, partly perhaps because it contained too much narrative for his taste and partly too because he would have chosen to make his film about the elephants instead of about the boy (Sabu) who looked after them.

When Michael Powell's *The Edge of the World* was released *World Film News* described him as the first director of English 'quickies' to show signs of knowing how to make a good film. Produced on the Shetland island of Foula the film told a melodramatic story based on the evacuation of impoverished St Kilda. Andrew Buchanan hailed the film as fictional-documentary, and suggested that its popularity with cinema audiences showed how they wanted realist films to be made. *World Film News*'s further comment was that, 'when film companies go on location with a bunch of actors and a story, we usually shudder in advance at the hotchpotch of bogus sunsets and studio afterthoughts which will inevitably make the bulk of the film. But not so in *The Edge of the World*; almost every shot counted.'

One of the most often revived films of 1937 was directed by an American, Rowland V. Lee, for the disparaged Max Schach. It was *Love from a Stranger*, based on Agatha Christie's early stage play about a girl, acted by another American, Ann Harding, who won a fortune in a lottery and then married a homicidal maniac, brilliantly portrayed by Basil Rathbone. No doubt it was the cleverness of the script that made the film, but nevertheless the picture's success was a score for Max Schach against his detractors.

Stephen Watts thought Victor Saville's first production for his independent unit, 'within the Denham organization', the most intelligently amusing picture made in England for years—'it is positively un-British in its independence of slapstick and absurdity, or of characters with *comedian* written on their brows'. This was *Storm in a Teacup,* adapted from a German comedy by Bruno Frank and transported to Scotland by the dramatist, James Bridie.

As 1937 pursued its uncertain way and the alarming possibility became increasingly clear that scores of new British films might never recover their production costs, George Formby joined Gracie Fields at the top of the popularity pool. His *Feather Your Nest* and *I See Ice* came up beside her 1937 contribution, *The Show Goes On.* Taking up a point made by Alan Page that 'there are thousands of filmgoers in this country to whom George Formby means a rattling good evening's entertainment and to whom Robert Taylor is a pain in the neck', *World Film News* observed that the record of these relatively cheaply made films with music hall comedians is a lot better than that of more pretentious ones. If inferior in production values, such as fine camera work, elaborate settings and expensive stars, they are better in essence. Their slapdash breeziness is in the vulgar tradition of the British music hall.

These films were made, of course, for the home market, and in particular for one part of it, the North of England. But one British star appearing in these fairly inexpensive films had become as popular in the United States as in this country. She was Jessie Matthews, and the 1937 film *Head Over Heels*, produced by Michael Balcon, was perhaps her best. It demonstrated that good light musical films could be made in this country while eschewing some of the banalities of the British music hall. Perhaps it would be more accurate to say 'could have been made', because British studios never tried to make this kind of film again.

THE YEAR OF DISILLUSION

This, the *Kinematograph Weekly* said at the end of 1938, has been the Year of Disillusion. The total number of feature films made in Great Britain fell from 225 (in 1937) to 116: and it was clearly going to plummet in 1939. Whatever might be said in favour of the new Cinematograph Films Act as drafted, one fact was evident. It had already failed in one of its principal objectives.

In spite of those excellent films produced in 1937 British films had few showings overseas. Few were seen outside the small 'art' cinemas in the United States where audiences had a taste for foreign films. (British films seemed as 'foreign' as French or German films.) The Commonwealth provided the only substantial overseas market, and it was selective too.

Herbert Wilcox, returning from the United States where his *Victoria the Great* had been so successful only a few months before, told the press that 'British pictures have never been so scornfully despised in the United States as at this moment'.

There is no simple explanation of this almost hostile attitude, but American feelings towards this country were far less cordial just before the outbreak of the war than they have been since 1940.

In one important respect, however, the new Cinematograph Films Act did achieve the end in view (or might have but for the gathering of the war clouds). It stimulated American production in British studios, although not without a further attempt being made to out-manoeuvre influential British opinion. The new stratagem was based on a grading of feature films which is still remembered and continues to have some influence as trade policy. 'A' films were those that had been classified as having top entertainment value. 'B' films were considered suitable as supporting films for double-feature programmes. Considerable differences were envisaged in the conditions (and methods of payment) for booking these two kinds of films.

The system had good points, but the composition of the grading committee was of key importance. Here, it seemed, the large

11. In Compton Bennett's *The Seventh Veil*, James Mason was the
tyrannical guardian of a youthful pianist, Ann Todd. This film
had psychological undercurrents.

The Noël Coward–David Lean adaptation of *Brief Encounter* (1945)
was particularly liked on the continent, where it is still regarded as
one of the finest of all British films, partly because of the superb way
in which Celia Johnson and Trevor Howard underplayed their parts.

12. David Lean's *Great Expectations*, the best of all Dickens films, was made in 1946. It encouraged the hope that the British cinematograph industry would retain its high place gained during the war. In this episode the actors are Alec Guinness, Bernard Miles and John Mills.

Confidence grew during 1947 when Carol Reed's Belfast tragedy, *Odd Man Out*, was received enthusiastically. Here James Mason is taking part in a memorable snow storm incident with F. J. McCormick.

renters were to have the predominant voice, and most of them either were American or had American affiliations. Thus they would have the power not only to relegate British films to the 'B' category but to give them summer release dates—in the 'off season' when cinema takings were lower.

The charge was specifically made in the British press, now thoroughly vexed, that the scheme would squeeze more money out of the British cinema, since it was to this country that Hollywood was now having to look for most of its profits. The American producer, not content with taking £10 million a year out of the British market, still, so it was alleged, wanted more: and it mattered not to him that by using his near monopoly he could (and would) send the British film-making industry again on to the rocks.

AMERICAN PRODUCERS IN LONDON

Responsible American opinion realized, however, that the wishes of Parliament were not to be flaunted this time, and all the leading companies continued with their plans for producing worthwhile feature films in this country. Threats of war discouraged some of them later, but MGM went ahead and made three splendid films before war was actually declared. What effect these films might have had on the future of the British film industry can be a matter only of surmise; but a parallel can be drawn with the situation brought about by the First World War, when the original American film colony in London broke up.

A Yank at Oxford was directed by Jack Conway, who had been instructed by his employers before leaving for England 'to make it good'. The story concerned an American college boy entering Oxford with the intention of shaking up the dump. He is won over by Oxford's traditions and leaves with some of his American brashness softened by English diffidence.

John Grierson disliked the spurious schoolboy nonsense, but felt that the film went with a lick and had witty dialogue. The general view was that Robert Taylor gave a persuasive portrayal of the gay and charming hero. It was, indeed, good that a Hollywood star could make a film in Great Britain and gain rather than lose in face. John Grierson added somewhat wryly that he was not worried because Robert Taylor beat the Limeys in all branches of sport, but because he was given every opportunity to out-act a cast that included not only fine British players such as C. V. France, Edmund Gwenn and Vivien Leigh, but competent Hollywood players such as Lionel Barrymore and Maureen O'Sullivan.

King Vidor's *The Citadel*, based on A. J. Cronin's controversial

K

novel, is about an an idealistic young Scottish doctor who, after struggling to do his best in poor practices, finds himself picking up easy money among London's fashionable consultants. King Vidor approached the plot with effective directness, and made one of the best acted films ever to come from a British studio. Not only was it among Robert Donat's outstanding films, but it had a supporting cast of quite remarkable strength. This included Rosalind Russell, Emlyn Williams, Ralph Richardson, Rex Harrison and Cecil Parker.

It was the third MGM film, however, which won the greatest public support. Even today requests are received endlessly to show Sam Wood's *Goodbye Mr Chips*. Based on James Hilton's sentimental novel about a life of service, it tells of the hopes and disappointments of an unassuming pedagogue, and of the affection showered on him in his later years by his pupils and former pupils. Robert Donat's portrayal of Mr Chips endeared the film to the public, but Greer Garson's exquisite grace in the brief love episode also contributed materially to the film's success.

THE LAST OF THE PRE-WAR FILMS

The more strictly British pictures produced during these overcast twenty months before the outbreak of the war included three featuring Charles Laughton. They were made for distribution by ABPC, John Maxwell having financed a company headed by Erich Pommer with £750,000. *The Vessel of Wrath* was based on a story by Somerset Maugham about a besotted South Seas beachcomber who toys with the virtue of a devout missionary, marries her, and brings her home to help run a pub in Sussex. John Grierson was delighted to find in it the gusto and sense of sophistication lacking from slapstick British comedies with, as he said, their occasional odd departures into drama and sentiment. Alan Page thought it a highly civilized production, Laughton's performances resembling a tropical plant of riotous growth and high-coloured flowers (even if needing pruning). Elsa Lancaster was superb as the well-intentioned ninny.

Vivien Leigh was with Laughton in *St Martin's Lane*, in which they were buskers entertaining the queues—and so the film has a nostalgic appeal for people who want to recall the London theatre of the years between the wars. It is doubtful if Hitchcock can be altogether happy about his *Jamaica Inn*, based on Daphne du Maurier's novel on smuggling and shipwrecking in Cornwall two hundred years ago. He was apparently unable to control a star-studded cast, 'drawn from every theatre in London', and was said to have given Laughton his head to indulge in overacting. The film was spectacular rather than subtle, and is now remembered chiefly because it gave Maureen O'Hara her first important part.

Hitchcock had already made his last film for Gaumont-British, *The Lady Vanishes,* undoubtedly one of his best British films. The action takes place aboard a transcontinental express. A seemingly ingenuous old dear, fluently played by Dame May Whitty, suddenly disappears. Two young people, Margaret Lockwood and Michael Redgrave, persist in trying to find out what has happened to her and become involved in espionage and counter-espionage. Paul Lukas was very sinister as a spy but perhaps the most often recalled members of the cast were Naughton Wayne and Basil Radford. They were two cricket fanatics hurrying home for the last days of a test match at Manchester (where they found that play had been abandoned because of rain). *Jamaica Inn* was Hitchcock's last British film (until he directed *Under Capricorn* in London in 1948). On completion of *Jamaica Inn* he signed a contract with David Selznick and went to Hollywood. Although he was out of Great Britain during the war he must have reflected with pleasure on the success of his last British films in American cinemas. John Maxwell's three films were among this country's best dollar earners in the first years of the war.

Some of the more publicized films of 1938 and 1939 are now almost forgotten. Korda continued to sell the Empire and went back to India, this time to the North-West Frontier. *The Drum,* directed by Zoltan Korda, was adapted from a novel by A. E. W. Mason. The public was attracted by the film's magnificent use of Technicolor. Sam Goldwyn, who was in close touch with Korda at this time, was so impressed that he was reported as saying that he would never make another film in black and white. Another Korda patriotic film was based on an A. E. W. Mason story. Set in the Egyptian Sudan it was *The Four Feathers* (white for cowardice), John Clements being the young officer who redeemed himself. The Korda production which won most praise from the critics was, however, a less expensive work. Based on Winifred Holtby's novel about local politics in the Yorkshire *South Riding,* it was directed by Victor Saville. It had many qualities of a documentary film, telling a story about various people who lived in a housing estate.

Possibly the two most significant British films of this unhappy period were *Bank Holiday* and *This Man Is News.* The former described the experiences of a dozen characters during an August weekend at a popular South of England seaside town. Conceived with warmth and humanity it had a variety of humorous touches and moments of sadness. The different items were integrated with great skill by the director, Carol Reed. C. A. Lejeune wrote that 'he is beginning to do things well because he has learned from the start to do things simply'.

Credit for the speed and slickness of *This Man Is News* was given to its two authors, Alan Mackinnon and Roger MacDougall; and, as the importance of script writing had at last been recognized in this country, a leading rôle in British cinematography was forecast for them. However, they did not continue as a team for very long, although MacDougall went on to become one of the London theatre's leading playwrights.

The last of the outstanding British films from the 1930s was *Pygmalion*. An unknown Hungarian with limited financial resources, Gabriel Pascal, persuaded Bernard Shaw to give him permission to turn some of his plays into pictures. Anthony Asquith and Leslie Howard had to force the *Pygmalion* words into filmic form and they were surprisingly successful, possibly because the theme itself was about words—about language barriers between the classes. *Pygmalion* was not a particularly good film—as in the play the third act had awkward moments—but it was enormously diverting.

In his assessment of the British cinematograph industry's achievements in the 1930s the American, Arthur Knight, author of *The Liveliest Art*, criticized the studios for imitating Hollywood's offerings. And yet, he added, behind the scenes, techniques and skills, courage and resourcefulness were growing steadily in both the documentary units and the studios. When the war finally brought together these two divergent groups, the result was not a clash but a fusion that marvellously transformed the entire British film.

AESTHETIC ASPECTS OF DOCUMENTARY

The seeker after information about any of the lesser British feature films of the 1930s must prepare himself for a long and possible fruitless search. Not so, however, if it is a documentary film that has aroused his interest. There are several authoritative books and articles to which he can refer on the documentary films made during that decade, besides journals such as *Sight and Sound* and *World Film News*, which devoted relatively more of their space to actuality films than to the fictional films. The explanation is that the directors and other men who made these realist films had a sense of purpose lacking elsewhere. They felt themselves part of a new movement concerned with the 'creative treatment of actuality'. Not only had they plenty to say about it; they encouraged other people to have plenty to say too.

In effect, John Grierson, the founder of the documentary movement, had introduced a social use into the 'interest' films which had always been one of this country's specialties. Paul Rotha explained in his book on the subject that a documentary film does more than record. It reports and interprets—and, while doing so, other characteristics are acquired, notably form and style.

When in the summer of 1937 John Grierson resigned from the GPO Film Unit to become a 'film consultant' and to form Film Centre with Arthur Elton, tributes were paid by Basil Wright and others to the part he had played in building up the realist film movement— to his forceful personality, his far-sighted production policies, his complete integrity and not least to his genius for film-making and for training film-makers. These tributes included references to the part played by a distinguished civil servant, Sir Stephen Tallents, who first at the Empire Marketing Board and then at the GPO had supported Grierson while he 'battled against incomprehensions and suspicions'.

Between January 1930 and July 1933 the Empire Marketing Board increased its film unit staff (with Grierson as director) from two to over thirty and produced one hundred films. Soon the Unit was supplying film directors to other Government departments, to the Travel Association and to commercial undertakings, notably the Shell Marketing Company which had in its turn set up a film department.

In 1933 the Unit passed to the Public Relations Department of the General Post Office. Grierson's terms of reference were changed from 'bringing the Empire alive' to presenting the story of the Post Office's activities—and this he interpreted as comprising communications in its widest sense. Outside sponsors were now coming to him in considerable numbers not only for advice on production policy but to recruit personnel. Realist film-making companies were formed, the Strand Company being the pioneer.

No fewer than 300 documentary films were made during the 1930s by men and women who had derived inspiration from John Grierson. Some were of such outstanding merit that their titles would be included in any selection, even if limited in number to about half a dozen.

In this group of Empire Marketing Board and GPO films are Arthur Elton's *Upstream* (1931), about salmon fishing in Scotland; Basil Wright's *O'er Hill and Dale* (1932), a study of a Border farmer's care for his flock; Robert Flaherty's *Industrial Britain* (1933), an impressionistic study of various aspects of craftsmanship; Evelyn Spice's *Weather Forecast* (1934), tracing the events leading up to the issuing of a gale warning; Edgar Anstey's *Six-thirty Collection* (1934), describing the handling of the evening's mail in London;

Cavalcanti's *Pett and Pott* (1934), a jolly film advertising the telephone service; *Night Mail* (1936) in which Harry Watt and Basil
Wright accompanied a postal sorting carriage on its railway journey
from London to Scotland; and Harry Watt's *North Sea* (1938),
which was particularly concerned with the ship-to-shore radio
service.

Among the films made under the auspices of large industrial
undertakings were Basil Wright's *The Song of Ceylon* (Ceylon Tea
Propaganda Board, 1935), a poetic study of the influence of Western
civilization on native life; *Housing Problems* (Gas Association,
1936) in which Arthur Elton, Edgar Anstey, Ruby Grierson and
John Taylor used interviews with slum dwellers in a manner adopted
later for televised documentaries; and a group of seven films made
by the Films of Scotland Committee for the Empire Exhibition in
Glasgow (1938), the best remembered being perhaps *They Made the
Land,* directed by Mary Field and Basil Wright's *The Face of
Scotland.*

With so many virile people actively participating in the British
Documentary Movement changes in outlook were inevitable. At
the beginning of the decade it had seemed to some critics to have
an almost preciously impressionistic point of view, seeking to exploit
various aspects of art form—fancy montage, odd camera angles
and the like. By 1939 its perspective had become more strictly
realistic and its numbers had been augmented by such men as
W. H. Auden the poet, Benjamin Britten the composer and Len
Lye the colourist.

Shortly after the outbreak of the war Ernest Lindgren, who had
been amongst the most enthusiastic supporters of the documentary
movement and its artistic conceptions, was turning over the pages
of journals linked with it. He recorded some of his impressions.
In particular he mentioned three magazines, *Close-up* (1928-33),
Cinema Quarterly (1932-35) and *Film Art* (1933-34). They covered
what seemed to have been a period of daring experiment and often
too daring theorizing, a period of aesthetic ferment. But by 1940
they had already become, he thought, quaintly outmoded. The age
in which the cinema had become fully conscious of its potentialities
as an art form was over.

'The film society movement,' he continued on this theme of passing
of an age, 'has long since lost its pristine glory. The documentary
movement would have lost its identity in the maw of commercialism
had it not breathed new inspiration from the Continent through
the work of Cavalcanti, the only genuine artist working on any scale
in the British cinema today.'

In some respects these views were well founded, but the men

and women who had worked with Grierson were now spreading over a wider field. They were, as Arthur Knight observed, becoming the makers of feature films, of fictional films about real people set against a documentary background rather than in formal film sets.

CHAPTER FOURTEEN

Europe at War Again:
America Neutral

....

IN THE BLACK OUT

Few could have supposed during the first two years of the war that the renaissance of the British cinematograph industry was at hand. Members of the documentary movement, and particularly those who were (or had been) members of the GPO Film Unit, raged in their impotence. They could find no way round the official disinclination to use their services or, indeed, the services of anyone else connected with the cinema. Apparently the risk of halls being bombed during air raids made it necessary for the British public to shut themselves up during the evenings listening to the radio. Picture houses were compulsorily closed at the outbreak of war and were not allowed to reopen until factory managers had made strong representations to the Government about the effect on morale of this pathetically negative attitude.

The trade pointed out that the chief form of recreation of possibly thirteen million people could not be written off in a moment, and that, incidentally, closed cinemas lost the Exchequer £200,000 a week in taxation. Another point was that, if the industry were shut down for a long period, no fewer than 75,000 people would lose their employment.

After the policy had been changed the cinemas carried on splendidly throughout the war, making considerable use of part-time staff. They had to cope with many difficulties caused by restricted hours of opening, fire-watching and ARP, shortage of carbons and valves for projectors, newsreel change-overs between neighbouring cinemas and increases in Entertainments Tax on three separate occasions during the war.

They fell in with the Government's wishes on many matters ranging from putting a short propaganda film in every programme to setting aside seats at low prices for members of the Forces. They made their halls available to organizers of local charity appeals (and helped to run their shows).

Fewer films were available. Representatives of the industry told the Government that they needed 550-600 American films each year and at least one hundred 'good' British films. In the first year of the war, while a considerable proportion of the American people was more concerned with remaining neutral than with rallying to the aid of Great Britain and France, the Treasury was determined to limit dollar expenditure. It fixed the allocation of new American films at 400 and warned the trade that this annual total would fall, not rise, in the ensuing years.

As happened during the First World War more people went to the pictures. Indeed, a quite spectacular increase took place, weekly attendances rising from nineteen million (in 1939) to thirty million (in 1945). Cinema managers had to cope with that too.

So confused, however, was Government thinking during the eight months of the 'phony war' that Board of Trade policy (greatly influenced, no doubt, by the disappointing achievements of the recent Cinematograph Films Act) seemed to favour abandoning the quota requirements and—as was alleged in the trade press at the time—'handing over British screens to American films for the duration'. Studios were requisitioned right and left—including Arthur Rank's Pinewood and Amalgamated and John Maxwell's at Elstree. Michael Balcon saved Ealing only after a most determined fight. Most of the personnel was directed into the forces or the engineering industry.

Consequently the industry had to carry on during the war with one-third of its technicians and with only nine instead of twenty-two of its studios (thirty instead of sixty-five sound stages). A fall in production figures was inevitable. By 1940 the number of new British feature films had tumbled to a quarter of those released in 1937 (56 instead of 225). The annual total remained in this region until 1946.

LEFT-OVERS FROM THE 1930s

The renaissance of film-making in Great Britain did not take place over night, although during the 'phony war' and the following few months several interesting films were produced in the remaining studios; although perhaps it would be more accurate to say that they were completed during this period. For instance, Gabriel Pascal's second Bernard Shaw film, *Major Barbara*, took a long time in the making and, as Michael Balcon has explained, the fact that it was still on the floor at Ealing was of considerable use to him in persuading the Ministry of Supply not to requisition that studio.

There was also *The Thief of Bagdad*, made on a 'lavish scale' even for a spectacular Korda presentation. During the intermittent stages of its production (it was not released until 1941) the film had no fewer than three directors—Ludwig Berger, Tim Whelan and Michael Powell. The film was little more than a pantomime with startling effects, but if not viewed with too critical an eye it is still found very entertaining. It has had several reissues.

Several of the British films which appeared in the cinemas for the first time during these months could be described as 'left-overs from the pre-war years', but some were of very good quality, such as Brian Desmond Hurst's *On the Night of the Fire*, described by Dilys Powell as a brilliant essay in realistic fiction. It contained two splendid psychological studies, one by Ralph Richardson as a man tormented by memories of a foolish but tragic theft he had committed while a big fire was raging in a Tyneside town, and the other by Diana Wynyard as his despairing wife. There were also Carol Reed's adaptation of A. J. Cronin's novel about the opening of a notoriously unsafe coal mine, *The Stars Look Down*, and Herbert Wilcox's *A Widow in London*, with its plot focused on the building of the new Waterloo Bridge.

In this period of uncertainty the studios turned once more to the theatre and films were made of such pieces as *The Farmer's Wife* (directed by Norman Lee and Leslie Arliss); *Spring Meeting* (directed by Walter Mycroft), the Irish racing story in which Margaret Rutherford was a decrepit spinster who backed horses on the sly; *The Ghost Train* (directed by Walter Forde) with the popular radio team, Arthur Askey and Richard Murdoch, in the cast; and *Quiet Wedding* (directed by Anthony Asquith). These would be described, no doubt, as 'escapist', but some now seem rather odd choices for these months when enemy bombs were raining down on this country— for instance, *Jeannie* (directed by Harold French) about a Scottish girl who came into money and dashed off to the (pre-war) Continent for a good time, and *Love on the Dole* (directed by John Baxter) set in Lancashire during the depression.

One film put in hand at this time—and adapted from a play—was nevertheless of outstanding importance, and would be included in some selections of the dozen best British films. This was Thorold Dickinson's *Gaslight*. Patrick Hamilton's play with its late Victorian setting, in which a murderer returns to the scene of his crime still searching for the rubies he missed, and then tries as an incidental exercise to drive his wife out of her mind, was superbly interpreted by Anton Walbrook and Diana Wynyard. After the war the film became a subject of bitter controversy. An American company bought the film rights of the play, which necessitated Thorold Dickinson's film

being scrapped. Protests came from many quarters but the Hollywood lion was immovable. And there was small comfort later when
the new version turned out to be unquestionably inferior to Thorold
Dickinson's.

On the whole, however, Dilys Powell was thoroughly justified
in her assertion that there was little in this group of films released
late in 1939 and in the early 1940s 'indicative of new orientation in
the British cinema; nothing to reflect the spiritual and emotional
changes which the British people were undergoing at the time'.

GOOD INTENTIONS

Another category of productions of 1939-40 comprises 'worthy'
films with themes related to the war, made with the best intentions.
The first was the 'star-studded' *The Lion Has Wings*, directed by
Michael Powell, Brian Desmond Hurst and Adrian Brunel for
Korda. Conceived in the pre-war months it was subsequently
sponsored by the Ministry of Information, the intention being 'to
inspire quiet confidence in the hearts of those who saw it'. In fact
it was an ill-conceived, jumbled film beginning with Lowell Thomas
describing how the shadow of Nazi Germany fell over this peaceful
country. After this is switched to an unconvincing demonstration
of the strength of this country's defences against enemy air attack.
Public reception here was regrettably apathetic but the film had over
a thousand bookings in the United States. Less pleasing was a
report in *Documentary Film News* that the Germans had procured
a copy—not a difficult thing to do in those early days—and were
showing it in Berlin 'for laughs'. In particular they were entertained
by a sequence showing a German air attack on London being driven
off by a balloon barrage.

If the purpose had been to show how different we were from
the Germans the contrast could not have been drawn more admirably. The Nazis were at this time acting on Goebbels's principle
about the cinema being Germany's fourth offensive arm and were
terrifying neutrals with films, such as those showing air raids on
Poland, demonstrating that the Germans at war were irresistible. The
enemy's studios were also turning out competently-made narrative
themes purporting to be based on historical fact. Some glorified
national heroes such as Frederick the Great. Some showed the
British in a despicable light as in the South African War and at the
loss of the *Titanic*.

In several respects John Sutro's and Michael Powell's *49th Parallel*
might be regarded as an effective reply. It was the first major British
feature film financially supported by the Ministry of Information.

Early in the war the Ministry had decided to spend £500,000 on making feature films. After *49th Parallel* was finished not a great deal was said to be left of that first half million. Of epic length, the film was produced principally in Canada—hence the reference in the title to the boundary between that country and the United States. Its subject was the personal clash of representative democrats and representative Nazis. It was composed of several episodes as six Germans from a submarine sunk by aircraft near the Canadian coast eluded capture. *Documentary News Letter* described it as being not only one of the few films of a purely episodic character to 'come off' but also as one of the best films ever sponsored in this country. It brought out various aspects of British democratic social life as it had taken root in the Dominion. The film had a splendid cast including Leslie Howard as a defeatist English intellectual, Laurence Olivier as a French Canadian trapper, Anton Walbrook as the leader of a German Hutterite settlement and Raymond Massey as a tough Canadian soldier. It is best remembered, however, just for two members of the cast. Eric Portman brought out the resource and courage of the Nazi Commander, the last survivor of the six, so powerfully as to dominate the film, and many feared that the picture had unintentionally become better propaganda for the enemy than for ourselves. Elisabeth Bergner, the German émigrée, is the other whose name will also be associated with the film. She had a leading part but, after the filming had been completed in Canada, she was said to have declined to return to this country, where some of the studio work had still to be undertaken. Glynis Johns substituted for her and several of the Canadian scenes had to be repeated. This might have contributed materially in causing a most disheartening delay in showing the film. It would have served a more useful purpose in the autumn of 1940, when it was greatly needed, than in 1941 when the worst days were over.

Other well-intentioned films of this period have been almost forgotten. There was, for instance, Roy Boulting's *Pastor Hall*, a biographical drama inspired by Ernst Toller's play about Pastor Niemoeller, the denouncer of National Socialism. It was probably Wilfrid Lawson's best film. Judged by its reception in the United States this must be regarded as having been in some respects the most satisfactory of the early films in this group.

Thorold Dickinson's *The Prime Minister* had John Gielgud as Disraeli. It was a painstaking film, accurate in detail, but the cinema-going public in the English-speaking world already knew that Disraeli was really George Arliss. Walter Forde directed Michael Redgrave in *Atlantic Ferry,* the theme being the institution of regular steamship sailings between this country and the United

States. It made much of the uncomfortable sailing conditions in the early nineteenth century. The commendable design behind this film was obvious—so, alas! was the use made of ship models. *Penn of Pennsylvania* was a biographical study of the Quaker who, after leaving this country in Charles II's reign, founded Philadelphia. Clifford Evans was particularly right-minded as Penn, and the young star, Deborah Kerr, played her part very charmingly. But as one United States periodical observed, if the British thought these slow and ponderous films would appeal to Americans, they did not know what they were playing at.

During 1940 several narrative films put in hand had themes related to the war. They were in no sense propagandist but in an indirect sense they might have contributed not only in lifting morale in this country but in making the American public's attitude more realistic. They included Leslie Howard's *Pimpernel Smith*, derived from a novel by A. G. McDonnell about a Cambridge professor, an 'academic knight-errant' in Europe, pretending to be absent-minded while helping eminent Jews and others to escape from Germany. By the time this film was released, however, the British people were too deeply immersed in the harsh unpleasantness of the war as it affected them personally, to accept the rather preposterous legerdemain employed in this tale. Brian Desmond Hurst's *Dangerous Moonlight* is often recalled because of Anton Walbrook's portrayal of a distinguished Polish pianist, also qualified as a pilot, who fought the Germans in his native country's skies, escaped and then participated in the Battle of Britain. The 'Warsaw Concerto' comes from this film.

Michael Powell and Emeric Pressburger made an ingenious spy film, *Contraband,* which retains considerable interest today because it was set against a background of the London docks in the early days of the war. Anthony Asquith directed two films at this juncture —*Freedom Radio,* in which a Hitler speech was sabotaged; and *Cottage to Let,* about a master spy who lived in a Scottish glen. At Ealing they had become nautically minded. Pen Tennyson, who lost his life later in the war, made *Convoy* and gave a splendid impression of conditions aboard a ship engaged in a convoy operation. The film had love interest in its story and one critic claimed that it had a moral too—the good sailor prefers ships to women. Sergei Nolbandov directed *Ships With Wings* at Ealing. It was woven around the romances of three Fleet Air Arm pilots, although the central character, the *Ark Royal,* was always in the picture.

For the rest the British studios were given over principally to music hall comedians making farcical comedies of the all too familiar type, calculated to divert the unenlightened. Familiarity, it is said, gives a sense of comfort and security.

FORTHRIGHT PROPAGANDA

On this showing it would seem that the British film-making industry had gone far by the summer of 1941 to get itself into the same jam as in the summer of 1918. But most happily this is an instance of history not repeating itself.

The general background is not particularly creditable. When historians evaluate the preparations made for the coming war the Government will be sharply criticized for lethargic complacency in the face of the devastatingly thorough use the Nazis made of cinematography for propaganda purposes. Virtually nothing was ready, partly apparently because of skirmishing between the embryo departments of the Ministry of Information and of the British Council. Following the outbreak of war the only actuality films put in hand were by the GPO Film Unit and by the five newsreel organizations (who assembled a joint newsreel for screening abroad).

John Grierson had by this time crossed the Atlantic to join the Canadian Government's Film Commission, but Alberto Cavalcanti continued to be an inspiring influence in the Unit until in the middle of the war he joined Michael Balcon at Ealing to make narrative films. To him are due acknowledgments for an invaluable record, *The First Days*, about the atmosphere of London in those fateful early weeks of September 1939.

Shortly after the war began the GPO Film Unit was transferred to the Ministry of Information. Cavalcanti and Harry Watt made a racy film, *Squadron 992*, about barrage balloons serving as a protection for the Forth Bridge during a brilliantly staged raid. Then they had to endure what they described as persistent delaying action by diligent members of the Ministry who had unearthed a security reason why the film shouldn't be shown to anyone. This was followed by *Men of the Lightship*, produced by Cavalcanti and directed by David Macdonald, which recreated the savage German machine gunning of the Suffolk lightship.

Many urged the Films Division of the Ministry of Information to bring home to the British people the Government's aims in the war, making some of its films instructive and some of them morale-building. The Films Division of the British Council could then be left to put the British point of view across in foreign countries, notably in the United States.

After various eminent but unsuitable gentlemen had been tried as chief of the Ministry of Information's Film Division, Jack

Beddington, formerly an oil company's head of publicity, was appointed director with Sidney Bernstein as honorary adviser. They put the house in order. In particular they instituted the production of five-minute propaganda films, which never pretended to be anything else than propaganda films, even when telling a tolerant if sceptical public about the delights of Woolton Pie. They were made available to cinemas free of cost and, with the co-operation of managers throughout the country, were seen by millions of people, including those in out-of-way places visited from time to time by the Ministry's 150 travelling units.

By the end of 1941 the Ministry of Information's Central Film Library possessed over eighty films on such subjects as Britain in Arms, Ack-Ack, and the Polish forces in this country. Neville Kearney was appointed Director of the British Council's Films Division and he made his contribution by initiating a programme of films on the characteristics of the British people. The British Council put out films on such subjects as shipbuilding (*Steel Goes to Sea*), the Green Belt, London's buses, and Lloyd's. Some of its industrial films, such as *Queen Cotton* and *Harris Tweed*, were produced in Technicolor.

Considerable doubt existed, however, as to the acceptability of these films abroad, and there was a suspicion that they were getting few if any showings outside this country. *Documentary News Letter*'s American correspondent commented in the autumn of 1940 on the extent to which we were deluding ourselves. He said that, apart from *The Lion Has Wings*, few British films had been shown in New York (and presumably elsewhere in the United States). Even *Pastor Hall*, in spite of the praise it had won from the New York press, was rarely seen outside the art cinemas. Neither *Squadron 992* nor *Men of the Lightship* had been released to American cinemas. He concluded by saying that he had not seen a single British wartime short that would be acceptable as a commercial proposition in the American market without considerable alteration.

LONDON CAN TAKE IT

It was in November 1940 that Jack Beddington rushed the first copy of the new ten-minute film to the United States, *London Can Take It*. Made by the Crown Film Unit in two weeks during the winter following the Battle of Britain its commentary was spoken in simple terms by Quentin Reynolds, *Collier's Weekly* war correspondent. Americans lapped it up as a first-class feat of journalism. As Dilys Powell has pointed out, it was the skilful editing and the effective use of commentary and dialogue which made the film so acceptable, and opened the way for its epoch-making successor, *Target for Tonight*. No longer could it be said that the Germans' use of film propaganda was far ahead of ours. Now it was their turn to worry.

So the documentary directors succeeded where accredited feature film directors had failed. For ten years, as Roger Manvell observed, the makers of actuality films had been studying the British character and the British scene. The qualities of under-statement, of pride revealed by implication rather than by display, were now injected into British narrative films. The stories themselves dwelt on such personal issues as comradeship, bravery, fear, tension, endurance, skill, boredom and hard work. And they did not have to be adapted from books or plays. The tales were there for the taking. 'A quiet sense of national feeling, of reticence and of wry humour became part of the tradition that was to guide the conception of the remarkable films that were to follow in the period 1942-45.'

Basil Wright made, as he had often done, a penetrating comment. He thought that the documentary directors had benefited greatly from working for 'sponsors' during the 1930s instead of from having to make films for the uncertain and temperamental markets of the film trade. So they had had much greater freedom not only to experiment with the filmic presentation of social problems, but also to experiment with technique and with difficult and apparently intractable subjects. They had acquired the sureness, the forthrightness that a wartime propaganda policy demanded.

DOCUMENTARY TO THE FORE

Although the particular appeal of *Target for Tonight* was derived simply from its description of a raid on Germany—it came at the moment when the British stopped taking it and began giving it back—the film's effectiveness not only in this country but abroad derived from its manner of presentation. By seeming to be no more than a documentary record it was fundamentally magnificent propaganda. In the course of a few months the film was shown in over 12,000 theatres in the United States, Canada and South America, and was seen by 50 million people.

The consequence of this fantastic triumph was that for the next two years the influence of the documentary school predominated throughout British film-making. By now almost every film-making unit in the country contained members of the pre-war documentary films in school.

Arthur Rank supported this policy wholeheartedly and the majority of the feature films about the war, mentioned in the following paragraphs, were made and distributed under his auspices. What John Maxwell's companies would have done if their studios had not been requisitioned is a matter for conjecture but some of his colleagues point ruefully to the millions of pounds these companies were paying away at the time on various forms of exceptional taxation based on their profits as exhibitors.

During the next two years, 1942 and 1943, the British cinema was at its peak. Some might be inclined to say that these were its finest hours. It is no easy matter to choose some productions for special mention from among the narrative films produced in the documentary manner during this period. But interpreting 'documentary' in the broadest sense, the following films would be included in most selections: 1942, Charles Frend's *The Foreman Went to France*, Michael Powell's *One of Our Aircraft is Missing*, Thorold Dickinson's *The Next of Kin*, Lesile Howard's *The First of the Few* and Noël Coward's *In Which We Serve*; and, in 1943, Launder and Gilliat's *Millions Like Us* and Charles Frend's *San Demetrio, London*. These films provide a most effective riposte to the suggestions of American critics that film-making is not indigenous to the British.

The Foreman Went to France was produced by Cavalcanti and has been called his 'impeccably exciting film'. Based on a story by J. B. Priestley, describing an actual incident following the collapse of France, and blessed with one of the finest scripts written by Angus Macphail, it had Clifford Evans as a resolute foreman who persuaded his manager to let him cross the channel to retrieve some special purpose machines just delivered in France. He encountered incredible difficulties but with the help of an American girl, played by Constance Cummings, and two Tommies, superbly played by Tommy Trinder and Gordon Jackson, he brought the machines back to this country. This was, incidentally, one of the first films to have specially composed music, in this instance by William Walton.

There was no love interest in the accepted sense in *One of Our Aircraft is Missing*. Sentiment replaced sentimentality in its account of the escape, with the courageous help of the Dutch people, of a bomber crew led by Eric Portman who had baled out over the Netherlands. The film was particularly interesting because it gave an impression of life in Occupied Europe—an aspect of the war about which people in this country were very curious and necessarily ignorant.

In some quarters *The Next of Kin* is regarded as the finest British film of the war. Its purpose was to warn troops against careless talk and to bring home to them the possible consequences of thoughtlessness. It was almost unique among long feature films in being made

L

without an eye on the box-office; the fighting services were intended to provide its audience. The story traced a German agent, played by Mervyn Johns, from the time he landed in this country assigned to obtaining details of a Commando raid on the French coast which the enemy suspected was being organized. Rarely have the incidents in a crime film of this kind been so succinctly fitted together. Because of the information picked up through careless talk the loss of life in the raid was exceptionally heavy. And at the end of the film the spy is seen, travelling quite nonchalantly in a railway carriage on the way to his next job.

Noël Coward's *In Which We Serve* was chosen by the United States National Board of Review of Motion Pictures as the outstanding film of 1942. It told the story of a destroyer, HMS *Torrin*, and of those who served in her until she was sunk by dive bombers in the Battle of Crete. There were no heroics. Dilys Powell said that the film's emotional impact was immense. The experiences of civilian and fighting men were presented as essentially bound by ties of home, love and devotion; nobody failed to feel that he had a stake in this drama.

The first outstanding success of 1943 was Harry Watt's *Nine Men*, about a group of soldiers stranded in the Libyan desert. They found their way to an old tomb and turned it into a fort. The plot was fictional but the documentary treatment made the whole episode seem factual. Leslie Howard directed and spoke the commentary for *The Gentle Sex*, but did not appear in it. Seven girls of different backgrounds and temperaments were followed during their training in the ATS. Leslie Howard was commended for the skill with which he 'brought together the threads of the seven lives, separated them, and then reunited them'.

Millions Like Us was about civilians employed in an aircraft factory—to which most had been 'directed' They were essentially people in whom other people could believe, and their experiences were confidently accepted as genuine. The four leading parts were taken by Eric Portman, Gordon Jackson, Patricia Roc and Anne Crawford, who represented people drawn from different social classes and with different outlooks. It was the best narrative film made during the war showing the workers in the munitions factories and the way they lived. Launder and Gilliat, who directed *Millions Like Us,* had been among this country's leading scriptwriters. It was their first essay in direction. By contrast *San Demetrio, London*, told a true story with intensely dramatic qualities. A boat crew from a shelled and blazing tanker come across their ship again after three days. They reboard her, put the fires out and bring her into the Clyde. Played by a professional cast, headed by Mervyn Johns, Walter Fitzgerald and Robert Beatty, the film continues to grip its audiences when shown today.

Having compiled this list there is a temptation to add other films, such as Humphrey Jennings's lucid account of the work done by the National Fire Service on a night during the 1940 raids on London. This film, *Fires Were Started*, was noteworthy too because of William Alwyn's musical score. Then there was Jack Holmes's *Coastal Command* which also had an impressive score, provided in this instance by Vaughan Williams. But so many other films would have to be cited that it is probably best to resist the temptation to begin.

One important aspect of these and other feature films of the middle-war period has still to be mentioned. The departure of the 'foreign help' at the beginning of the war had cleared the way in the studios for promising young British artists and technicians. How well they took their chances is illustrated by *In Which We Serve*, quoted by Alan Wood as the starting point of many careers. The associate director was David Lean, the art director David Rawnsley and the cameraman Ronald Neame. All have since established considerable reputations.

Before production began Del Giudice, who persuaded Coward to make the film, failed to awaken any Wardour Street interest in the venture, and the film was begun without a distribution contract. In particular the renters had objected to the cast of 'unknowns' chosen to support Coward, himself virtually a stranger to cinema audiences. These unknowns included John Mills, Richard Attenborough (in his first film part), Bernard Miles and Celia Johnson.

CHAPTER FIFTEEN

The Last of the War Years

....

THE RANK EMPIRE

During the war, and the years which immediately preceded it, the control of the British cinematograph industry passed into new hands, and it has in effect remained in them since. Alan Wood in particular has explained how this came about. The Rank empire, with which they were particularly concerned, was not, they say, built by any deliberate planning, calculated aggrandisement for Machiavellian scheming. Arthur Rank simply inherited the fruits of other people's financial skill and put the results together. Most of the opportunities that came his way did so by chance. But he took risks. He was most courageous and showed outstanding capacity for making up his mind and for giving decisions quickly.

Perhaps it should also be said that he was more willing than most people to come to aid of members of the industry when they found themselves in trouble. Several of his ventures in these difficult years would not be incorrectly described as 'rescue operations'.

In 1937 he backed C. M. Woolf's renting company, General Films Distributors, and became virtual owner of the immense new studios at Pinewood. Gaumont-British were proposing to go out of production (except for Gainsborough's small studios at Islington). He fell in with C. M. Woolf's proposal to transfer the remnants of GB production to Pinewood (the GB studios at Shepherd's Bush remaining closed). Almost immediately he had an outstanding success, Gabriel Pascal having not only persuaded Bernard Shaw to allow him to film *Pygmalion*, but Arthur Rank to contribute materially in financing the film.

The result was a box-office triumph which contrasted unhappily with some of Alexander Korda's current failures. Korda gave up his five new studios at Denham, and the Prudential Assurance

Company, one of his principal financial backers, participated in a deal by which the studios passed to Arthur Rank. A new company called D. and P. was set up to administer the Denham Studios and the neighbouring Pinewood Studios. Arthur Rank also acquired the new Amalgamated Studios at Elstree. They had been built by a continental family, the Soskins, who found themselves unable to make adequate use of the facilities, and John Maxwell was reported to be negotiating to take them over. According to Alan Wood, Arthur Rank's advisers assured him that this additional studio space at Elstree would place John Maxwell in an overwhelmingly strong position. So Arthur Rank stepped in and personally bought Amalgamated Studios.

Now he owned three of the largest studios in the country, but with relatively little production to put in them. Alan Wood's comment was that they were relieved when the Government requisitioned most of the space. 'For the first time the buildings were earning a steady income for their owners.'

Arthur Rank was by now thoroughly convinced that he must have a larger circuit of cinemas to support the increased number of films he intended to make. An unexpected opportunity presented itself through the mortal illness of Oscar Deutsch. He was only forty-eight years old. Realizing that his death (from cancer) was near he asked Arthur Rank to become chairman of Odeon Cinemas and to ensure that they remained under British ownership.

Arthur Rank did this by buying the Odeon circuit of 306 cinemas. He kept it separate from the 251 Gaumont-British cinemas recently acquired from Isidore Ostrer, who had decided to leave England because of his wife's ill-health. In October 1941 Arthur Rank became chairman of Gaumont-British. C. M. Woolf rejoined Gaumont-British (but, because of his own death, for only a short time) as joint managing director with Mark Ostrer. The two American companies with substantial holdings in the company did not intervene on this occasion to 'stop the deal'.

The third great circuit was John Maxwell's ABPC. He had recently obliged the Government by selling a substantial block of his company's shares (for almost £1 million) to the Americans, Warner Brothers—so making a most acceptable contribution of dollar exchange to the Treasury. But in 1941 John Maxwell also died, and shortly before the five-year option became due by which he was to acquire Isidore Ostrer's voting shares. So ended that strange episode which had had Wardour Street agog with excitement in 1937, and the British cinematograph industry entered the post-war world with three large circuits—two owned by Arthur Rank and his associates, and the other by John Maxwell's successors.

LIMITING THE MONOPOLIES

In 1944 this concentration of power was frowned on by some of the groups which were planning (with or without official support) the new Britain that was to emerge from the war. They pointed out that the Rank Organization had 619 cinemas (of which 90 per cent had survived enemy attacks and were open), while ABPC had 442 cinemas (of which 94 per cent were open). The two groups together controlled one-third of the cinema seating capacity in this country. Pressed to give an undertaking they assured the Board of Trade that they would not buy any more cinemas without its prior consent.

On the production side they owned two-thirds of the available stages, and the Rank Organization alone controlled considerably more than half the supplies of equipment and accessories. The Government appointed a new committee, known as the Palache Committee, to consider whether anything should be done to check the development of monopoly in the British film industry. The Committee reiterated the feelings of the Moyne Committee. A cinematograph film represents something more, it said, than a mere commodity to be bartered against others. 'Already the screen has great influence both politically and culturally over the minds of the people. Its potentialities are vast, as a vehicle for expression of national life, ideals and tradition, as a dramatic and artistic medium, and as an instrument for propaganda.'

The Government was told that it was not sufficient to ensure that the British production industry survived; part of it must remain independent of the combines. The creation of a film finance corporation was recommended, as in the Moyne Report, but with direct Government sponsorship. Indeed, the Committee went further in proposing that this Corporation should set up a distributing organization to help the small producer. The Committee hoped too that the Corporation would establish an organization to promote the export of British films. These and other suggestions did not have a good reception from the trade press, *The Kinematograph Weekly* observing that, contrary to the Committee's views, 'every organization, except the Technicians' Union, wishes to avoid every kind of Government control'.

A secondary issue raised by the Committee was that the limited (available) studio capacity was being wasted by producing 'super films'. It would be preferable, the Committee thought, to make several medium-priced films than just two or three expensive films. They expressed concern that when the war ended the British film industry should not be lured yet again into the trap of making costly 'prestige' films, instead of economically-priced films. The trade press replied that the Committee had omitted to tell the producers how to make cheap films that would sell abroad.

MORE STUDIO PRODUCTIONS

The kind of feature film produced in this country changed considerably during the latter years of the war. The public, going to the pictures in greater numbers than ever, was seeking entertainment. With the United States completely involved in the war, an ample supply of American films had become available to the cinemas—and among them were many war films made in the transatlantic manner. Some aroused resentment and caused trouble. But others were liked by sections of the British public with a taste for bustling activity, harshness and over-statement. The country's attitude to the war was different too. Few had any doubts about the outcome. What they wanted to know was when the war would be over. And they could not get the answer to that question at the pictures.

After the enthusiasm shown for films about the war in North Africa—*Wavell's 30,000, War in Libya, Desert Victory, From El Alamein to Tripoli* and *Tunisian Victory*—interest in documentary films about the war tended to decline, although some splendid productions were still to come, such as *Burma Victory* and *Western Approaches*. Indeed, these films from the last battles of the war will be greatly prized by later generations.

From 1941 the fighting services made considerable use of films, the Army adopting them wholeheartedly for training, educating and entertaining the troops. The Director of Army Kinematography was Paul Kimberley, whose association with Cecil Hepworth was mentioned earlier. Many of the training films were made by the Army Film Unit, which had not only become closely associated with the Films Division of the Ministry of Information, but was recruiting prominent directors, including Carol Reed. The Army possessed many projectors which were used partly for instructional and educational purposes but partly also for entertainment purposes—in roughly a fifty-fifty proportion.

Most of the entertainment films made in 1942 and 1943 still had themes related to the war. For instance, Leslie Howard and David Niven were in a sensitive biographical film, *First of the Few,* about R. J. Mitchell, the designer of the Spitfire. Leslie Howard lost his life during the war and this was the last film in which he appeared. Carol Reed's *Young Mr Pitt* is probably the finest historical moving picture ever to be staged in this country. Its theme, basically propagandist, was that the events of the early 1940s were remarkably similar to those of the 1790s—the implication being that the outcome would be victorious. The story of the Younger Pitt's life was presented in a succession of episodes, and such personalities were materialized as George III, the Older Pitt, the Younger Fox (played by Robert Morley), Talleyrand, Napoleon and Nelson. To the historian the film's principal defect was probably the utter dissimilarity between the appearance of Pitt and Robert Donat. But this too must be said—Robert Donat delivered extracts from some of Pitt's speeches quite admirably.

Carol Reed's other film of this period, *Kipps,* had little to do with the war, except that 1941 (when the film was begun) might seem a pertinent moment for telling the story of a simple soul. No one was really villainous. The atmosphere was homely. And Michael Redgrave made Kipps a lovable little man. 'Given two years more of productions of this kind of film,' *Documentary News Letter* observed, 'and the British film industry should be back on its feet again.'

The Boulting Brothers' version of Robert Ardrey's play *Thunder Rock* was notable as a somewhat rare example of a film being decidedly better than the original stage play. This re-creation of an escapist's dream world will be recalled particularly because of a touching performance by Barbara Mullen. Michael Redgrave was splendid as the man who hides away from the war by confining himself in a lighthouse, and imagines it haunted with the ghosts of European emigrants wrecked on the rock many years ago.

In 1944 and 1945 some more splendid narrative themes related to the war appeared on the screens, and stood up magnificently to competition with Hollywood's best productions. *The Way Ahead* was directed for the Army Film Unit with impressive efficiency by Carol Reed, from a script written by the experienced Eric Ambler and the novice Peter Ustinov. It was intended for showing to the public rather than to the troops. The Army was inclined to resent public adulation of the 'glamour boys' in the Royal Air Force and the Royal Navy. The film corrected the perspective by telling the story of a British Army unit in which seven individualists are transformed into part of an integrated military group. Now ready for sacrifice, they go to the North African landings and thence to the way ahead.

Anthony Asquith's *The Way to the Stars* is one of the great films of the war. He had seemed less at ease than some other directors while making films about the fighting services, and even in this picture he concentrated on the people rather than on the war. Dilys Powell referred to Anthony Asquith's strong poetic feeling and said the film held an incomparable quality of regret for the massacre of youth. Terence Rattigan wrote the script, the story being about an airfield used in the Battle of Britain which is transferred to a United States Air Force Bomber Squadron. Michael Redgrave headed the cast, which included Douglass Montgomery, John Mills and Rosamund John. Jean Simmons made a brief but memorable first appearance, singing 'Let Him Go, Let Him Tarry'.

Some months before directing this picture Anthony Asquith made a satirical comedy, *The Demi-Paradise*. Laurence Olivier, in his best film part so far, was a Russian engineer who had been in England in 1939 supervising a shipyard job and had disliked the assignment, being quite unable to comprehend the local idiosyncrasies. He had been glad to go home. Returning during the war he had adopted a more understanding attitude towards the English. The film provided many opportunities for quiet gibes at English foibles, and had some delightfully funny moments when Margaret Rutherford organized a local pageant.

The most remarkable film of the period was *The Life and Death of Colonel Blimp*, the first production by Michael Powell and Emeric Pressburger for their new company, The Archers. Powell was principally responsible for the direction and Pressburger for the script. The impression persists that they did not make the film they had intended, and many still ask what was the point in turning Low's Col. Blimp, previously a subject for ridicule rather than for fun, into a sympathetic character. Roger Livesey's theatrical make-up as Col. Clive Candy, a Boer War VC, was amusing rather than realistic. Anton Walbrook played the part of a German officer, with whom Candy had once fought a duel. Now Candy's friend and a hater of Hitlerism, he came to this country as Candy's permanent guest. The film's message was presumably that mankind unites to resist brutal intolerance. Neither of these men was, however, the star of the film. This was Deborah Kerr, charming and sympathetic as three women of different generations who had won Candy's affection.

Alexander Korda, who had crossed the Atlantic many times during the war, returned to his director's chair in this country in 1944 and made a delightful comedy, *Perfect Strangers*. A dyspeptic clerk, played by Robert Donat, and his dowdy wife, another part brilliantly interpreted by Deborah Kerr, both join the Royal Navy and do not see each other for three years. When they meet again each has divorce in mind. They have enjoyed romantic if harmless affairs and have changed in many ways. They quarrel but soon begin to like each other's personality and decide to resume their married life. This MGM film has a particular significance in that it was directed by Korda after he had decided to resume his production activities in this country. He set up MGM-London and, as Ian Dalrymple explained in his tribute to Korda, he 'put the top writers of the day under contract to prepare a colossal programme; and started to recover, improve and equip the MGM Studios at Elstree, still being used as a depository. But although he intended to make the studios the best in England, he was never himself to enjoy their use. In 1946 he broke with MGM, and all he had to show for his three years' work was *Perfect Strangers*.'

After 1941 several directors urged their employers to allow them to make studio productions of the kind with which they had been associated. Sometimes their representations were successful. The total number of films made in these circumstances was, however, small, and they included several more adaptations of plays from the London theatre. J. B. Priestley's sociological fantasy advocating universal friendship, *They Came to a City*, was among them.

The Englishman's foibles were gently satirized in David Lean's version of Noël Coward's imaginative pictorial study of the ways in which a group of Londoners fared during the two decades between the war, *This Happy Breed*. Robert Newton had one of his best rôles as the father whose family presented him with plenty of problems while growing up. Another genial film was *Tawny Pipit*, although perhaps rather too whimsical to be popular. Directed by Charles Saunders and Bernard Miles, it described the ferment which followed the discovery near a Cotswold village of a rare pair of migrant birds mating in a meadow. Aristocratic traditions were the butt of the humour in *Don't Take it to Heart* by Jeffrey Dell, another script-writer turned director. An enemy bomb which had demolished part of an old mansion house brought some old manuscripts to light, but also stirred up a ghost who felt most keenly about the contents of those manuscripts.

Comparatively few of these narrative films of 1944 really broke away from the war. Sidney Gilliat's *Waterloo Road* was set among some of the shady characters thrown up by the war in the humbler districts of South London. It is remembered principally because of a tremendous fist fight between Stewart Granger and John Mills—an early pointer perhaps to the new 'toughness' making its way into the cinema. Basil Dearden's *The Halfway House* was very eerie. Several embittered people chanced to stay for a night in an old Welsh inn and discovered in the morning that the building had been destroyed in an air raid a year ago.

The war was, in fact, still far from over, but much was being said about the British film industry's newly-won reputation and the rosy future. Perhaps this explains why Powell and Pressburger's production, *A Canterbury Tale*, caused so much disappointment. It

contained some beautiful photographs of the cathedral in its wartime surroundings, but inadequate use was made of its evocative
story about three men and a girl who go to Canterbury to do
penance, as Chaucer's pilgrims had centuries before. Eric Portman
can never have had a more distasteful film part than that of a
neurotic who smeared glue on girls' hair during the blackout. One
of the leading critics still shudders whenever she thinks about it.

CHAPTER SIXTEEN

Melodramas, Tough and Tearful

••

It was another film, released as early as the summer of 1943, that set the pattern for some of the principal British feature films of the next years. It was the prototype of a succession of expensive melodramas, tough and obsessed with sex problems—novelettes, as one critic remarked, elaborately presented on glossy art paper.

The film was Leslie Arliss's *The Man in Grey*. Based on a novel by Lady Eleanor Smith, it was set in the Regency period with a cast headed by four of the leading British stars of the period, Margaret Lockwood, Phyllis Calvert, James Mason and Stewart Granger. Its complicated plot was almost wholly concerned with their comings and goings. Towards the end of the film Margaret Lockwood stood aside leaving her friend and benefactor to die. James Mason, when he realized this, beat her to death.

Twenty years earlier Cecil Hepworth, who also had a taste for melodrama, was criticized for being too refined and for deleting 'nasty bits' from his scripts. It seemed that we were now headed the other way. But, if critical opinion was far from happy about the sadistic line taken in this film, there could be no questioning the film's tremendous popularity with the cinema-going public. It was followed by half a dozen other melodramas. Anthony Asquith's *Fanny by Gaslight* was adapted from Michael Sadleir's novel about London music hall life in that boisterous decade, the 1880s. Phyllis Calvert was a Cabinet Minister's illegitimate daughter, brought up by a saloon keeper. Stewart Granger, as this politician's secretary, loved Fanny and fought a duel for her. James Mason, now specializing in sinister parts, was a dissolute peer who emerged from time to time to spoil everybody's happiness. Margaret Lockwood and Stewart Granger were the leading players in Leslie Arliss's *Love Story*. She was a famous pianist with a weak heart and with a few months to live; he was a mining engineer going blind through war injury. They fell in love in Cornwall—where Margaret Lockwood played the 'Cornish Rhapsody'—and had various misunderstandings which could have been cleared up in a moment had they confided in one another.

In Arthur Crabtree's *Madonna of the Seven Moons* Phyllis Calvert had a dual personality. She was a wealthy wine merchant's saintly wife and also a jewel thief's mistress in the house of the Seven Moons in Florence. Stewart Granger was only one of many baffled by her dual personality. Margaret Lockwood was beset in Bernard Knowles's *A Place of One's Own* by the spirit of a girl who died 40 years previously. Phyllis Calvert was joined by Anne Crawford and Dulcie Gray in Arthur Crabtree's *They Were Sisters*, a film which was almost entirely concerned with their post-marital difficulties. James Mason was one of the husbands.

All of these films were liked by the public and attracted very large audiences. They were dwarfed towards the end of 1945, however, by two more films made for the Rank Organization, Compton Bennett's *The Seventh Veil* and Leslie Arliss's *The Wicked Lady*. In the former Ann Todd gave one of the outstanding performances of her career as a pianist, depressed after her hands had been burned in a car accident. A psychiatrist, played by Herbert Lom, helped her to relive incidents from her past, and so brought to the surface her vital relationship with her tyrannical guardian, played by James Mason. One critic commented that Mason was becoming 'a Victorian maidservant's conception of a rich, romantically overbearing lord'.

The Wicked Lady lived in the reign of Charles II. She was played by Margaret Lockwood, whose décolletage made quite an impression in this pre-bikini year. After stealing her best friend's bridegroom she became bored and turned highwayman for the sport of it, or as the modern generation would say, just for kicks.

All of this was dismissed by Richard Winnington as 'an ugly hodge-podge of servant girls' lore'. And Alan Wood in his book about Mr Rank says that it was made with 'a considerable admixture of salacity and raw dialogue. It was condemned by newspaper critics, but made a fortune at the box-office, and is constantly cited by Arthur Rank's critics as a triumph of his business instincts over his Methodist principles.'

Looking back at these films after the passing of twenty years it becomes clear that they were made with a formula not dissimilar to that of many of Hollywood's dramatic films of the 1930s. Their provocative plots do not stand up to analysis, but the incidents were plentiful and the pace never let up. They were tough and tearful. Their heroes did not hesitate to resort to fisticuffs. Their heroines were virtuous only within reasonable limits.

This much must be said, however. These films were in the tradition of the cinema. They had popular stars. They had 'loads of action'. They had no subtleties and no pretentions. Furthermore they were not excessively costly ventures, and they showed most satisfactory profits. So far as the public was concerned British films were off to a good beginning in the brave new world.

DEL GIUDICE MAKES HIS ENTRANCE

The story of the British film industry has some resemblance to the script for an episodic play in which characters come, make a contribution to the plot, and make way for someone else.

Filippo Del Giudice was such a character. He was an Italian lawyer, an émigré to this country from the Fascist régime. In a few years he became almost as influential as the absent Alexander Korda had been, but the similitude between the two men did not go very far, because Korda was a man of the cinema, a producer and a director. Del Giudice was an impresario. Korda had been widely known through his publicity flair to the British public; few had ever heard of Del Giudice.

Del Giudice established himself in British studios through his acquaintance with a wealthy Italian nobleman, living in London, Toeplitz de Grand Ry, who backed film productions. The upshot was that Del Giudice formed a company, Two Cities Films (the two cities were London and Rome), and they had a quick success with Anthony Asquith's comedy, *French Without Tears*, based on Terence Rattigan's popular play.

Del Giudice's master stroke was persuading Noël Coward to write, direct and act in *In Which We Serve*. The film cost much more (£240,000) than had been estimated, but it took £300,000 in British cinemas, two million dollars in the United States, and much in other countries. The new *Henry VIII* was at last begotten.

Del Giudice's reputation stood high, especially with the Ministry of Information, which had a financial interest in the film and was gratified with the publicity it achieved. The Ministry now suggested that he should sponsor a film about the ATS, to be called *The Gentle Sex* and to be directed by Leslie Howard. Arthur Rank put up some of the money for this commendable film and an association was formed between the two men. A series of brilliant films followed— some already mentioned, others to be mentioned later: the Noël Coward-David Lean films, *This Happy Breed, Blithe Spirit* and *Brief Encounter*; Carol Reed's *The Way Ahead* and *Odd Man Out*; Anthony Asquith's *The Way to the Stars*; and Laurence Olivier's *Henry V* and *Hamlet*.

Shortly before the war Laurence Olivier had played in the

Elisabeth Bergner-Paul Czinner version of Shakespeare's *As You Like It*. It left him with a strong desire to produce a better Shakespearian film, and the opportunity came his way in 1943. The proposal for making a moving picture of *Henry V* had been canvassed since the outbreak of the war (it was thought that the Battle of Agincourt sequence and the stirring speeches would be good for morale) but Del Giudice was the first impresario capable of procuring the finance for the production (with a distribution contract from Arthur Rank) and willing to face the technical and other problems likely to be encountered—as, for instance, when the battle itself was fought by a thousand Irishmen on an estate near Dublin.

Few would dispute the claim that *Henry V* was one of the most important British films ever made. They might hesitate, however, before including it among the best half a dozen. Some critics were carried away with enthusiasm. Keith Bean, for instance, declared that 'Olivier has presented the spectacular drama as Shakespeare conceived it but could not present it. It demonstrates magnificently the authentic derivation of the cinema from earlier dramatic forms. Here is dramatic literature of high excellence translated with high technical competence to a medium which can reach millions.'

Others while admiring the décor and pageantry, the vigorous realism of the battle, and other aspects, such as the splendour of William Walton's music, were conscious of weaknesses. The pictures made it difficult to concentrate on the words. It was, in fact, half a play and half a film, and as such it was disappointing, they thought, both to theatregoers and to cinemagoers. The extent to which those millions were won over to Shakespeare was doubtful.

The film cost more than had been expected (£350,000) and was rescued by Arthur Rank offering to meet all the bills. The final cost is given by Alan Wood as £475,000, plus overheads. Eventually, however, its entire cost was covered by its earnings.

Unfortunately that could not be said of some of Del Giudice's other presentations, mentioned later. His successes have been attributed to his appreciation of the scope of the scriptwriter's work. He recruited the best and gave them their heads. He failed because he allowed other (and less responsible) people in his employment to have their heads too. Only too often his productions cost far more than he had expected—hence, Alan Wood's remark, when commenting on the large losses incurred by some of Del Giudice's later films, 'it is certain that any account of British films, during the war and early post-war years, would be churlish and ungenerous indeed if it did not stress the tremendous importance of Del Giudice's part: and it would be equally unfair if it did not mention that much was done at Arthur Rank's expense'.

After a brief period in the United States, Del Giudice returned to Italy in 1952. He went to a Benedictine monastery, waiting, so it was said, his recall to help the British film industry. He died ten years later in a Florence hospital.

DECEMBER 1945 AND A NEW BEGINNING

One of the many differences between the first and second world wars is that everyone knows the date of the Armistice which brought the former to its end; but comparatively few can say when the latter finished and when we entered into the post-war world. From the point of view of British film-making it would be pleasant to say that the new beginning was made in December 1945. No fewer than four major productions were released and one of them—the Noël Coward-David Lean adaptation of a thirty-minute play, *Brief Encounter*—remained the best-known British film on the Continent for a decade.

It was the fourth of Noël Coward's films of this period, the rather farcical comedy *Blithe Spirit* having already been very well received by discriminating audiences, delighted by Margaret Rutherford as a spiritualist whose incompetence brought acute embarrassment to a happily-married husband by materializing the ghost of his first wife.

Brief Encounter is about a passing romance. A housewife in her thirties, vaguely discontented with her humdrum existence and disturbingly conscious that life is passing her by, meets a married doctor, first by chance and then by appointment. But they decide it would be best if they did not meet one another again, and the brief encounter ends.

The photography was imaginative, the symbolism subtle and acceptable, the dialogue taut. Celia Johnson and Trevor Howard underplayed the leading parts quite brilliantly, especially at the moment when they realize that this affair has no place in the restricted pattern of their lives. Denis Forman observed that the housewife becomes a suburban Everywoman. 'They built up, under Lean's guidance, a film about a moment in the history of human emotion that was stronger than Coward's conception of it.'

Even if Powell and Pressburger's *I Know Where I'm Going* was not quite such a remarkable picture it still has a habit of cropping up in critics' selections of their favourite dozen British films. Denis Forman, for instance, has described it as 'a gem of a film'. It was, incidentally, the first major feature film shot against the enchanting background of the Western Isles although, as it was not in colour, this tends to be overlooked. Wendy Hiller was the self-possessed girl who plans to marry wealth but cannot rid herself of the affection

13. *The Red Shoes* (1947) is the only non-American production that has a place in the list of films which have earned over five million dollars in the United States. Produced by Powell and Pressburger, it had Moira Shearer, the ballerina, as its star. She is seen in this picture with Marius Goring and Anton Walbrook.

The last great British film of the 1940s was Carol Reed's *The Third Man*, set in post-war Vienna. Joseph Cotten went there seeking his lost friend, Orson Welles.

14. The lively Ealing Comedies had some years of considerable popularity. One of the films was *Whisky Galore*, directed in 1949 by Alexander MacKendrick. Here Wylie Watson is finding a temporary repository for his precious hoard on the approach of the Excise Man.

The favourite British comedy of the 1950s probably Henry Corn *Genevieve*. The four competitors in the ve car race to Brighton having one of their s disagreements. They Dinah Sheridan, John Gregson, Kay Kenda Kenneth More.

she has just formed for an impoverished laird. A delightful tune written for the film—an earlier generation would have called it a theme song—has kept the title alive.

Both of these films were aimed, as with wartime films, at the more intelligent cinemagoers. That could also be said of the cynical *The Rake's Progress*, Rex Harrison being the charming but callous Rake who progressed from one appalling incident to another. 'Swindling and seducing to the last,' Denis Forman said, 'he goes off to war and expiates all by a self-sacrificial death.' As a social satire the film just missed greatness by 'postulating that wartime heroes can be made out of peacetime cads'.

The fourth film released in December 1945 was Gabriel Pascal's adaptation of another Bernard Shaw play, *Caesar and Cleopatra*. It too was intended for discriminating cinemagoers, but this time they did not set much store by it. James Agate said that he had thought of reviewing it under the title *'Cheops and Tomato Sauce'*.

Caesar and Cleopatra was far from being the best film ever made in Great Britain but (after allowing for the changed value of the pound today) it was certainly the most expensive.

Shooting began at Denham in June 1944, six days after the Normandy landings, the cost of making the film having been estimated as £250,000. When it was completed well over a year later its actual cost was £1,278,000—three times that of *Henry V*. Even Bernard Shaw's compassion had been aroused. 'My dear Gabriel,' he wrote, 'I pity poor Rank. The film will cost him a million.' Gabriel's reply, as quoted by Alan Wood, was, 'What does it matter? Mr. Rank can sell a few more bags of flour.'

Not only did Gabriel Pascal go to incredible lengths to achieve perfect authenticity (in colour) of his settings, he quarrelled with Brian Desmond Hurst, his associate director, and completed the film himself. At one time he was not on speaking terms with Caesar (Claude Rains). And, when Bernard Shaw—to quote Alan Wood again—remarked, after seeing the completed production, 'You know, Gabriel, that is a very bad film,' Gabriel is said to have replied, 'Yes, I always knew it was.' If he really did make this remark he was doing the film less than justice. It has some very good features including a charming portrayal of Cleopatra by Vivien Leigh.

Arthur Rank took his losses philosophically but would not give Gabriel Pascal support for a proposed production of *St Joan*. He also wrote off *The Snow Goose*, on which £30,000 had already been spent.

British film-makers, Denis Forman wrote at this critical period at the end of 1945, have 'emerged from the war full of confidence in their new-found powers; for the first time there is a truly British

M

school of production which had gained world-wide recognition'. And Roger Manvell spoke in the spring of 1946 of the 'dozen or more directors who are the imaginative strength of our cinema's renaissance'.

Sam Goldwyn in an interview commented that 'the chief reason for the success of British films is that they have stopped trying to imitate us. They have applied a viewpoint that is broader and more international than ours. Yet they are closer to the people by reflecting the intimate universality of everyday living.' And H. H. Wollenberg, when surveying the reception of British films abroad, was pleased by an observation he chanced upon in an Indiana newspaper—'The more intelligent people here like English films.'

Yet doubts persisted. Paul Rotha, for instance, thought that 'the realism and fidelity to life of the best of the wartime films have been replaced by an escape into romanticism and historical set pieces. Once more we have turned back to the adaptation of successful plays and novels instead of stories written for the screen. For all their cunning use of camera magic these new films are theatrical and literary in conception. They are as claustrophobic as the early German studio creations.'

CHAPTER SEVENTEEN

Much Less than was Hoped For

•••

EXPORTING BRITISH FILMS

There can be no dubiety in naming the central character in the history of the British cinematograph industry during the next two years. He was Arthur Rank himself. He now owned a very large circuit of cinemas in this country and had extensive interests throughout the Commonwealth. (Eventually he was to have 200 Odeons in Canada.)

He also owned large and splendidly-equipped studios with personnel capable of turning out perhaps one hundred feature films every year. He still had to ensure, however, that these films—or, at least, a considerable proportion of them—were shown in the United States; and implicit in that, because he was so often told that the American public did not like British films, he had to make films which they would want to see.

His guide and friend, C. M. Woolf, was dead. He had a young team, including John Davis, 'coming up'; but in grappling with these problems he was to quite a considerable extent isolated, as described in Arthur Wood's biography, from which much of the information in the following pages is derived.

He was filled with the enthusiasm, the determination, the zest with which great British businesses (including the Rank milling business) had been built in the past. And he was resolved that, if the film-making industry was not to collapse in the same shameful way as after the First World War, the American market must be opened up. So he entered into various arrangements for exhibiting his films and formed a new company, Eagle-Lion Distributors. He rented the Winter Garden to provide a shop window in the centre of New York. He thought even of acquiring a chain of cinemas in the United States.

In these enterprises he was encouraged by members of the Government, and this is one of the most significant aspects of the situation as it developed. The Labour Party was in power and its members tended to be picturegoers, unlike members of the Conservative Party who preferred (if they had any taste for this form of indoor entertainment) to go to the theatre. The 'left wing' had made greater use of films about social issues than other groups. More than one member of the new Cabinet was intimately aware of the part which films played in the lives of the British people and of the extent to which the production of British films had been thwarted by American interests.

The diversity of Arthur Rank's attempts in 1946 and 1947 to build up the British film industry were almost stupendous. But it is impossible not to deplore the absence of a perspicacious adviser of C. M. Woolf's calibre to give him guidance. At the end of financial year for 1946 the Rank Organization was known to have lost £1,700,000 on its recent productions. This included, according to reports, almost £1 million on a disastrous attempt to make a musical, *London Town*, to rival Hollywood's spectacular achievements in this field. The film was, in fact, never released in the United States.

Another venture, which according to Alan Wood cost £500,000, was intended to establish film cartooning in this country. Arthur Rank had to start from scratch and he engaged David Hand, one of Walt Disney's ablest assistants. Unfortunately David Hand was too steeped in the Disney tradition to evolve anything very fresh, and the major British development in this field, by John Halas and Joy Batchelor, was to come from quite a different source. It is in film cartooning that Europe, including this country, has made some of the greatest strides relative to America in recent years.

The shortage of studio space led Arthur Rank to sponsor a new method of film production, supposed at the time to be of a revolutionary character. This was the Independent Frame method, devised by David Rawnsley. It called for detailed preplanning. Instead of building elaborate sets in which the players were to act, parts of sets were built around them particularly in the foreground. The rest of the picture was filled by means of back projection and other devices. Several feature films were made in this way, but the method fell out of favour. Directors and players declared themselves unable to do their best work in such artificial surroundings. And with the derequisitioning of more studios the need for economizing in the use of space was less clamant. The method was eventually abandoned after, according to the press, £600,000 had been spent on it. The Independent Frame method might conceivably have begun in television studios where conditions tend to be very much more cramped than in cinema studios.

Some other of Arthur Rank's innovations met with more success. *This Moden Age*, a series in the *March of Time* manner, headed for four successive years the Exhibitors' Poll for short films made in this country. He had been keenly interested in making feature and other films for children. Mary Field came from Gaumont-British Instructional to take charge of the project and her films became very popular with young cinema club audiences in other countries besides Great Britain. As Arthur Vesselo remarked, about one of her early films, *Bush Christmas*, it was constructed better than many films made for adults, came more clearly to its dramatic climax, and achieved its end more effectively. Children do not pay very much for admission to Saturday morning shows and these films were usually expected to do little more than meet production costs. But they have pleased everyone so much that they are still being produced, even though Mary Field herself has gone over to television.

Arthur Rank had to accept disappointments in the rapidly developing branches of television too. He had inherited from far-sighted Isidore Ostrer considerable interests in television (originally through J. L. Baird himself) and in radio (through the Bush Company). In the months before the war televised items had been part of the ordinary programmes in Gaumont-British's Dominion Theatre. Now he wished to renew his company's activities in this field and Alan Wood says quite bluntly that he was obstructed by Government departments in the interest of the BBC's monopoly. Indeed, he suggests that the politicians were more concerned with limiting Arthur Rank's monopoly than with one or two other monopolies that had come into being in the studios and which they chose not to notice.

The public knew surprisingly little about Arthur Rank personally. Few realized the extent to which the British film industry's renaissance resulted from his courage, from his sense of social responsibility, from his patriotic feeling, and incidentally from his willingness to risk a considerable amount of his own money. Senior men in the trade were fully aware of this, however, and several attempted to enlighten the great mass of picturegoers. They pointed out, for example, that the Rank Organization was responsible for approximately half of all the first-feature films made in Great Britain during the vital period folowing the spring of 1941 to 1947, and that its successes included *Gaslight, The Foreman Went to France, In Which We Serve, The Next of Kin, San Demetrio, London, Millions Like Us, The Way Ahead, The Way to the Stars, Blithe Spirit, Brief Encounter, I Know Where I'm Going* and *Henry V*.

Michael Balcon stated that Arthur Rank's bid to put British films over in the world market is 'the most ambitious yet attempted in this country and also the most thoroughly planned and organized'. David Lean wrote that 'Arthur Rank is often spoken of as an all-embracing monopolist who must be watched lest he crush the creative talents of the British film industry. . . . I doubt if any other group of film-makers anywhere in the world can claim as much freedom. We can make any subject we wish, with as much money as we think that subject should have spent on it. We can cast whatever actors we choose, and we have no interference at all in the way the film is made. No one sees the films until they are finished. . . . Such is the enviable position of British film-makers today and such are the conditions which have at last given our films a style and nationality of their own.'

THE GOVERNMENT IS FIRM WITH HOLLYWOOD

The American industry took Arthur Rank's incursions most seriously, partly because the large number of cinemas under his control put him in a strong negotiating position, but partly also because his unorthodoxy—so far as the film world was concerned—made his motives obscure. The American industry, knowing the extent to which their own Government supported them in getting American films into cinemas overseas, supposed that he must be similarly backed. This misunderstanding was to have unfortunate consequences.

Arthur Rank soon learned how the Americans could, and did, hold up the showing of his films in the United States—for instance, by censorship quibbles about an adjective in a piece of dialogue, or by holding up his stock for printing his films. Responding to the challenge he showed *Blithe Spirit*, *The Way to the Stars* and *Henry V* during his lease of the Winter Garden in New York. Whether this was an effective method for getting his films shown throughout the United States might be doubted; but it unquestionably caused quite a stir.

Indeed, by the early months of 1947 Hollywood seemed disposed to come to terms. But, while Arthur Rank was in the United States negotiating with leading members of the industry, the newspapers reported that the British Government was proposing, because of our dollar shortage, to impose a special duty on American films being imported into this country. Quick to react the Americans came forward with an alternative offer to freeze part of their dollar earnings in Great Britain.

The subsequent course of events has been detailed by Alan Wood, but any attempt to explain what happened must inevitably be politically controversial. Guided, so it is said by Hugh Dalton, the Government decided to be tough and imposed a 75 per cent *ad valorem* duty on all American films coming into this country. Being an import duty, it had to be paid beforehand. Perhaps the Government hoped that the American industry would come forward with a further counter-proposal improving on the proportion of their earnings they were willing to have frozen. But if such was the expectation, the Government had underestimated their opponents' intransigence. Hollywood instantly placed an embargo on films going into Great Britain. For several months afterwards, and during the boom period, cinema programmes had to be drawn from a rapidly dwindling store of new American films that had been squeezed into this country before the embargo, from reissues and from an altogether insufficient supply of new British films.

What happened then is highly controversial. According to Alan Wood the Government assured British film-makers that here was their chance. Now they could establish themselves in the home market by producing a great many more films. The trade was sceptical, but Arthur Rank's response was different and in November 1947 he announced his production programme to cost over £9 million. To provide the financial support for this venture he made his Odeon Theatres the parent company for his other undertakings. Thus the Odeon shareholders, whose money had been invested in the profitable business of showing films, found that their dividends would be affected by returns from production—a less rewarding line. For this arrangement Arthur Rank was sharply criticized in the financial press. He also merged the Odeon and Gaumont circuits to form the Circuits Management Association (CMA). However, films booked for one circuit were shown only rarely by the other and this principle was applied for another dozen years while the circuits continued to be fairly independent of each other.

As the months passed the Government learned that the stratagem, designed to halt the flow of between half and a million dollars a week out of this country, had been ineffective. Almost as much was still going out. It was being earned principally through the reissue of old films, an unexpected windfall for the Americans. This led, according to Alan Wood, the Government to negotiate an agreement with Hollywood's representatives under which the *ad valorem* tax was withdrawn. The Americans were to take a maximum of seventeen million dollars out of this country each year. They had to invest the rest of their profits in British enterprises (not necessarily connected with the cinema).

Soon after this the Government, acting on the advice of the Cinematograph Films Council, raised the Exhibitors' Quota for British films from 20 to 45 per cent. Eric Johnston, President of the Motion Picture Association of America, reflecting the strains of the times described this as a gratuitous affront to the American picture industry. No less gratuitously he added that Great Britain had not made one new film recently good enough to attract American cinemagoers.

No limitation was placed on the rate at which American films were to be admitted into this country, and the floodgates were opened just when Arthur Rank's own films were being released in this country.

GREAT EXPECTATIONS INDEED

And what of the films themselves made during this exacting post-war period? The first point about them is that the grand total was still small. During the year March 1947 to March 1948, this aggregate for feature films (over 4,500 feet in length) rose only to seventy-four.

They included two of the finest of all British films. David Lean's *Great Expectations*, released towards the end of 1946, had a magnificent press in the United States as well as in this country. 'It is a landmark in the history of British film,' Richard Winnington said, 'not only because it is taken from the most shapely, mature and filmable of all Dickens's novels, not because it has the best photography I've seen for years, or because the casting is nearly perfect, or because of its knife-edge cutting or its furious pace, but because it casts a complete spell derived from some inner power. . . . Several sequences belong to the handbook of cinema—the feverish journey of Pip in a state of near delirium through the streets to his bed, the dreadful end of Miss Havisham, the death sentence in the jail . . . *Great Expectations* deserved all the screaming publicity that *London Town* and *Caesar and Cleopatra* embarrassed us with.'

Carol Reed's *Odd Man Out* was quoted by Roger Manvell as an example of what a prestige film should really be like, 'intense and powerful, an experience rather than an entertainment, achieving most of its effect without final dependence on mere words—and so making a good film to export to foreign-speaking countries'.

Based on F. L. Green's novel about the tragic last eight hours in the life of the leader of an illegal political organization in Belfast, it was blessed by having a superb cast of Irish and other actors, with F. J. McCormick of the Abbey Theatre giving one of the most brilliantly etched character studies in the history of cinematography.

There was much more to *Odd Man Out* than just an account of a gangster's downfall. 'In a single afternoon and evening of rain, snow and grime are condensed all the events of the plot, whose symbolic account of man's pursuit by furies is unfolded amid scenes familiar to every dweller in a populous, industrial city.'

Denis Forman reproved those who cast about for a message in the film, some even seeing Johnny McQueen as a symbol of the Christ figure. 'The drama is not derived from internal conflict within the leading character, nor from moral issues involving right and wrong. . . . On Reed's stage the players move within the framework of circumstances, neither seeking to control their fate nor questioning it, and in this sense, for all its poetry, it can best be described as a documentary study based on a fictional thesis.'

Apart from these two films the years 1946 and 1947, of which so much had been hoped, produced little that is memorable. There was the beautiful *Black Narcissus* by Powell and Pressburger. Its theme was the spiritual conflict between a Himalayan community's paganism and the Christian resolution of an invading group of nuns. Little of this is recalled today but memories persist of some quite remarkable studio achievements photographed in Technicolor.

There was also the astonishing *A Matter of Life and Death.* A wounded airman, undergoing a brain operation, imagines that he is being tried by a Heavenly Court, and that he is defended by various historical characters. This fantasy was witty and technically remarkably clever. Dilys Powell described it as having technical audacity without parallel in Great Britain. But, as Denis Forman remarked, its pretentions were a shade too heavy for most sensibilities and it left an almost distasteful impression. It did please some discriminating people very much, however, and Bosley Crowther of the *New York Times* put it among the best ten films of the year—a notable achievement for a British film at this juncture.

War themes were still being employed (unlike the period after 1918 when for almost a decade they were taboo). Some of these films are still being revived, such as Basil Dearden's *The Captive Heart*, in which the moods of British prisoners of war were studied, and *Night Boat to Dublin*, telling a spy story with reflections on the Irish attitude to the war.

These were not easy years in which to identify public tastes. For instance, Roy Boulting's *Fame is the Spur* aroused less interest than might have been expected. It was based on Howard Spring's account of the career of an idealistic Labour politician with character defects. Frank Launder's urbane *Captain Boycott,* in which Cecil Parker had one of his finest parts, dealt with aspects of recent Irish history about which the public was found to be surprisingly uninformed or uninterested, or both.

Several more highly melodramatic films were made, but their tenor was changing. Plots were less novelettish; but, if not so tearful, they were getting even tougher. Some critics were expressing concern about the amount of crime and sadism entering into British films. In

The Upturned Glass, for instance. James Mason was a deranged brain specialist consumed with a ruthless desire for revenge. Margaret Lockwood had to submit in *Jassy* to one of her not uncommon experiences of flagellation. The relationship between *The Brothers*, played by Maxwell Reed and Duncan Macrae, in the film version of L. A. G. Strong's novel set in the Western Isles, was far from agreeable. Robert Hamer's *It Always Rains on Sundays*, about an escaped convict who turned up in Bethnal Green, was said by Arthur Vesselo to leave an impression of gloom and of subterranean violence, even though it had vitality, humour and more than a gleam of atmospheric magic as well as back-street squalor.

Leonard Mosley complained at the end of 1947 about 'the fierce and horrible faces that still peer at me—Kieron Moore about to have a schizophrenic attack, Rosamund John moaning over the loss of her child, Margaret Lockwood bracing herself to enter the dock on a murder charge, Dennis Price leering over the writhing form of the girl he is beating'.

One of the more widely circulated film magazines conducted a poll to choose the best picture of 1947. Among the films from which its readers made their selection were *Great Expectations* and *Odd Man Out*. But they gave first place to Herbert Wilcox's *Courtneys of Curzon Street*. Arthur Vesselo said that its hokum content was obvious but that it was put together by a practised hand according to a well-tried sentimental formula. In an interview, after his success was announced, Wilcox said that the film appealed to British audiences because it was 'about nice people. The public appreciated a change from gloomy horrors. They wanted sentiment not sadism, and certainly not studies in psychiatry.'

It was not, however, of the *Courtneys of Curzon Street* that René Jeanner and Charles Ford were thinking in their recent *Cinéma d'aujord'hui*, when they gave 1946 and 1948 as the finest years of the British cinema.

CHAPTER EIGHTEEN

Swept Aside in the Flood

....

ARTHUR RANK'S RIVALS

Until 1948 ABPC's production was virtually confined to the small stages at Welwyn. Then the studios at Elstree were reopened, greatly altered and supplied with much new equipment. The first productions were not notable, but before long Elstree had resumed its former rôle as the training ground of directors, technicians and stars. Lee Thomson was there, directing his first film for ABPC, *Murder Without Crime*. Michael Anderson, who was to direct *The Dam Busters*, was already under contract. Soon afterwards the youthful dancer, Audrey Hepburn, was too.

Robert Clark was now in charge of production. Carrying on in John Maxwell's tradition, he was described as blending a realistic business sense with an occasional flash of considerable daring. It is an interesting thought that Elstree, in spite of its Scottish affiliations, avoided the Bonnie Prince Charlie theme. That was left to Alexander Korda. As soon as the Elstree studios were running smoothly, Robert Clark continued to keep them fully occupied. The Corporation's chairman, Sir Philip Warter, stated their policy as 'to produce a reasonable number of films for our own distribution and at the same time to provide first-class facilities to outside companies, both British and American, for making films in this country. In this way we hope to maintain a steady level of employment at the studios without taking unnecessary financial risks.'

At the beginning of 1947 Alexander Korda, having parted from MGM, re-established London Films as a separate organization. He acquired controlling interest in a distributing company, British Lion, in which he had a new associate, Sir Arthur Jarratt, formerly of Gaumont-British. He then bought the studios at Shepperton, which he extended to five stages and equipped so thoroughly over the next few years that they were perhaps the best in Europe. He also had an interest in the Isleworth Studios, giving him altogether eight stages

—11,000 square feet of studio floor space. So he possessed facilities which were larger than ABPC's, although still considerably smaller than Arthur Rank's.

During these post-war years Arthur Rank and Alexander Korda were often likened to Mr Gladstone and Disraeli, the one Methodist with a nonconformist conscience, the other Bohemian with an artistic conscience. But the feeling of rivalry was in no way as intense as that between the politicians. Alexander Korda was not impressed by the Government's appeal to step up his production. He was dismayed when Arthur Rank announced his proposal to make thirty-eight films and urged him to reconsider his plan; he forecast inevitable disaster because of the lack of creative and technical talent in this country. Arthur Rank's programme was, in fact, never completed.

Alexander Korda was as well known in Hollywood as Arthur Rank was unknown, and he was able to make an agreement with 20th Century-Fox to distribute his films throughout the American continent. But even his organization could not escape the increased prejudice which had grown up in the United States against British films.

His first major production, now that he really was settled down in this country again, was a new version of Oscar Wilde's *An Ideal Husband*. It was also the last film that he directed personally. An elegant production, elaborately staged by Vincent Korda (with a reconstruction of Hyde Park Corner in the 1890s), it was superbly dressed by Cecil Beaton and photographed by Alexander Korda's favourite cameramen, George Perinal. Trade reviewers described it as 'a lavish production that never ceased to dazzle the eyes'.

The cast was distinguished too and included Paulette Goddard, Hugh Williams, Michael Wilding and Diana Wynyard. But Oscar Wilde is the stagiest of playwrights. His wittiest epigrams need delicate handling instead of the inevitable over-emphasis on the screen. And the coincidences in his plots, seemingly of secondary importance in the theatre, become embarrassingly apparent in the cinema. Except with select audiences *An Ideal Husband* was a comparative failure in this country as well as overseas.

Nor could it be said that Alexander Korda's other films at this stage were outstandingly successful. He plunged into melodrama with *A Man About the House*. It was directed by Ted Black and Leslie Arliss, the first of the more important members of Arthur Rank's team to transfer their services to him. They had been responsible for such highly profitable Gaumont-British ventures as *The Man in Grey* and *The Wicked Lady*. They did not quite repeat these triumphs, however, with *A Man About the House*. It described the distressing experience of two British spinsters, played by Margaret Johnston and Dulcie Gray, who became involved with a scheming Italian, played rather inadequately by Kieron Moore. The critics were not impressed by the film. They thought that the earlier parts inclined to the satirical and that the later parts became turgid.

Another director who joined Alexander Korda in this post-war period was Anthony Kimmins, and his version of Nigel Balchin's novel, *Mine Own Executioner*, was more to the critics' liking. Burgess Meredith gave a sensitive portrayal of a psychiatrist grappling with a mentally-deranged RAF pilot's problems; but the subject could not have been expected to appeal to what the trade press sometimes called the masses.

Indeed, it was one of Arthur Rank's films, *The Red Shoes*, which eventually re-established British films in the American as well as the continental markets.

It was written, produced and directed by Powell and Pressburger. The essential part of the film was a ballet based on the fairy story and danced with 'fragile loveliness' by Moira Shearer, making her first appearance on the screen. Conceived in a modern idiom it was well received, although it had critics. Arthur Vesselo said that 'however much it may be claimed that the *Ballet of the Red Shoes*, as performed on the screen, represents the subjective attitude of the dancer to the music and to her dance, the fact remains that the method has more than a passing resemblance to that of the spectacular Busby Berkeley type dance sequences'. This might explain why the film, when shown in the United States, had such an enthusiastic reception—a success which reflected well on the resistance and determination of Arthur Rank's organization overseas. Indeed, the film's success in the United States considerably influenced the public support which built up more slowly for it in Great Britain. Few if any who first saw it towards the end of 1946 would have forecast that it would eventually be included in the list of films that have earned most money in United States' cinemas—the only non-American film on the list. Its gross total is given as over five million dillars.

FOUR FILMS THAT WILL BE REMEMBERED

If Arthur Rank had had more films of this calibre available in 1948 the shape of the British film-making industry would be different now. But in this year, when his large output of new films had to stand up to the sudden unloading of a mass of American films, he had only a few 'winners'. So unfortunately did other British film-makers.

Stephen Watts maintained that 1948 would be remembered

because of just four films, *Hamlet, The Fallen Idol, Bonnie Prince Charlie* and *No Orchids for Miss Blandish.* The first two were splendid films, the former coming from Arthur Rank, and the latter from Alexander Korda. *Hamlet* had, on the whole, an even better reception from American than from British critics. Indeed, it is one of the few British films which has won an Oscar of the Academy of Motion Picture Arts and Sciences.

Not many films can have been given so much care in preparation as *Hamlet,* perhaps to such an extent that in its final form it looked just a little pretentious—hence C. A. Lejeune's estimate that, although it was a valiant adventure in Shakespeare, it was an ultimate failure. Arthur Vesselo admired the film's excellent patches but said that it was also in patches tedious, and that its methods raised the whole question of how best Shakespeare can be translated into film terms, if the thing is to be done at all. . . . The producer who concentrates on being faithful to the original cannot also concentrate on making a film.

Among the film's many technical features was its use of deep-focus photography, keeping both foreground and background sharply in focus. By extending the length of shots it ensured that the flow of the dialogue was not interrupted by camera switchings from one face to another. Inadvertently, as Alan Wood observed, this emphasized the film's main fault, its theatricality.

Arthur Rank's other outstanding film, David Lean's version of *Oliver Twist,* was a tremendous achievement with by far the best representation of mid-Victorian London ever seen in the cinema. But it ran into heavy weather. There was a bitter disagreement at the time between the American and British Governments about the admission of European Jews to Israel, and Alec Guinness's portrayal of Fagin was assailed with such hostility that the film was not shown in the United States. Alan Wood quotes this representation of Fagin as an example of the freedom Arthur Rank allowed his directors. He says that these possible developments were perceived long before the film was completed, but Arthur Rank resisted the pressure brought to bear on him to intervene. He let the director have his way.

Like all other British films in this unhappy year, *Oliver Twist* ran into competition head on from several excellent American films released almost simultaneously in this country. Alexander Korda's disaster with *Bonnie Prince Charlie* can be explained, however, by admitting that it was a poor film. Apparently several of his directors had at various times been attracted to the subject, but eventually Anthony Kimmins was drafted reluctantly to make it, and after many authors had had a hand in writing the script. Although beautifully photographed the film lacked excitement. It just plodded on. Its major weakness was, however, in some incredible casting errors, notably in the choice of David Niven as the Prince. Niven had never emphasized his Scottish ancestry and he was associated in the public mind with the character of a society playboy. Scottish cinemagoers were outraged by his interpretation of the Prince, and English audiences found the film uninteresting. David Niven is reported to have felt unhappy in the part and to have declared afterwards that acting in the film was an experience he would prefer to forget. The production is said to have cost Alexander Korda half a million pounds. It had a dreadful reception from the critics and for once he made an error in arguing with them, saying that they had written their reviews with hatchets instead of pens. He also launched an expensive publicity campaign to support the film and that just added to the losses.

He had another disappointment with *Anna Karenina*, directed by Julien Duvivier from a script by Jean Anouilh. A costly effort, it too did not have a good press. The story had been filmed shortly before the war by MGM, with Greta Garbo and John Barrymore in the leading parts, and the new film was compared unfavourably with it, although admitted to be more in sympathy with Tolstoy's novel. Vivien Leigh acted splendidly, but her coldness and general lack of emotionality did not adequately explain the eccentricities of Anna's behaviour.

Alexander Korda had more success with two other films produced on a less spectacular scale. They were Carol Reed's *The Fallen Idol* and Anthony Asquith's *The Winslow Boy*. The former was summed up by C. A. Lejeune as a beautiful and touching picture about a small boy's disillusion. Perhaps the film had a weakness in that Ralph Richardson made the family butler, the lad's hero, too sympathetic a character. But Michèle Morgan, in a more restrained performance, was very effective as the housekeeper and young Bobby Henrey registered his loss of faith lucidly. This was the first film that Carol Reed directed for Alexander Korda after leaving Arthur Rank and, according to Paul Tabori, 'of all the producer-directors working with Korda, Reed was the most successful and his relationship with Korda the most harmonious'.

Unlike *The Fallen Idol*, which was based on one of Graham Greene's lesser known short stories, *The Winslow Boy* kept fairly close to a familiar plot, derived from a current stage play by Terence Rattigan. The Archer-Shee case was a newspaper headline story of the pre-First World War years—a naval cadet was expelled from Osborne charged with theft, and his father fought determinedly and successfully in defending his honour. The trial was not included among the scenes in the play but it was one of the highlights of the film. Robert Donat took the opportunity to give an excellent performance, but some critics thought that seeing the trial instead of just hearing (as in the play) about the result really took away from the film's conviction.

MANY ORCHIDS FOR MISS BLANDISH

The box-office triumphs of *No Orchids for Miss Blandish* may have had more influence at this period on the future of the industry in Great Britain than the achievements of any other film. This sex-crime piece was directed by St John L. Clowes and based on a story by James Hadley Chase. It had a spurious American gangster setting although produced in Great Britain. It was dismissed by one critic as a piece of calculated nastiness, a disagreeable excursion into the brutal and vicious. Some other British films of the year also contained a suggestion that tastes were changing. For instance, Arthur Vesselo commented on the bleak depressionism of the Boulting Brothers' version of Graham Greene's *Brighton Rock*. 'It is a sordid tale of razor-slashing racecourse gangsters in Brighton between the wars. The atmosphere is chilled and overhung by a mood of craven fear and disillusion.' Another film—one of Alexander Korda's —*Night Beat*, directed by Harold Huth, was said to descend to the realms of spivvery and hooliganism. David Birt's version of Joan Temple's *No Room at the Inn* occasioned some eyebrow raising too.

Those who were gazing with dismay at the English music hall as it made its death throes hideous with gross vulgarities wondered whether here were the first indications that the English cinematograph industry might head in the wrong direction too. One feature was, however, puzzling. The assumption had been that women rather than men choose the film show when having an evening out. It seemed incredible that women should prefer these films to others with more romantic themes.

STAGGERING LOSSES

Some of Arthur Rank's films were of a much higher standard— Peter Ustinov's burlesque of Frederick Anstey's farce *Vice Versa*, for instance, Ken Annakin's amusing trifle, *Miranda*, with Glynis Johns as an alluring mermaid; his adaptation of Joseph Shearing's *Blanche Fury*; and *Quartet*, derived from four more of Somerset Maugham's short stories. But in October 1948 Arthur Rank had to tell his shareholders that their borrowings from the bank had reached £13½ million, and that film production might have to be given up altogether. *The Economist* declared, 'the Odeon group is stripped and bare'.

15. In the critics' opinion *Richard III* (1955) was the most mature of
Laurence Olivier's three Shakespearian productions. It greatly
pleased discerning cinemagoers. With Olivier in this scene is Ralph
Richardson.

Outstanding among all retrospective British war films, particularly in
distribution abroad, was David Lean's *The Bridge on the River Kwai*
(1957), in which Alec Guinness reminded the public that he is
primarily a dramatic actor and not a comedian.

16. Jack Clayton's *Room at the Top* was said to have been made from the standpoint of the angry young man. It opened a new phase in British cinematography. The players here are the French actress Simone Signoret and Laurence Harvey.

The decade ended with Basil Dearden's *Sapphire* winning the British Film Academy Award for 1959. Detectives Nigel Patrick and Michael Craig are visiting a club during their inquiries into Sapphire's death.

While many different factors had contributed—and Arthur Rank took much of the blame to himself—the Government's retention of the Entertainments Tax at an incredibly high level—no less than £40 million was being paid out of the total box-office receipts of £109 million—was one of the greatest. But Arthur Rank had no doubt about the principal source of his discomfiture. As recently as at the 1959 annual meeting of the Rank Organization he said that 'Great Britain would now have a very successful market in the United States if it had not been for the *ad valorem* duty imposed by the Government on American film imports in 1947'.

CHAPTER NINETEEN

The Year When Everything Went Wrong

••

GREAT BRITAIN'S MOST PROFITABLE CINEMA BUSINESS

There was more to worry about in 1949, however, than the losses on British-made films. It was in 1949, according to Fred Majdalany, that most people stopped going to the pictures regularly, and went only to see particular films. Box-office receipts took a downward trend. Probably most exhibitors realized that the post-war boom must eventually end. For almost a decade they had queues almost every evening. Now they had queues only on Saturday evenings, and sometimes even then they were late in forming.

The trade wondered when the slide would end—perhaps in 1950, they thought, or even in 1951—and, how much higher would the average attendance total be when things settled down than in 1938 and 1939. They had no inkling that the downward trend would go on throughout the 1950s.

The immediate crisis in the Rank Organization, still controlling two of the country's three largest circuits of cinemas, focused attention on the greater prosperity of the Associated British Picture Corporation. The *Financial Times* warmly commended its directors for paying a dividend of 20 per cent year after year. The secret of the company's success, according to *The Economist*, was that, while it both exhibited and produced films, it saw that the balance was well weighted towards exhibition. Frederick Ellis, the City journalist, attributed its success to 'keeping largely to film-showing at its 450 cinemas and to keeping its expenditure on film-making down to a modest budget'.

This was the company founded by John Maxwell twenty years before. One of the great doubts which must be faced in a history of the British film industry is whether John Maxwell would have played a greater part in the early years of the war if his health had been better and if his studios at Elstree had not been taken from him. There is another doubt too—about what would have happened if the studios had been derequisitioned soon after the end of the war. How would he have reacted to the Government's appeals in 1946 and 1947? There are some who hold that the ABPC directors were fortunate because Elstree's non-availability made it unnecessary for them to make any agonizing decisions at that juncture. In the summer of 1949 they had the satisfaction of releasing a very successful film, *The Hasty Heart*, based on John Patrick's wartime story about an embittered Scots soldier dying in a Burma hospital. It was directed by an American, Vincent Sharman, and had an American, Ronald Regan, as its leading player. But it was one of their own young actors, Richard Todd, who won the notices and became a star almost overnight.

John Davis set about the formidable task of getting the Rank Organization's film-making activities back on a business footing— the press reported that £6 million had been lost in the course of the last four and a half years. Some of the independent producers and directors that Arthur Rank had gathered in the war and post-war years did not take well to John Davis's notions about planning and economy. Ted Black from Gainsborough and Del Giudice from Two Cities soon made their departure, Earl St John taking over responsibility for production. Powell and Pressburger went early, then in turn Launder and Gilliat, David Lean and Carol Reed. They seem to have liked working with Alexander Korda and to have benefited from his astute counsel. They were all sufficiently well established not to be overawed by his personality.

This was the year of one of Alexander Korda's outstanding successes, Carol Reed's *The Third Man*. A crime film, written by Graham Greene and set among the ruins of Vienna just after the war, it had several vignettes that are still recalled—such as Orson Welles's first leering appearance in a dimly-lit doorway and Alida Valli's last appearance walking along an avenue on an autumnal day. Arthur Knight rightly observed that the film is probably best known for the economy of its nostalgic zither accompaniment, but he added that behind the zither was the echo of fleeing footsteps across a cobble-stoned square, the laboured breathing of pursued and pursuer in the climactic chase through the cavernous sewers beneath the city.

David Selznick was associated with the production and with its distribution in the United States. Dilys Powell was among those who sensed danger in this arrangement. The film was being accepted, she said, as the creation of British talent and technique. Yet three of its leading players came from America—came not to settle and to work at Shepperton, but to lend their box-office lustre to a single film. Co-production might lead to the use of American directors for

English subjects, and American stars for English characters. 'If the English cinema is to be worth saving it must be allowed to handle the English subjects in the English way.'

Knowledgeable cinemagoers were becoming disturbingly aware that the post-war group of young directors was not living up to its early promise. David Lean's adaptation of H. G. Wells's *The Passionate Friends* had only beautiful Alpine photography to commend it. Launder and Gilliat's *The Blue Lagoon* was, in spite of box-office success, just a pot-boiler. Powell and Pressburger began well with a version of Nigel Balchin's novel about boffins and a dangerous bomb, *The Small Back Room*, but their *Gone to Earth* (a joint Korda-Selznick production) was less distinguished.

Indeed, apart from *The Third Man*, the best films of the year came from other quarters; Thorold Dickinson's *The Queen of Spades*, with Edith Evans superb as Pushkin's elderly Countess who knew how to win at cards; Ian Dalrymple's satirical *Dear Mr Prohack*, about a Treasury official who did not know what to do with his inheritance; and Peter Ustinov's adaptation of Eric Linklater's novel about an Italian soldier, *Private Angelo*, who abhorred war.

Famous British directors returned from the United States to make films for their employers, but it is doubtful if they recall their productions with much satisfaction (such as Alfred Hitchcock's *Under Capricorn* and Victor Saville's *The Conspirator*). George Cukor was with us too making *Edward, My Son*. But it was Michael Balcon who did most to save the British cinematograph industry's reputation.

THE EALING COMEDIES

His new film, *Hue and Cry*, delighted the critics. Set among the bombed buildings of London's East End it accompanied a group of children in tracking a master criminal. Denis Forman remarked that it combined three happy elements. Its story had an unsophisticated gusto which romped into the cinemas like a tomboy into a cocktail party. Its background was three-dimensional (it was shot almost entirely on location). 'There was St Paul's as real as life, and Covent Garden, and the City with street names and landmarks that millions could recognize with a sense of being at home. And most importantly there was robust yet high fantasy, a schoolboy's daydream perhaps, but the real stuff, getting bigger, finer and fiercer at every step.'

During the next months Michael Balcon made other films with the same lively spirit. The summer months of 1949 were quite memorable for three other Ealing Comedies, released in rapid succession: *Passport to Pimlico*, directed by Henry Cornelius, in which a fifteenth-century charter showed that the London district of Pimlico was and is Burgundian, and hence not subject to the many irksome restrictions then being endured by the rest of the country; *Kind Hearts and Coronets*, directed by Robert Hamer, in which Dennis Price was a polished scoundrel and Alec Guinness portrayed each of the eight members of an aristocratic family earmarked for extermination; and *Whisky Galore*, directed by Alexander MacKendrick, based on Compton Mackenzie's account of bibulous events following the wrecking near the Hebridean island of Toddy of a ship with a cargo of whisky. The last of these films became, under the title *Tight Little Island*, a most remunerative British film (in relation to its cost) in the United States as well as in the Commonwealth.

The patronymic, *An Ealing Comedy*, was becoming familiar to cinegoers throughout the English-speaking world. And Arthur Rank, who distributed these Ealing films, must have derived solace for the loss of his galaxy of young directors to Alexander Korda.

'EADY MONEY'

The Government appointed a Working Party under Sir George Gater to look into the cost of making films in this country and to suggest ways of setting the producers' house in order. A Committee was appointed under Professor Sir Arnold Plant to examine the way in which films were being distributed and exhibited in Great Britain.

While these two bodies were taking evidence and preparing their reports the situation turned critical. Lord Archibald told the House of Lords of an estimate that the cost of producing feature films in Great Britain during 1949 would be £15 million. The companies which made these films might receive £7 million from the home market and perhaps another £4 million from overseas markets. So it would seem that another £4 million was going to be added to the deficit.

It was clear that the film-making companies must recover more of their costs from the home market. The Plant Committee showed that, of the £44 million earned annually by British films in British cinemas, 34 per cent was removed by Entertainments Tax, 39 per cent was taken by the exhibitors, and 6 per cent went to the distributors. Allowing another 2 per cent as the cost of the supporting programme only 17 per cent was left for the companies that made the first feature films. The Plant Committee said that the share of the total proceeds of the industry taken by the Exchequer in the form of entertainments duty was so high as to constitute a serious handicap to British production.

The Gater Committee thought that the film production industry lived 'in a general atmosphere of extravagance and unreality, leading to a disregard of expense which would not be tolerated in other forms of business'. The report added that towards the end of the war and in the following years the industry 'encouraged by the exceptional success of certain British films and by the boom in the cinema attendances made films with an ever increasing disregard of cost'. (And this, it was noted, was virtually an 'exact description of what had happened once before in the 1934-37 situation'.) The Gater Committee was concerned not only about waste in the studios but about the absence of planning ahead. It labelled the film production methods as the most serious deficiency in the industry.

During 1949 the number of people employed in British studios fell by almost one half—from 7,700 to 4,400. Studios closed down and, as a foretaste of things to come, the former Gaumont-British premises at Shepherd's Bush were sold by the Rank Organization to the BBC for conversion into television studios.

In midsummer, 1948, the Government announced its intention of creating the National Film Finance Corporation to provide short-term finance for film production. In effect the Corporation was to be a means of preventing the British film-making industry from going bankrupt by lending money to producers.

The Corporation was to have a statutory obligation to pay its own way. Accordingly, its loans (up to 30 per cent of the film's total budget) were based upon the prospective return of the cash. This was probably a wise decision in the prevailing circumstances, but in trying to pick out good box-office bets the Corporation was, as its critics pointed out, making popular taste the sole criterion. 'Content and style did not count.' Lord Reith was appointed the Corporation's chairman and James Lawrie its managing director.

The National Film Finance Corporation was provided with working capital of £5 million, and this was increased in 1950 to £6 million.

ABPC and Ealing made no applications to the Corporation during its first year, and the Rank Organization preferred to cut down its production schedule. Of the larger groups only British Lion asked for a substantial loan to help provide the £2 million (later increased to £3 million) estimated for financing their production programme as planned. Several independents were helped, and makers of second feature films came in for sympathetic consideration (a total of fifty-one applications was approved in the Corporation's first year, from April 1949 to April 1950). The subsidized films ranged from *The Third Man* to *Old Mother Riley, Headmistress*.

Government intervention in the industry was to go even farther. In midsummer 1950 the Eady Plan, called after Sir Wilfrid Eady, Second Secretary of the Treasury, was accepted by the Government with minor amendments. The original proposal was made by the trade and the levy was in theory 'voluntary'. The proposal was to adjust Entertainments Tax rates while raising seat prices. This was expected to add £3 million to the industry's earnings, but in return the exhibitors were to pay one farthing for every ticket sold into a new fund, the British Film Production Fund. Film-makers were to receive payments from this fund 'on a purely automatic and objective basis'. A small percentage was to be applied in financing other bodies such as the Children's Film Foundation, whose executive head was Mary Field.

It was soon found that the sum being collected was inadequate to cover the producers' losses and so, in the next midsummer (1951), an augmented Eady Plan had to be introduced. Raising seat prices again was approved, and this enabled the Chancellor of the Exchequer not only to give a further measure of Entertainments Tax relief, but also to increase the amount going into the Eady Fund.

It was estimated that the scheme would cost cinemagoers an additional £12½ million a year. Of this slightly over half would go to the Treasury as taxation. The exhibitors, who by this time were also flying distress signals, would get £3·7 million, and the producers a further £2·3 million.

Although devised as a temporary measure the plan has become a permanent form of Government financial support, and the Corporation has assisted about half of all British first feature Quota films made since it was set up in 1949. But for the Corporation the British industry have virtually disappeared by now.

Eady money is paid out according to the box-office receipts of all British films qualified for Quota. Separate groups were formed to deal with the leading companies. Another, officially called Group 3, was set up to make second feature films each costing about £20,000. John Grierson was appoined executive producer of this Group and John Baxter production controller.

With the industry coming to rely on Eady Money to quite a considerable extent, criticism grew about the basis on which it was being distributed. The complaint was that the successful producers were being subsidized—and the more successful they were the greater the subsidy—while little was done to help producers who were trying to get off the beaten track.

CHAPTER TWENTY

On the Wrong Side of Fifty

IS HOLLYWOOD LOSING ITS TOUCH?

In one highly significant respect the situation which developed in the late 1940s differed from that of the late 1930s. Acute disappointment was felt on both occasions over unfulfilled hopes and wasted opportunities. But before the war Hollywood was producing so many first-class films that British films, even those of fine quality, had difficulty in procuring an adequate number of showings. But by 1950 it was not only the British who were flagging. So were the Americans.

Indeed, while we were lamenting our failures, *Time* magazine was rebuking Hollywood producers, suggesting that they had lost their touch. It compared their unsatisfactory recent achievements with the excellent thrillers and comedies coming from British studios. Among those mentioned were *The Third Man* (described as 'a mood-saturated melodrama of black-market intrigue of post-war Vienna'), *Kind Hearts and Coronets* ('with Alec Guinness taking the year's honours for irony, urbanity and impudent wit'), *Tight Little Island* ('a comedy, almost perfect of its kind, which applies character, insight and cinematic ingenuity'), *The Rocking Horse Winner* (based on a D. H. Lawrence story about a small boy's life being sacrificed through a woman's pathological greed), *Trio* (from three of Somerset Maugham's short stories, in one of which Nigel Patrick gave his brilliant portrayal of an insufferable cad shielding a foolish lady), and *The Winslow Boy*. On this showing British films were at least occupying a place in the United States comparable to that which French films held in this country.

On the other hand, *Sight and Sound* thought we had still to discover the secret (an open one, it said, in Hollywood) of making cheap films discreetly. 'Ruthless economy over here means palpable shoddiness. Good technique in British films is usually restricted to the prestige pictures, and these display almost an infatuation with it, as if high-grade craftsmanship were something only recently discovered and textbook proficiency exciting in itself. The result is that prestige pictures have tended to be cold and self-conscious, lacking in human values, and sometimes not even satisfying the minority at which they are particularly aimed.'

There was one gratifying feature—the triumphant successes of two more Ealing comedies, overseas as well as at home. They were *The Lavender Hill Mob*, directed by Charles Crichton, and *The Man in the White Suit*, directed by Alexander Mackendrick. In the former Alec Guinness is a bank clerk who has evolved a scheme for stealing a vast quantity of bullion and for smuggling it into France. In spite of amateurish bungling his plan is successful, although in the last sequence the law is allowed to catch up with him. In the latter film Alec Guinness is a laboratory assistant in a textile factory who invents a fabric that will not get dirty and, in fact, will not wear out. The consequence is that tens of thousands of people are doomed to lose their jobs.

These two comedies finally clinched Ealing's position—and not only in the English-speaking countries but in France and Italy, and especially in Germany. Francis Koval, writing in *Sight and Sound*, emphasized the opportunities for British film-makers on their continental doorstep. Since the war, he said, people had been satiated by American films and were becoming either bored or irritated with the unvarying repetition of certain themes, the over-emphasis put on crime and glamour, the relentlessly smooth technique so characteristic of even the average Hollywood product. Apart from *Brief Encounter* and *The Seventh Veil* (and in Germany, *The Third Man*), the first British films to impress discriminating cinemagoers on the Continent were the Ealing Comedies.

Gavin Lambert attempted an analysis and found that the Ealing Comedies had methods if not values in common—ingenuity of situation and narrative twists, a blend of irony and slapstick, and a fairly exact observation, behind all the junketings, of social background. He also noted the absence of romantic sentiment. Freda Bruce Lockhart's view was that Ealing Films depend 'on story-idea rather than treatment, on a fortunate blend of spontaneity, social conscience and cheerful vitality, rather than on style'.

No other films up to their standard were made in Great Britain at this time. The popular and financial success of 1950—and the British Film Academy winner—was *The Blue Lamp*, directed by Basil Dearden for Michael Balcon. It is chiefly of interest today as a precursor of various television series. The critics, while appreciating the neatness of the film's construction, were never enthusiastic. Possibly a better indication of the high regard in which the film was held at the time is given by the months which passed between its release at the beginning of the year and its gaining major awards at the end of the year. Public memory is not usually so retentive, prizewinners tending to be drawn from recently shown films.

The Festival of Britain was to be held in 1951, and the British cinematograph industry decided to make a worthy film as a combined effort. It was to be produced in the ABPC studios at Elstree. The Rank Organization would distribute it. The producer was to be Ronald Neame and the director John Boulting. The script would be written by Eric Ambler, the photography would be undertaken by Jack Cardiff and the music by William Alwyn. There could have been no finer team.

The subject was to be *The Magic Box*. Its inventor, William Friese-Greene, was to be played by Robert Donat, and he was to be supported by a cast of sixty, drawn from most of the leading actors and actresses in the industry.

Eric Ambler was probably troubled when he ascertained that the claims about Friese-Greene having invented cinematography had been pitched too high. In the long run he had to be presented quite candidly as no more than one of the industry's many pioneers— which was hardly in keeping with the object in mind when the film was first mooted.

Eric Ambler must also have been disconcerted by the descent of Friese-Greene from a successful 'Court photographer' to a discard on the fringes of the trade. Anti-climax is not usually favoured by story-tellers. Nor could the plot be linked with any astounding developments in cinematography because he had made virtually no contributions to them. Eventually the theme had to be centred on Friese-Greene's two marriages to give it acceptable dramatic form.

Many other problems were encountered, and the film was so late that it was not released until the end of 1951, when enthusiasm for the Festival of Britain had almost evaporated. The result did not appeal to the public. No other major production can have played to so many half-empty houses.

The best films of the period included the Boulting Brothers' production for Alexander Korda of *Seven Days to Noon*, telling a tense story about a deranged scientist's proposal to blow up London. In some respects it was just a cleverly-made thriller with the police searching the emptying city for their man; but as a study of mounting anxiety it has been rarely surpassed. There were also some good war films such as Ian Dalrymple's adaptation, also for Alexander Korda, of Eric Williams's *The Wooden Horse*, about the escape of three British Servicemen from a prisoner-of-war camp.

Another Dickens film, *Scrooge*, was made, this time by Brian

Desmond Hurst, and a third collection of Somerset Maugham's stories, *Encore*, including a splendid episode in which Kay Walsh was a garrulous spinster on a winter cruise. Anthony Asquith directed a discreet version of Terence Rattigan's tragedy, *The Browning Version*, and ABPC presented a slick musical, *Happy Go Lovely*, centred on the Edinburgh Festival, featuring Vera-Ellen and David Niven.

MORE ANGLO-AMERICAN PRODUCTIONS

In one respect the Government's policy now met with notable success. This was in encouraging American companies to produce major films in Great Britain. MGM, Fox, Warner and RKO all made pictures here in 1951, usually with stars from both countries and sometimes with continental stars too. During the decade these 'international' films became so common that they rarely attracted any particular comment—not even when the practice was reversed and, instead of American directors taking charge of British productions, it was British directors who took charge of American productions.

John Spraos reviewed this development ten years later in *The Decline of the Cinema*. Among the factors he mentioned in bringing about this American change of heart were: to take advantage of cheaper costs in the British studios; to spend 'blocked' earnings; to qualify for the Quota of British films which exhibitors are legally obliged to attain; and to benefit from the Levy on box-office receipts imposed to aid film production in this country. Another factor was that several leading stars found it convenient to live part of each year in Europe so as to reduce the amount of American taxation they had to bear.

Anglo-American films of 1951 included Raoul Walsh's *Captain Horatio Hornblower*, made at Elstree for Warner Brothers. By selecting various episodes from C. S. Forester's trilogy a film was concocted that could be truly described as 'packed with action'. One inevitable consequence perhaps was that Gregory Peck's irascible and nervous Hornblower was turned, as Penelope Houston noted, into an impassive, infinitely resourceful superman. Ray Bolger's musical, *Where's Charley?*, had a most unusual history. Based on a successful Broadway musical comedy, yet to be produced on the stage in this country, it did rather poorly in British cinemas. But subsequently when the original musical comedy was produced in the Palace Theatre in London, with Norman Wisdom as Charley, it had a long run. Presumably the film had been made primarily for American and not British cinemas.

Nunnally Johnston's *The Mudlark*, which he produced for 20th

Century-Fox with Jean Negulesco as director, was honoured by selection for the Royal Film Performance. According to the film Queen Victoria, played by Irene Dunn, abandoned her isolation in Windsor Castle because of an encounter with a ragamuffin, and Disraeli, played by Alec Guinness, used the incident to further his social reform policy.

The American producer who has been most consistent in using British studios is unquestionably Walt Disney. At this time he made *Treasure Island* for RKO-Radio, with Robert Newton as Long John Silver. Although it attracted large audiences in this country the film could also be said to have been conceived with an eye on the international market.

BACK TO DOCUMENTARY

Most members of the documentary movement had returned by the end of the war to making actuality instead of narrative films. Perhaps too much was expected of them, now that their reputation was so enhanced, but disappointment was openly expressed with some of their achievements. Perhaps, therefore, it would be sufficient to mention here the four pictures that the National Film Theatre chose to represent the British documentary film after it had passed out of the wartime atmosphere. The first was *The Undefeated* (1950), directed by Paul Dickson. Describing how a legless ex-pilot overcame his disablement the film was summed up by William Whitebait as 'cool, energetic, sensitive and restrained'. Next came *David* (1951), made by the same team and sponsored by the Film Section of the Festival of Britain. In it an elderly Welsh miner relived his life. Gavin Lambert spoke of 'its touching dignity and simplicity, its quiet sympathy and warm perception'. It was criticized by others, however, as excessively drawn-out. Anthony Simmons's *Sunday by the Sea* (1953) won a Grand Prix at the Venice Festival as the best short film of its year. C. A. Lejeune spoke of its 'sense of vulgarity seen from a highbrow viewpoint'. And last was Edgar Anstey's *The Elephant Will Never Forget* (1953), a cheerfully sentimental film about London's farewell to its trams.

In some respects the most noteworthy aspect of this period was the almost overwhelming public support given to the British Film Institute's Telekinema at the South Bank Exhibition of the Festival of Britain. One of the most popular sections of the Exhibition, its audiences totalled no fewer than 500,000.

The need for changing audiences quickly and frequently precluded showing long feature films—in any event *The Magic Box* was not ready—and the programmes were composed of short films, mostly experimental. Stereoscopy and stereophony were demonstrated, as well as large screen television projection. The feature which attracted many people was the possibility, when entering the cinema, of seeing themselves on the screen as they had been some moments before when passing through the foyer.

Films produced particularly for the Telekinema included *A Tour of the Zoo*, made by the Pathe Documentary Unit, and Brian Smith's *Royal River*, 'designed to show the visual impact of stereoscopic cinema'. Norman MacLaren experimented abstractly with stereophonic music and four short cartoon films were produced by John Halas in a series called *Painter and Poet*—the most often recalled being a visual accompaniment drawn by Ronald Searle to the narrative poem on *John Gilpin's Ride*. The Telekinema building was retained for several years as the National Film Theatre. When the site had to be cleared for the Shell office block the new National Film Theatre was located nearby.

CHAPTER TWENTY-ONE

Losing the Cinema Habit

∙∙∙

FILMS NOW GO TO THE PEOPLE

The post-war era ended for the British cinematograph industry almost indeterminately during 1952 and 1953. The Labour Government fell and the Conservatives were returned to power. The sympathies of cinema people had veered long ago towards the left —in certain instances far to the left. The documentary movement had proclaimed its radicalism, and had certainly made some contribution to the defeat of the Churchillian Government in 1945. Film society cinéastes often disclosed an attachment to the left. And in the trade itself several independent cinema owners as well as studio technicians had declared their preference for red as a policital colour.

The new Government promptly closed down the Crown Film Unit. Perhaps there was some justification for Sir Stephen Tallent's observation that this was in no sense a calamity because the country now had several other good units; and for John Grierson's reaction that the best of Crown was now to be found more or less everywhere.

In 1952 the country had a new monarch. Her Coronation provided the Rank and ABPC organizations with the opportunity to make superb films of the ceremony and the processions. These created a most favourable impression throughout the world, especially perhaps in the United States and in the Commonwealth. Nevertheless, it was television and not the cinema which benefited most from the Coronation. The people of this country gathered in their millions around television sets to watch the proceedings. Not only did the enthralling experience make them enthusiastic about television, but the innovation became linked in the public mind with the opening of a new Elizabethan Age. That meant much to the younger generations; but older generations were pleased to recall that television had unquestionably been a British invention.

Queen Victoria at the end of her career had given the cinematograph industry its start; Queen Elizabeth did a similar service for television. But there was an important difference; Queen Elizabeth was at the *beginning* of her career, not at its end.

John Spraos in his *The Decline of the Cinema* has suggested that 1955 was really a more significant year than 1952, because it was then that 'the dramatic expansion of television started among the working class'. He shares the common view that much of the blame for the decline of the cinema must be attributed to television; but he is less inclined to support another opinion which more specifically would substitute ITV for television, the contention being that ITV appeals more to people in the lower income groups, from which a considerable percentage of picturegoers come (or came).

Perhaps too it was not television as such which was primarily responsible for the calamitous fall in cinema attendances but hire-purchase debts. Domestic economy may explain why many people go to the pictures less often than they used to; and why so much attention has been diverted in the film industry to young wage-earners who are said to have most 'spending money'.

Up to 1955 the exhibitors had been able to compensate (at least, to a considerable extent) for their loss of clientele by the raising of the admission prices. During the second half of the decade things went from bad to worse. The decline became precipitate, the only significant variation in whether it was plus or minus 10 per cent annually, being related to the hours of sunshine (and the inches of rainfall) in the holiday months. Bad weather in the summer was still one of the showman's best friends. Attendances had reached their peak in 1946, when the average weekly total was 31·4 million. The fall by 1949 to 27·5 million disturbed no one. Indeed, in comparison with the 19 million of 1939 it seemed more than satisfactory. There was little realization in January 1950 of the tribulations ahead. Few greater contrasts can be found anywhere than between the sentiments expressed in the trade press at the beginning of the 1950s and of the 1960s.

The collapse is shown in all its starkness in the table of average weekly admissions and gross box-office takings:

1955	22.7 million	(£2.03 million)
1956	21.2 million	(£2.00 million)
1957	17.6 million	(£1.79 million)
1958	14.5 million	(£1.60 million)
1959	11.5 million	(£1.33 million)
1960	10.0 million	(£1.26 million)
1961	8.9 million	(£1.17 million)
1962	7.9 million	(£1.13 million)

The number of cinemas in the country was also dropping, although relatively more slowly—a cinema does not necessarily have to close down because it has lost half of its audience. In 1950 Great Britain had 4,600 cinemas with a seating capacity of $4\frac{1}{4}$ million. By 1959 the figures had fallen to 3,600 cinemas and $3\frac{1}{2}$ million seats.

By then many halls were feeling the pinch sorely, especially the small individually-owned halls, and this in spite of the extensive development of sales services for dairy ice-cream, squash drinks, frozen confections and salted peanuts. It was one of Wardour Street's mordant jokes that the industry was being sustained—and, indeed, kept alive—by ice-cream. Statisticians thought that soon only 3,000 cinemas would be open in the country, with 3 million seats.

In lesser towns, particularly in farming districts, the only local cinema closed down. If the municipal or county council needed a public hall they might acquire it—the reverse of what had happened fifty years before. Otherwise it stood empty, moribund, with a tattered notice, 'for sale', mocking middle-aged passers-by who nostalgically recalled many happy hours and jolly moments spent there when young. Times had indeed changed. In larger towns cinemas were gutted and turned into dance halls to cater for the requirements of the new generations, and early in 1960 British cinemas were leased for the first time for conversion into bowling alleys. Then came adaptation for 'Bingo', save the mark! By the end of 1962 the number of cinemas still being used for their original purpose had dropped to 2,400.

Although various other factors besides those already outlined had contributed to the disaster, such as better housing (fewer people were seeking refuge in the cinemas) and the location of new suburbs some distance from the central picture houses, nevertheless television was blamed for having ousted the cinematograph as the 'medium for mass entertainment'. Going to the pictures was ceasing to be a social habit.

By 1959 the combined television and radio licences issued in this country had passed 10 million. (In 1947, the first year in which licences were issued, the total was 18,000.) Now, indeed, instead of people going to the pictures, the pictures were going to people. And, according to some statisticians, every new television licence taken out in this country represented a loss of perhaps 100 cinema attendances for *each year* in the foreseeable future.

THE BIG SCREEN AND THE DWARF SCREEN

This meant that it was the exhibitors who were most affected—producers, scriptwriters, actors and technicians were flocking to television. New ideas were tried out in cinemas almost in desperation. The industry was justified in regarding the introduction of stereoscopy just as a novelty, unlikely to be of permanent value unless a method could be devised for discarding the polarized glasses. More interest was taken in the enlargement of the screen being developed by 20th Century-Fox with their CinemaScope. Gavin Lambert amusingly quipped that people had complained in the past about many aspects of the cinema, but not about the screen being too small. But these 'new ratios' really did expose the inadequacies of television's dwarf screen, and henceforth the trade emphasized the definite advantages it possessed in, as Dilys Powell said, 'the beautiful, big public screen'. And there was colour into the bargain.

In 1960, when C. A. Lejeune discussed the lost audiences, she said that film chiefs 'often wonder, more in sorrow than in anger, why in Britain, it has been so hard to crack the nut of educated people. I can tell them in a word. Vulgarity. England is not, and never has been, dependent on films for entertainment. We are a small country. Books and ballet, music, art exhibitions and some form of the theatre are within most people's reach. These give us the standards of comparison. We know by instinct what is badly done. By instinct we recognize and avoid vulgarity. The cinema hasn't learned this yet.' Cinema businessmen might comment, however, that she was really writing about the middle-aged and most of them were now irretrievably lost.

MIXED FORTUNES IN THE OVERCAST FIFTIES

This is the background against which that 'galaxy' of outstanding young directors, and their achievements during the 1950s, have to be judged. Outstanding in at least one respect was David Lean, winner of the British Film Academy Award for the Best British Film on no fewer than three occasions: 1952, *The Sound Barrier*; 1954, *Hobson's Choice*; and 1957, *The Bridge on the River Kwai*.

The Sound Barrier was an exciting film with superb aerial photography, about flying faster than sound. It emphasized the accompanying mental as well as mechanical strains and tensions. *Hobson's Choice* was based upon Harold Brighouse's Lancastrian play. Charles Laughton, John Mills and Brenda de Banzie gave what Dilys Powell described as solid and sympathetic performances. The following year David Lean directed *Summer Madness*, in which Katharine Hepburn was a lonely, puritanical spinster from the Middle West caught in an escapade during a holiday in corrupt, sophisticated Venice. Then in 1957 he made his epic film, *The Bridge*

O

on the River Kwai, about prisoners-of-war who under the insistent but misguided lead of their colonel built a bridge for the notorious death railway.

Carol Reed is one of the industry's three directors to be knighted (the others being Alexander Korda and Michael Balcon). He was an international director during this decade, but the films which he made in this country, while well regarded, did not arouse a great deal of enthusiasm. His *Outcast of the Islands* was based on a Conrad novel. As Gavin Lambert pointed out this was not really an adventure story set in a Far Eastern Port. Its many incidents illuminated atmosphere and character. But, if the film were neither good Joseph Conrad nor good Carol Reed (Basil Wright thought the film divided against itself), it was a fascinating piece of work, photographed against an exotic background.

A Kid for Two Farthings, based on a fable of Whitechapel life written by Wolf Mankowitz, had a cool reception which puzzled Dilys Powell who said that she found it beautiful and moving. *The Key* (of the flat) in which Sophia Loren comforted two men, Trevor Howard and William Holden, masters of Liverpool tugs that rescued torpedoed ships in the Western Approaches, also failed to be entirely satisfactory. Carol Reed's work at this period was being criticized as out of touch with human experience. The craftsmanship was there in abundance but the warmth of feeling was not. It was not until 1960, when *Our Man in Havana* was shown, that he displayed the brilliance which had led to his being described as the greatest of all British film directors.

Frank Launder and Sidney Gilliat tossed off several light-hearted comedies and were particularly successful with two anarchist films about Ronald Searle's ferocious delinquents, the Girls of St Trinians. They made some more serious films, such as the underrated *The Story of Gilbert and Sullivan,* but they became associated in the public mind with fun.

Powell and Pressburger did not have any notable successes with their spectacular films, such as *Oh Rosalinda!,* but the rewards were greater from two war films, *The Battle of the River Plate,* which followed the sequence of events leading to the scuttling of the German pocket battleship, the *Admiral Graf Spee,* and *Ill Met by Moonlight,* concerning a most exciting exploit to kidnap a Panzer General in Crete during the German occupation.

After adapting a play about Anglo-American co-operation in naval research, *Seagulls Over Sorrento* (1955)—Gene Kelly played a straight part as an American lieutenant—and a light comedy, *Josephine and Men* (1956), the Boulting Brothers struck a rich seam with the 'unfortunate but coyly artful' Ian Carmichael, beginning with an irreverent farce about Army procedures, *Private's Progress*. This was followed by *Brothers in Law* in which Carmichael was an inept young barrister; *Lucky Jim* in which he was turned into an academic misfit; and *I'm All Right, Jack*, a most successful comedy about factory life, in which he was a blundering intruder (and Peter Sellers rose to the heights as a shop steward). The Boultings also had Terry Thomas along with Peter Sellers in a rather prolonged joke about British colonial administration, *Carlton-Browne of the F.O.*

THE BRITISH COMEDIANS

It was in the field of comedy that the British film-making industry was most distinguished during the 1950s, although Alec Guinness, an actor of outstanding ability, chose to depart from the character in which he was being typed, that of an amiable but confused young intellectual. After his appearance in *The Bridge on the River Kwai*, the public accepted him in serious rôles.

During the decade Kenneth More established himself as the country's most popular star. He appeared in many pictures, some, such as Terence Rattigan's *The Deep Blue Sea*, *Reach for the Sky* (as Douglas Bader), *A Night to Remember* (about the *Titanic* disaster), and *Sink the Bismarck* (in which he was a high Admiralty official), being essentially dramatic. Yet it could be said that he never departed from one particular character, that of a bluff, hearty cynical, dominating 'RAF type'. Some of his films, such as *Doctor in the House* and *Genevieve*, were extravanganzas; in others his humour was rarely completely absent, even when he was being imperturbable, heroic or even brutal.

By the last years of the decade it was Peter Sellers who was coming to the fore, but in 1959 John Davis, speaking with the knowledge of the Rank Organization's box-office receipts, described Norman Wisdom, then completing his seventh film for that company, as the finest comedian thrown up since the war. He was continuing in the music hall tradition which had aroused much discussion in the early 1930s. Charlie Chaplin himself came from this source, but no one has suggested that Norman Wisdom is likely to fill that illustrious comic actor's shoes—and, incidentally, it was in London that Chaplin made his *The King in New York*, and so added it to the list of British comedy films made in the 1950s.

Times were, indeed, changing. A broad farce, directed by Gerald Thomas, called *Carry on Nurse*, achieved great success in the United States where it played in its first two years to 7,000 bookings and earned $2\frac{1}{2}$ million dollars. Those who recalled the American attitude to British knock-about farces in previous decades were astounded. A series of 'Carry On' films followed.

Several of the most successful British comedies of this period did not rely on any particular star to achieve popularity. For instance, one of the most enjoyable British films ever made was Henry Cornelius's *Genevieve,* described by Dilys Powell as the gayest, funniest and prettiest film for years. A brilliant script had been written around the annual veteran car race to Brighton. The driver of a 1904 Darracq was Kenneth More, and the film first raised him to the heights as one of the country's principal stars. John Gregson was his rival, and American audiences especially liked the way the pair pushed their womenfolk, Dinah Sheridan and Kay Kendall, around.

The 'Doctor' films began in 1954 with Betty Box's *Doctor in the House,* with the movie fans' favourite star, Dirk Bogarde, as well as Kenneth More, in the cast. Dilys Powell commented on the expert hilarity, the youthful high spirits and the 'smugly macabre professional jokes'. A series of 'Doctor' films followed, each tending to be more farcical than the last.

When other comedies of the decade are mentioned, such as Alexander Mackendrick's *The Maggie* (the name of a Scottish puffer boat); Charles Crichton's account of the closing down of a local railway line, *The Titfield Thunderbolt*; Herbert Mason's description of how John and Julie went to London to see the Coronation; and Launder and Gilliat's incursion into the early days of cinematography, *The Smallest Show on Earth*, it becomes increasingly clear that in the 1950s the British took the comedy line.

BOX-OFFICE SUCCESSES OF THE DECADE

Films with war themes had been made in every year since 1945 but it was not until Michael Anderson directed *The Dam Busters* (about the air attack on the Ruhr dams) that they became very popular. Several were made most appropriately by Michael Balcon with his able team of directors, including Charles Crichton, Basil Dearden, Charles Frend, Alexander MacKendrick and Leslie Norman, who had played a prominent part in making feature films during the brilliant years 1941-43.

Almost every aspect of the war was touched on, from the epic qualities of the struggle at *Dunkirk* to the achievements of the French Resistance (*Carve Her Name With Pride*) and to the sufferings of British civilian prisoners in Malaya (*A Town Like Alice*).

Some were grim, such as *The Cruel Sea,* adapted from Nicholas Monsarrat's aptly-named story of the life and destruction of a corvette. Some described little known episodes, such as Ronald Neame's *The Man Who Never Was*, with Clifton Webb in charge of a scheme for floating a corpse carrying concocted secret papers on to the Spanish coast, and J. Lee Thompson's *Ice Cold in Alex*, about an ambulance unit cut off in Libya.

There were several exciting pictures about escapes from prisoner-of-war camps, all 'packed with action', and there were others which saw the war as a rowdy romp, in which girls contrived to get involved. But eventually all of these war films were surpassed by David Lean's *The Bridge on the River Kwai*.

Fewer 'women's pictures' were made, but one of them, J. Lee Thompson's *Woman in a Dressing Gown*, won international honours in 1957. It dealt with a small scale human situation, with the pitiful courage shown by a frowsy wife, forcing domestic crises, and incapable of holding the affection of her husband and grown-up son. Yvonne Mitchell made a sensitive study of this confused woman who had stayed in her kitchen while her husband made his way in the world.

The romance of the decade was probably Anthony Asquith's *The Young Lovers*, with the thwarted sweethearts separated by the Iron Curtain. Gavin Lambert praised Charles Crichton's *The Divided Heart* as 'a likeable and sometimes impressive film that could be saluted as a British drama welcomely unafraid of an emotional response to an emotional situation'. Its theme was a struggle between two women for a Jugoslavian child reared in Germany as a war orphan. The women were played by Yvonne Mitchell and Cornel Borchers. Probably the outstanding 'weepie' (to use a trade term) of the decade was, however, Alexander Mackendrick's *Mandy*, a study of the rearing of a deaf and dumb child. C. A. Lejeune thought it 'half a wonderful picture, a slight thing but our own, and very sweet and true as long as it sticks to its subject'.

Although many second-feature films were devoted to crime detection (as also were the plays being presented for television), comparatively few major British films followed suit. The most notable exception was Basil Dearden's *Sapphire*, winner of the British Film Academy Award for 1959. Its well-sustained mystery was set against an unusual background as it touched on the ostracism of black people in this country.

Another film which was placed high among the critics' selection for the year (1959) was J. Lee Thompson's *Tiger Bay* in which a Polish seaman kidnapped a small girl (played by Hayley Mills) who had seen him commit a murder. The atmosphere of the Cardiff dockside was vividly represented and the piece was quite brilliantly constructed.

The close association between British studios and the London theatre continued and was responsible in the mid-1950s for Laurence Olivier's production of *Richard III*, the finest cinema adaptation of a Shakespearian play that has yet been seen. C. A. Lejeune described it as a 'mature' film and commented on Olivier's own presentation of that 'jaunty, scheming rogue, Richard III'. Others found it satisfyingly forthright and dynamic. William Whitebait observed that it has thrust aside for him any stage performances of the play he has ever seen, including Olivier's own. Gavin Lambert's comment was that 'Laurence Olivier's richly drawn portrait is surely one of the classic Shakespearian interpretations', and Derek Prouse added that the cast had acted with 'a general urgency and a welcome lack of ranting'.

Several other stage plays which have become in their various ways 'classics' were filmed during this period and with relatively little success collectively at the box-office. Pinero's *The Second Mrs Tanqueray* and Wilde's *The Importance of Being Earnest* were presented elegantly and literally. Their appeal was limited. Anthony Asquith's version of *The Doctor's Dilemma* was a polished piece of work although Bernard Shaw's satire on medical specialists is utterly out of date. Another Bernard Shaw play, *The Devil's Disciple*, was an Anglo-American production, and Laurence Olivier did not get top billing in the cast, although outshining a ponderous Burt Lancaster and an hysterical Kirk Douglas. Herbert Wilcox produced a confused version of *The Beggar's Opera* which Peter Brook directed without distinction, and George Hoellering tried most worthily to make a film of T. S. Eliot's verse play on the martyrdom of Thomas-à-Becket. His *Murder in the Cathedral* can only be regarded as a labour of love.

The British cinematograph industry became more international in this period than for twenty years. Foreign stars such as Odile Versois were included in the casts of British films to appeal to foreign cinemagoers and Simone Signoret, the dramatic French actress, won awards, including an 'Oscar', for her performance in a British film (Jack Clayton's *Room at the Top*). British versions of French films were produced, including René Clement's *Knave of Hearts*, a sophisticated comedy that was too cruel for many British cinemagoers, Gérard Philipe being the youthful Don Juan.

The Australian market came in for attention and two films made in the Bush about children were popular successes. They were Anthony Kimmins's *Smiley* and Leslie Norman's *The Shiralee*. The latter in which Peter Finch, as a swagman who had to take his deserted small daughter, Dana Wilson, along with him in his wanderings, was entertaining and warm-hearted too.

ALL BRITISH, PART BRITISH AND
JUST A LITTLE BIT BRITISH

The middle- and late-fifties will be particularly associated with the American penetration into British studios. In 1956 Dilys Powell observed that one-third of the British films made that year were wholly or partly financed by Americans. Some, she thought, were as British as Salt Lake City. A few American directors, including John Huston and John Ford, spent much time in London but most came just for their one film. It cannot be said that harmony always prevailed while they were in the studios, but British film-makers learned much from them and the industry benefited materially from their presence in this country.

John Huston's adaptation of C. S. Forester's *The African Queen* would probably find a place in any international list of the best films of the 1950s. Katharine Hepburn was brilliant as a prissy but spirited spinster in charge of a mission in German East Africa, when the First World War was breaking out. Accompanied by Humphrey Bogart as the sozzling Canadian captain of a diminutive river steamer she destroyed the patrolling gunboat at the river's mouth. Here, the critics said, was high adventure with a touch of fantasy. Another of John Huston's films *Moby Dick* (with Gregory Peck and Richard Basehart) would have a place as one of the most spectacular and brilliantly contrived films ever made in this country. Adapted from Herman Melville's novel it was, however, perhaps more concerned with 'man versus whale' than with the psychological issues behind their struggle. But it was a 'tremendous' film.

Otto Preminger's *Bonjour Tristesse*, with Deborah Kerr, David Niven and Jean Seberg, was adapted from Françoise Sagan's novel about an indulgent Paris widower, his adolescent daughter and his various mistresses, and so added further complexity to a supposedly British film; but Stanley Dixon's *Indiscreet* (with Cary Grant and Ingrid Bergman) was quite acceptable. It was about a philandering American in London who pretended to his girl friends that he was a married man. As Cary Grant who played the part is an Englishman this seems to have squared things.

The last of these hybrid Anglo-American films of the 1950s did, however, include two most noteworthy films. One was Mark Robson's *The Inn of the Sixth Happiness* (with Ingrid Bergman, Curt Jurgens and Robert Donat). A grim but romanticized study of the humiliations and hardships endured by an English girl held in a remote part of China by the Japanese invasion, it was derived from Alan Burgess's novel, *The Small Woman*. The second was the previously-mentioned *The Bridge on the River Kwai*.

There were many other Anglo-American films of this period, such as the ingenious Ruritanian comedy which Laurence Olivier directed for Marilyn Monroe, *The Prince and the Showgirl*; Otto Preminger's version of Bernard Shaw's *Saint Joan*, with the novice Jean Seberg out of her depth in the title rôle; and John Huston's *Beat the Devil* with Humphrey Bogart, Jennifer Jones and Gina Lollobrigida getting in each other's way on a Mediterranean tramp ship.

These Anglo-American films varied considerably in their Anglo and American content, as well as in their continental content. The best were successful and most cinemagoers did not even realize that they were looking at an international picture, so inter-mixed had British and American accents become. Some did come in for pastings from the critics, however, notably the period films which were apt to be dismissed as 'old fashioned Hollywood history, almost comic strip in approach'. Some films, such as Gene Kelly's three ballet studies, *Invitation to the Dance*, could be regarded as American films that just happened to be produced in this country; but most carried more evidence of their British origin. A few even had British directors, but American producers tended to dislike this arrangement. British directors failed, in their opinion, to curb their compatriots' proneness to move too slowly and to talk too quickly.

THE DOCUMENTARY MOVEMENT'S LOST SENSE OF PURPOSE

The Crown Film Unit had been disbanded, but some organizations, such as British Transport Films, maintained under Edgar Anstey a steady output of extremely well-made films. They depicted many aspects of British life—a snowdrift at Bleath Hill, the charm of the land of Robert Burns, aspects of Elizabethan buildings, and the coming of the seasons, including Ralph Keene's superb *Journey Into Spring*. The Shell Film Unit produced a picturesque *Song of the Clouds*, and the Petroleum Film Board made a fascinating study of the valley of the Tigris and the Euphrates, *Rivers of Time*.

Many individual films were shown: Richard Massingham's last productions, *The Blakes Slept Here* and *Brief City* (the South Bank Exhibition); Thomas Stobart's *The Conquest of Everest*; Jack Ramsden's *The Flight of the White Heron* (the Royal Tour of Australasia); Stuart Legg and Bert Haanstra's *The Rival World*; Anthony Asquith's *On Such a Night* (Glyndebourne); Hans Nieter's *A Song to Prince Charlie*; Basil Wright's *The Immortal Land*; James Carr's *Antarctic Crossing*; and Richard Cawston's *This is the B.B.C.*

At the end of the decade the pioneers had sharp things to say about the state of the documentary movement in this country. Sir Arthur Elton remarked that some of our recent films seemed dead-beat in comparison with films coming out of Asia, Africa, the Middle East and Latin America. Basil Wright thought that 'British documentary has followed the pattern of all creative movements in the world of art—experiment (achieving something aesthetically new and exciting); development and consolidation of style; hardening of the arteries; and finally decline (or rather the transmutation of the original impulse through influence on a new generation of film-makers or on existing styles). He recalled the creative excitement, the sense of unlimited horizons, thirty years before, and added that in 1946, after the Second World War, many documentary directors did not know where they were. After years of revelling in opposition they now had their own Labour Government. The cohesion of the earlier days had vanished. There was no longer unity of purpose, no longer a closely-knit group.

Perhaps some other less highly polished films of the period came a little closer at least in spirit to those of the 1930s—for instance, Lindsay Anderson's *Thursday's Children* (deaf children) and *Every Day Except Christmas* (Covent Garden), and Karel Reisz's *We are the Lambeth Boys* (youth club at Kennington). Some promising young directors, such as John Hawksworth, Robert Hamer, Lorenza Mazzetti and Tony Richardson, were also associated with the British Film Institute in directing a series of virile experimental films, described as Free Cinema and making clever use of the 'candid camera'. From these a revolutionary new movement in the production of feature films was about to emerge.

One very important film of the period has still to be mentioned. This is *Animal Farm* by John Halas and Joy Batchelor, the first full-length British cartoon film. It was unusual in having a serious theme, based on George Orwell's political fable. Catherine de la Roche summed it up as an angry satire on dictatorship, cast in the form of a simple and moving tale about animals, given symbolic rôles. The preparation of short cartoon films for television gave this branch of the industry a considerable lift and in 1960 it was reported that no fewer than fifteen companies were members of the animation group of the British Association of Specialized Film Producers.

Perhaps it will be said that not many of the short films of the mid- and late-fifties were of outstanding merit. But they did, as Paul Rotha pointed out, win more awards at International Film Festivals than British feature films of the period. And some passing consolation for the vanished documentation of social problems—now being made for television instead of the cinema—might be found in the increasing number of films made in Great Britain during the 1950s for schools, for industrial training, for scientific exposition, for various aspects of publicity, and for many other purposes.

CHAPTER TWENTY-TWO

The Uncertain Future

....

CHALLENGING AND EXCITING PROSPECTS

This book should end with the comforting assurance to which recourse has been made in so many films, when the maltreated and bemused hero smiles bravely, if wanly, from his hospital bed. 'He's going to be *all right*.' But whether in this instance he is going to be is another matter. A past president of the CEA put it this way at the beginning of the new decade. 'Something is sure to survive; but the cinematograph industry that I have known since my boyhood isn't.' Not that everyone has been feeling so desolated. Penelope Houston, for instance, was able to speak of 'the immense vitality of 1959' and of 'its amazingly confident contrast to the decade's earlier years'.

The point of view of the exhibitor was no doubt very different from that of the film-maker. He was taking the beating—attendances had fallen (another 10 per cent that year). There was cold comfort for him in *The Times* when it wondered 'whether the function of the cinema in our society during the last half century has partly been to provide an escape from drabness, and whether the rising standard of living, by making escape less imperative, is considerably weakening the cinema's attractions'.

Dilys Powell commented on a statement that one out of every ten cinemas in this country was being run at a loss. Her view was that the small family cinema was doomed to extinction. It was the local picture house, she thought, rather than the majestic house in the town centre that was being discarded. Others declared that they could see no evidence of the decline in attendances being arrested and one prominent member of the trade feared that eventually only 1,000 cinemas (instead of more than twice that number) would be left in this country. But John Davis of the Rank Organization wrote two articles—for the *Financial Times* and for the *Times Review of Industry*—in which he described the prospects as challenging and exciting. The instances he gave were in developing large scale television in colour to bring actuality to cinema audiences, and in opening up toll-television. He mentioned too the measures that his company had taken to secure an economically sound and probably unassailable future. These included launching divers schemes extending not only 'in the wide field of entertainment and relaxation, and also in the spheres of engineering, electronics, property development and consumer goods'.

The two large British groups, the Rank Organization, now converted into a compact and efficient unit, and ABPC, as ably administered as in the past, continued to be in good heart. Both had closed down many cinemas, but the buildings were often disposed of satisfactorily, and others occupying central sites in cities and towns were sold profitably because of their high site values. Undoubtedly the companies' interests in commercial television contributed to their rosy health but John Davis was able to point out that 63 per cent of the revenue earned by the Rank films came from overseas, now reaching millions of pounds annually.

It could not be claimed that the owners of individual and small groups of cinemas were as satisfactorily placed. Many had to go out of business and their empty halls, if off main streets, were a liability. Unemployment was the lot of elderly men and women who as cinema managers or as members of renters' staffs had served the industry well in its palmy days.

In January 1961 John Davis brought a story to its conclusion that had its beginnings in July 1929 (the time of the 'talkie' boom), when the two American companies, Twentieth Century and Fox, had acquired their substantial voting interest in Gaumont-British. Through a trust they had bought 2,915,000 of the 5,000,000 ordinary 10s shares and 4,449,856 of the 5s shares. The price was 19 million dollars. This was the deal that had cast a shadow over the British industry for thirty years, and had a significant place in the lives of the Ostrers, John Maxwell, C. M. Woolf, Oscar Deutsch and other leaders of the industry. Now the Rank Organization acquired these shares for £4 million.

They also acquired the Ostrers' interest in Bush Radio and in Rank Cintel, and the participating preferred ordinary shares in the General Theatre Corporation which they had not previously owned. John Davis spoke of these as steps towards his ultimate aim of merging all of the group's various interests into the Rank Organization, and described the successful Rank rights issue, on favourable terms, as putting the City's seal of approval on the Organization's policies.

Also in 1961 the Associated British Picture Corporation acquired for £2½ million the shares owned by Warner Brothers, and so the British cinematograph industry is now established in a highly independent position. A joint distribution company has been formed by Associated British-Pathe and Warner Brothers. It is called Warner-Pathe Distributors and handles the product of Warners' Burbank Studios, of ABPC's Elstree Studios and of Allied Artists. It also distributes Pathe News and Pathe Pictorial. In a joint statement Sir Philip Warter and Jack L. Warner said 'the changing phase through which the film industry is now passing necessitates effective consolidation of the UK distribution of the two companies in one compact organization. This will be in the best interests not only of the two companies, but also of the industry in general. The amalgamation will lead to increased British production, as there will be a great inducement to Warners to take part more fully with ABPC in joint production of British films at Elstree.'

FEW REMAINING 'FAITHFULS'

The state of business was surveyed in several analyses prepared in or about 1960, most being based upon audience studies. While some might be criticized statistically, no strong disagreement was expressed in the trade press with their findings.

The first point to be made is that admission totals are in one important respect misleading. Twenty years ago, when it was said that half of the people in Great Britain was going to the pictures every week, a qualification was needed. A great many people were going twice each week, and a fair proportion of addicts four or five times. So they were counted in several times. The total number of regular cinemagoers in the country was really much less than was sometimes suggested.

Between 1948 and 1960 the number of cinemas dropped by 34 per cent and the number of admissions by 66 per cent. Three-quarters of the people now going to the cinema are between sixteen and thirty-four years old—so the losses have come particularly from the middle-aged. No fewer than 54 per cent of the married women in Great Britain have stopped altogether from going to the pictures, and only 10 per cent are going once (or more) a week. This means that *proportionately* there are more men in audiences than formerly. According to one estimate half an 'average audience' today is male. In spite of the closure of many 'industrial halls' approximately 43 per cent of cinema audiences come from the 'working class'.

The cinema has retained, however, some of its ardent supporters and, according to one report, three-quarters of all the people who can be described as cinemagoers in this country still go to the pictures at least once a fortnight.

THE GOVERNMENT AND THE CINEMATOGRAPH TRADE

The Government has continued to take a lively interest in the industry and two new Cinematograph Films Acts were approved in 1957 and in 1960. A Consolidating Bill to cover all the Films Acts since the Edwardian era was said to be in preparation.

The two new Acts made no sweeping changes. The 1959 Act replaced the voluntary British Film Production Fund by a statutory agency to continue until 1967, and required the rate of the levy to be assessed each year according to current needs. It was to yield between £2 million and £5 million. The 1960 Act covered various aspects of co-production with foreign countries.

The National Film Finance Corporation also had its existence extended to 1967. Its capital is now £6 million, with an additional £2 million borrowed on Treasury guarantee. Changes were made in quota requirements but a proposal was dropped for limiting the number of foreigners who can be engaged in making a 'British' film if it is to be registered for quota purposes. In recent years most exhibitors have exceeded the first feature quota, which is fixed each year and is of the order of 30 per cent.

Another revealing happening at this period was the Government's decision to end the Anglo-American Film Agreement of March 1948. No longer was part of the earnings of American films shown in this country to be 'frozen'. Several factors influenced the Government in making this change, but one was the extent to which British films were now being shown throughout the Western Hemisphere.

To the trade's great disappointment the Government took a long time over dropping the Entertainments Tax. But the rates were steadily reduced. The tax on a half-a-crown seat was: 1956, 11½d; 1957, 9½d; 1958, 4d. It was not given up altogether until the 1960 Budget, when the relief was expected to add £6 million to the annual earnings of British cinemas.

Although exhibitors continued to grumble at having to pay the Eady Levy most readily agreed with the *Kinematograph Weekly*'s assessment. 'Both in its voluntary and statutory form the British production levy has been of immeasurable benefit in helping to maintain the supply of British films at a constant level. . . . The majority of exhibitors recognize that the continuance of the aid to production is for their own benefit as well as for the producers.' However, after the abolition of the Entertainments Tax some of the exhibitors, and particularly the owners of the small independent halls, began a campaign to get the levy abolished too.

More encouraging aspects come to the fore as soon as the discussion is switched from exhibiting films to making films. The first of these is the remarkable recovery made by British Lion. This was the company, closely associated with Alexander Korda, which turned to the National Film Finance Corporation for major financial assistance and procured a loan of £3 million. Subsequently it announced that business had been so poor that the entire share capital was lost. A receiver was appointed and a new company formed to continue the distributing side of the business and to retain control of the Shepperton Studios. So the Government found itself even more involved in some aspects of the cinematograph industry, and that was presumably far from what Conservatives would have wanted.

Ian Dalrymple, in his tribute to Alexander Korda after his death, described him as broken-hearted by the catastrophe and said that, after the first associations between British Lion and the Finance Corporation, Korda's position had been 'only that of Adviser on Production and that henceforth he had surrendered his artistic career to the service and fostering of others'.

Some of the leading men in the industry, including the Boulting Brothers, Frank Launder and Sidney Gilliat, were invited to join the Board. Sidney Gilliat became chairman and David Kingsley managing director. In 1959 they made a profit of £100,000 as against a loss the previous year of £150,000 (they had two outstanding successes in *Room at the Top* and *I'm All Right Jack*). Since then they have had substantial profits (*Saturday Night and Sunday Morning* being one of their later films). The company's recent achievements were attributed by David Kingsley in an interview with the press to: (a) 30 per cent of the company's earnings being in America; (b) the export markets' desire for British pictures reflecting British life; and (c) the fall in Hollywood's output having created more openings for British films.

The National Film Finance Corporation is doing well too. *Films and Filming* remarked that it had changed its face from a Universal Aunt to a Benevolent Uncle. 'It now uses the £4 million of Government money which it did not lose from the total Treasury advances of £8 million to tackle film investment in a very business-like manner.' It helps to finance half of the feature films made in this country, and has expressed a need for additional borrowing powers.

In a recent White Paper showing that the Corporation had made a profit in 1960 of £50,000, the main contributors to this result were given as: *Carry On Nurse, The Colditz Story, Dentist in the Chair, Expresso Bongo, Happy is the Bride, I'm All Right Jack, League of Gentlemen, Sapphire, Saturday Night and Sunday Morning* and *Tiger Bay.*

The Corporation's profit does not mean that British films are generally profitable, even with the aid of the statutory levy. A few very successful films attract an exceptional amount of levy, but others show substantial losses.

Sir Michael Balcon formed a new alliance, Bryanston Films, which brought together a score of active film-makers. Several other groups were also at work in three-stage studios at Beaconsfield, Bray (Maidenhead), Merton Park and Twickenham. Many of their films were cheaply made 'second features', but from time to time more notable films came from these sources.

At the end of the decade four large studios were still being used in making motion pictures. They were the studios at Shepperton (area of thirteen stages 116,000 square feet); at Pinewood (eight stages, 78,000 square feet); at Boreham Wood, Elstree, owned by ABPC (six stages, 75,000 square feet); and also at Boreham Wood, owned by MGM British (nine stages, 74,000 square feet). The total number of employees at each was in the region of 1,000.

ORGANIZED INTERESTS

Almost ninety different trade organizations are still performing their allotted tasks in the British cinematograph industry. Many have not changed materially in constitution during recent decades—such as the Cinematograph Exhibitors' Association and the Kinematograph Renters' Society, to which references have already been made in this book, as well as the industry's scientific and technical body, the British Kinematograph Society, founded in 1931.

The greatest changes have taken place, perhaps significantly, among the producers, who now have no fewer than three different associations—the British Film Producers' Association (founded in 1941), the Federation of British Film Makers (founded in 1957), and the Association of Specialized Film Producers (founded in 1947).

The BFPA is usually associated in the public mind with the larger groups, notably the Rank Organization and the Associated British Picture Corporation. The five organizations which founded the FBFM were headed by John and Roy Boulting, Sir Michael Balcon and R. P. Baker, Ivan Foxwell, Frank Launder and Sidney Gilliat, Irving Allen and Albert R. Broccoli. The ASFP has several sections covering such specialized branches as cartoon films, advertising films and educational films.

Over 4,000 members of seven trade unions are engaged in film production, almost three-quarters being members of NATKE (The National Association of Theatrical and Kine Technicians). The majority of the others are members of ACTT (The Association of Cinematograph, Television and Allied Technicians), or of the Electrical Trades Union.

The BFPA has had to concern itself with the film festivals proliferating throughout the continent, and indeed the world. The British cinematograph industry, like the American, has been hesitant in its attitude to many of these festivals, although it is conscious of the extent to which they can be used to promote the commercial disribution of favoured films. However, the standards by which some juries assess films are so much at variance with British (and American) notions—besides occasionally being biased politically—that the reluctance of British companies to participate has been understandable.

They cannot fail to be impressed by the frequency with which festival-winning continental films, when shown publicly in this country, do poorly at cinema box-offices, even at halls which specialize in exhibiting unusual films. Some festival-winning continental films are unable to procure any showings at all in this country, no distributing company thinking sufficiently highly of their chances with British audiences.

A Film Festival was founded in this country in 1947 which now forms part of the Edinburgh Festival. Its sponsors, the Edinburgh Film Guild, were particularly interested in actuality films and, although the Festival's scope has since been broadened, it continues to have a different conception from the continental cinemas —it does not, for instance, make awards, and so avoids the wranglings which are inevitable accompaniments of some other festivals.

In 1957 the British Film Institute inaugurated its Festival of Festivals, to show outstanding prizewinning and other films at the close of the season in the autumn. This Festival is held in the National Film Theatre, near the site of the Institute's Telekinema at the South Bank Exhibition.

The British Film Institute and the British Film Academy have been the principal organizations connected with the cinematograph industry, apart from the trade associations already mentioned and the trade unions. The British Film Institute has to some extent continued along the lines mentioned in Chapter Eleven, although it now concerns itself more with film appreciation and less with films as visual aids in teaching. It has had James Quinn as its director in recent years. The popularity of the National Film Theatre has been partly responsible for the growth of the Institute's membership which (with associates) now reaches the remarkable figure of 40,000.

P

The British Film Academy was founded in 1947 'by many leading British film-makers to advance film art and technique by discussion and research and to encourage creative film-making everywhere'. In 1958 it amalgamated with the Guild of Television Producers to form the Society of Film and Television Arts, with H.R.H. The Duke of Edinburgh as president.

The Academy is best known to the public through its annual awards to producers of outstanding films, and this is perhaps a convenient place for assembling the titles of the British feature films selected as the best of the year: 1947, *Odd Man Out*; 1948, *The Fallen Idol*; 1949, *The Third Man*; 1950, *The Blue Lamp*; 1951, *The Lavender Hill Mob*; 1952, *The Sound Barrier*; 1953, *Genevieve*; 1954, *Hobson's Choice*; 1955, *Richard III*; 1956, *Reach for the Sky*; 1957, *The Bridge on the River Kwai*; 1958, *Room at the Top*; 1959, *Sapphire*; 1960, *Saturday Night and Sunday Morning*; 1961, *A Taste of Honey*.

The various activities of the film societies brought them into close association with members of the film industry—with the exhibitors from whom they hired cinemas, usually on Sundays, with the renters who supplied them sometimes reluctantly with their films, and with the film-makers who were principally interested in their shows. The film society movement became a strong force in this country in the late 1940s, when the New London Film Society endeavoured to carry on in the tradition of the original London Film Society. At this period the total membership of film societies in Great Britain was put at over 50,000. Subsequently the societies were handicapped when films they had wanted for their meetings were diverted to local cinemas specializing in showing continental feature films. Rising costs have greatly reduced the ranks of the older film societies, but a most remarkable increase has taken place in the number of smaller societies operating on 16 mm. in halls and in works' canteens. The estimated strength of British film societies now is 65,000.

The principal use made of films for purposes other than entertainment is educational. Many schools now have their own projectors —and teachers to operate them. But, although a fair number of films are now being produced or adapted in this country primarily for showing in schools or colleges, some European countries, notably Germany and France, continue to lead the United Kingdom in applying these 'visual aids to education'. Similarly we are not in the forefront of industrial countries in using films for instruction and work study purposes in factories or, indeed, for sales promotion. It is impossible to point to any field in which the British, in spite of their early specialization in interest, documentary, actuality and other films of this genre, have been the pioneers—not even in the churches which were responsible for Lord Rank's incursion into the film world.

Many thousands of British men and women are amateur cinematographers, although most are content with family snapshots interspersed with holiday views. Some well-attended festivals are held in this country each year, but comparatively few of the films are of outstanding quality. British films rarely win awards at continental amateur film festivals. Possibly an explanation is that the splendid films which win the awards on these occasions are made by people who would be regarded in this country as professionals. There is a growing body of men in most industrial countries who shoot films as a sideline—and do it well enough to come by many orders. Recently television has increased the scope for their activities, and has encouraged some to form local film-making companies to which they devote the whole of their time. Almost all of their films are documentaries.

FEWER FILMS: GREATER EARNINGS

Although the number of feature films produced in Great Britain annually is smaller than in the pre-war years (70 against 200), they are being widely shown abroad and earn considerably more, especially in comparison with the pitifully small sums received from overseas sales in the late 1930s.

According to Board of Trade statistics recent overseas remittances (most coming from North America) have been:

1956	£4.0 million
1957	£4.6 million
1958	£5.1 million
1959	£5.0 million
1960	£6.3 million
1961	£5.1 million
1962	£4.0 million

Earnings in the home market in 1960 were £4.5 million and producers received an additional £3.9 million from the British Film Production Fund.

This partly accounts for the British film-maker's sanguine mood. But the British cinema owner has far less reason for equanimity, one of his incidental worries arising directly out of the shortage of feature films. He is not infrequently at his wit's end to know what to show in a week or two's time, in contrast to the 1920s when his bookings were made a year ahead.

Hollywood's output has fallen no less steeply than Great Britain's and John Davis has pointed out that in the heyday of the industry it was possible to provide 156 programmes each year, of which at least

100 would be profitable; now they have considerable difficulty in finding 100 programmes a year.

Nevertheless, it is the quality rather than the quantity of current films which worries many exhibitors. At the end of the 1950s several critics, such as Jympson Harman, deplored the virtual disappearance of the honest-to-goodness love stories which had contributed so much to the prosperity of the industry. He noted too that women film stars seemed to have lost some of their appeal. A trade representative was quoted as saying that 'we sell beef-cake now not cheese-cake'.

These journalists had been disturbed by two films expressing the 'angry young man's point of view'. The first was Jack Clayton's *Room at the Top*, which was described as bitter, bold, compelling, vigorous. It was also said to have 'brought sex to the British screen'. Tony Richardson's *Look Back in Anger* was adapted from John Osborne's play. In his review David Robinson said that it explored a contemporary state of mind. 'Jimmy Porter belongs to the culture of the fifties, typifying the malaise and frustration of a generation conceived out of the decades of the turmoil, the people whose roots are left bare and vulnerable in the disturbed top-soil of Victorian social organization.'

Sir Carol Reed contributed his views to the discussion. 'The audience would always be asking what's round the next corner? and if they can watch good artists in dramatic situations with colourful backgrounds in a way of life they may never experience for themselves, why should we drag them to the cinema to look for an hour or two at a kitchen sink, a one-set film, the greasy dishes and the mental and moral miasma of certain elements in society?'

Although some of the leading critics also expressed themselves about modern trends (C. A. Lejeune described one feature film as beastly and Dilys Powell said it was essentially vicious), and the CEA urged producers to go after the family market, not everyone agreed. For instance, in *Films and Filming* Ian Johnston welcomed the swing during the decade from complaisant *Genevieve* to the angry cinema. He noted the trend towards mocking middle-class conformist respect for authority or for authority figures, poking fun at self-important empire-builders, and being increasingly explicit in sexual candour.

The new cinema, it seems, is catering for people with adult minds in contrast to the old cinema which was concerned with juvenile minds. One critic observed that in the 1920s 'films were generally looked on as a low form of entertainment. Now they are the intellectual's delight.' This is certainly a little unfair to the intellectuals of thirty-five years ago, who were writing about the German silent films in the same terms as are being used today, although we are admittedly more lavish now in spicing horror films with sex, and sex films with horror. It is doubtful too if anything can be said about the aspect of 'the contemporary state of mind' which is gratified by nudist films, except to try to explain it away.

At a recent conference a distinguished lecturer, commenting on 'the approaching end of censorship', remarked to his audience that they all had 'double X minds' now. He was told that this might indeed be true of the people listening to him then, but it might also account for the cinema business having lost three-quarters of its customers.

Cinema managers, perturbed for their livelihood, are greatly concerned about this loss, especially when former patrons exclaim with mild surprise, 'You know, I haven't been to the pictures for ages'. Nor are they altogether happy about the kind of support which their houses have retained.

Seats are best filled when they show a film like *It's Trad, Dad,* but the audiences are drawn almost entirely from the groups described in the trade press as 'the blue jeans-pony tail contingent'. Managers see few potential 'loyal supporters' among them, and they believe that their behaviour discourages other teenagers from developing the cinema habit. Incidentally, they are not sanguine about getting more than infrequent visits from the group referred to in the trade press as 'intellectuals and pseudo-intellectuals'.

Whether regular cinemagoing would be re-established if more films were made in the 1930s' manner is doubtful. Television viewers do, in fact, see many old films, although not necessarily the best, and on a tiny screen, without enjoying the gregarious feeling of being part of a large audience. Penelope Gilliatt described the 1962 Venice Festival as 'a knockdown victory for the thirties'. A retrospective series of programmes had been arranged as *The Birth of the Talkies in the U.S.A.*

'When one sees the films of the thirties in a run,' she said, 'it is exactly their estimate of the audience's intelligence that is such a surprise. The dialogue comes out like a grapeshot, instead of at the speed of a railway announcement, and the laughs and plot-points go by in a flash; if you miss them, too bad. The heroines, too, are so different from ours that they are like another race; they have a character and a humour that makes most Hollywood women now look more like housewives in a television commercial.'

It is a sobering thought though that when the British produced films in the 1930s—and they made a great many more than they do today—nobody outside this country wanted to see them. British films which are being so widely acclaimed today are the tough, realistic productions, probably made by young and adventurous directors trained in the documentary school, able, as Penelope Houston remarked, 'to communicate a passionate concern about the medium they are using'.

The temptation to predict the course of the next few years must be resisted. Some critics have warned most emphatically against indulging in this exercise. In December 1959 they went over their files to remind themselves about what they had said in their last column of the 1940s, and were dismayed to find how far from the mark they had been. Movements expected to be of much consequence had petered out. Others treated as minor happenings, if noticed at all, had assumed astonishing proportions. No doubt, it will be so in the 1960s too.

INDEX

Q

GEORGE ALLEN & UNWIN LTD

London: 40 Museum Street, W.C.1

Auckland: 24 Wyndham Street
Bombay: 15 Graham Road, Ballard Estate, Bombay, 1
Bridgetown: P.O. Box 222
Buenos Aires: Escritorio 454-459, Florida 165
Calcutta: 17 Chittaranjan Avenue, Calcutta 13
Cape Town: 109 Long Street
Hong Kong: 44 Mody Road, Kowloon
Ibadan: P.O. Box 62
Karachi: Karachi Chambers, McLeod Road
Madras: Mohan Mansions, 38c Mount Road, Madras 6
Mexico: Villalongin 32-10, Piso, Mexico 5, D.F.
Nairobi: P.O. Box 4536
New Delhi: 13-14 Asaf Ali Road, New Delhi 1
Sao Paulo: Avenida 9 de Julho 1138-Ap. 51
Singapore: 63c Prinsep Street, Singapore 7
Sydney, N.S.W.: Bradbury House, 55 York Street
Tokyo: 10 Kanda-Ogawamachi, 3-Chome, Chiyoda-Ku
Toronto: 91 Wellington Street West, Toronto 1

JOHN MONTGOMERY

COMEDY FILMS

Comedy Films is the first history of screen comedy and the world's film comedians, tracing the development of humour in motion pictures since the first flickering shadows of the late nineties.

Starting in 1894 with Edison's sneezing film, the book describes the early pioneers such as Paul, Gaumont, Hepworth, Charles Pathé, Zecca, and their first comic films. The picture palace craze, the early Italian and French comedians, and the rise of the American film are all graphically described. The development of Hollywood is represented by the career of Carl Laemmle. The work of Al Christie, Mack Sennett and their rivals in the slapstick pictures which followed the knockabout comedies, is shown. A chapter is devoted to the Keystone studios. Then come Chaplin, Harold Lloyd and the roaring twenties, with America producing 85 per cent of the world's pictures, and Europe dropping back in quality and quantity.

The coming of sound films and their effect on the comedians is shown, and the story comes up to date through the thirties and forties, to 1953.

Demo 8vo.   *21s. net.*

JAY LEYDA

KINO

It is primarily in the Soviet Union that the film has been used with a consciousness of its persuasive powers, and this history gives a full account of the film's development as an art in the service of that society.

Concluding with the problems of the present, this first comprehensive history of the film in Russia begins with the Lumière's filming of the last tsar's coronation in 1896. For the first time full attention is given to the large and important Russian film industry before the revolution of 1917, and to its many links with the emerging Soviet film. The Russian film's continuing history is set against the connected background of Russia's social and artistic progress of the past fifty years.

The author's three years of work in Soviet film schools and studios gave him the opportunity to examine all Russian and Soviet films of importance, many never seen abroad, and his personal acquaintance with the leading film-makers of all Soviet nationalities makes his account of their careers colourful and authoritative.

The history's appeal is to the general reader as well as the specialist. It is fully documented, both with newly translated statements by creators and critics, and with rich illustrations, many published for the first time.

Small Royal 8vo.   *42s. net.*

ERNEST LINDGREN

THE ART OF THE FILM

The Art of the Film presents to the filmgoer and the student, in a clear and readable form, a survey of the established canons of film criticism and a general outline of the development of film technique which is designed to enrich their knowledge of filmcraft and their enjoyment of outstanding film work. It includes chapters on work in the studio, the structure of the film story, the film-maker's tools, editing, the use of sound, film music, the photography and the art of the actor.

There are 32 pages of excellent half-tone plates and, in the appendices, an historical chart of famous films of the main producing countries. Included also are a specimen film script, a select bibliography and a glossary of over 400 technical terms.

'Will enlighten both the amateur and the professional. A very important book.' *Anthony Asquith*

'The most complete and satisfying book on the subject yet to have been published in this country.' *Roger Manvell*

'I only wish Mr Lindgren's excellent book had been in existence long ago; it would have saved me, for one, a great deal of hard, solitary work.' *Dilys Powell*

'Fills a long-felt gap in literature dealing with the cinema.' *Paul Rotha*

'A genuinely "authoritative work", by a man who knows the subject thoroughly and can describe and explain every corner of it with clarity and skill, it makes fascinating reading for all interested in films and is besides of the utmost value to anyone either making or writing about them . . . entertaining as well as enlightening; almost any reader will find his pleasure in films widened and deepened by it.' *Punch*

'An admirably useful guide to the making and criticism of films which everyone who likes films and is curious about them ought to read. It covers everything on the practical side. . . . To those who wish to write for the films the book will be invaluable.' *The Bookman*

'General outline of the development of the film, in all its branches, which cannot fail to enhance one's understanding of the cinema.' *The Listener*

Demy 8vo. *New Edition* *30s. net.*

GEORGE ALLEN AND UNWIN LTD